Forum for Protest

Forum for Protest

THE BLACK PRESS DURING WORLD WAR II

Lee Finkle

RUTHERFORD • MADISON • TEANECK
FAIRLEIGH DICKINSON UNIVERSITY PRESS
LONDON: ASSOCIATED UNIVERSITY PRESSES

Associated University Presses, Inc.
Cranbury, New Jersey 08512

Associated University Presses
108 New Bond Street
London W1Y OQX, England

Library of Congress Cataloging in Publication Data
Finkle, Lee.
Forum for Protest.
Bibliography: p.
Includes index.
1. Negro press. 2. World War, 1939–1945—Negroes.
I. Title.
PN4888.N4F5 071'.3 74–4973
ISBN 0–8386–1577–5

PRINTED IN THE UNITED STATES OF AMERICA

for

Cathy and John

Contents

Preface

With some notable exceptions such as A. Philip Randolph's *Messenger* and Marcus Garvey's *Negro World,* the black press has played a consistent role from its inception in 1827 to the period covered by this study. It has been an organ based on assimilation and protest; a medium through which white America's ideals and institutions have been upheld and its deviations from these denounced.

This study concentrates on World War II, a period when the black press reached its zenith, and one in which the integrationist-civil rights movement began to attract consideration from prominent white liberals. It was also a time when white America "discovered" the black press. The initial reaction of nonblacks to the black press was usually one of alarm and hostility, most notably in the South, but also in the North. This reaction, whether hostile or favorable, indicated that the black press was recognized as a distinct element of influence and power in the black community.

During the war years the black press continued to denounce the government for discriminating against blacks. At the same time, it viewed its role as supportive of the national ideals, and it sought to encourage its readers to join wholeheartedly in the country's war effort despite racial proscriptions. Black editors believed that an exemplary war record would aid the black community in gaining equality. But the black masses, frustrated by discrimination, were apathetic about the war. The black press solved this dilemma by becoming more militant and calling for a double struggle—the "Double V," victory at home and abroad. The primary aim of the militant "Double V" rhetoric was to encourage blacks to "fight for the right to fight" against the country's enemies. It was not, despite the alarm of many whites, a call for a massive attack on the segregation system at home while the country was fighting for its survival. This study evaluates the use of militant rhetoric by a conservative press in trying to channel the activities of an oppressed minority into seeking change within the existing institutions.

This analysis is based upon opinion and news disseminated by the black press. Emphasis is on news content, editorials, and columnists. Other aspects of the black press are not considered here. The society news, sports, church, and entertainment sections are omitted since they do not relate directly to wartime problems, and are better situated within journalistic and sociological studies.

Though this study emphasizes black newspapers, the entire black printed media is utilized as it pertains to the black wartime experience. Black magazines, academic journals, organizational journals, and intellectual reviews have been surveyed. Also, writings in the white media by or about blacks are included.

In 1940 there were approximately 210 black newspapers in print, of which 155 reported circulation figures to the Census Bureau. All except one were weeklies. The total circulation of those reporting was approximately 1,200,000 per week. In order to obtain volume and geographical representation, this study concentrates on those papers having the largest circulation, plus leading papers from various sectors of the country.

Newspapers that had a large or national circulation, and a generous selection of leading regional papers are available. Certain papers with less circulation, but nevertheless regarded as leading papers, are not readily accessible. However, the views of these important editors have not been ignored. The ideas expressed in black papers that are now unavailable have been culled from various other sources. Many editorial reprints appeared in newspapers that were examined. Their opinions were also expressed in the black press trade journals, at press meetings, in black magazines and public statements. During the war various journals and magazines appeared that served as a digest for the black press. The views expressed by editors of those papers not found in the bibliography all lend support to the general thesis presented here concerning the wartime role of the black press.

Previous histories of the black press have been journalistic or sociological. Shorter historical sketches often tend to concentrate on growth and protest aspects. Too often, these accounts have measured the decibel level of protest and from this assumed that the black press was seeking black equality in a radical manner. In 1943 E. Washington Rhodes, publisher of the Philadelphia *Tribune,* told a group of the leading white journalists in America that "people don't read the Negro newspapers. You ought to read them; don't read just the headlines." I have followed Rhodes's advice and discovered that almost all accounts of the wartime press, along with those studies of other aspects of the black wartime experience which use the press as a source, have missed the true nature of the black press during World War II.

Acknowledgments

Portions of chapters 2 and 3 first appeared in my article "The Conservative Aims of Militant Rhetoric: Black Protest during World War II:" *Journal of American History* 60 (December 1973), and portions of chapter 4 first appeared in my article "Quotas or Integration: The NAACP versus the Pittsburgh *Courier* and the Committee on Participation of Negroes in the National Defense Program," *Journalism Quarterly* 52 (Spring 1975). I would like to thank the editors of these journals for permission to use this material.

I am indebted to the staffs of the following libraries for their assistance: the Schomburg Center for Black Research and Culture, the New York City Public Library, the Franklin D. Roosevelt Library, the Howard University Library, the Oral History Research Office at Columbia University, and the Yale University Library.

Financial assistance from the Ford Foundation aided in the initial draft of this study.

I am grateful to Ernest Angell and Conrad Lynn for consenting to personal interviews and to Mr. Lynn for allowing me to examine the unpublished manuscript of his autobiography.

Several people have read the manuscript at various stages of its preparation. I would like to thank David M. Reimers, Albert U. Romasco, Irwin Unger, and Amritjit Singh for their many valuable suggestions. None of these people are, of course, responsible for the interpretations in this book, which are entirely my own.

My special thanks to my wife, Sylvia, who aided me through every stage in the preparation of the book.

Forum for Protest

1
The Development of the Black Press

We shall ever regard the Constitution of the United States as our polar star.[1]

Origin and Early Years

Until 1827 his cause was at times taken up in the press by friendly white writers, but the black man was seldom allowed to express himself in the white man's media. In 1827 the New York City black community was the object of continuous invective from several newspapers owned by Mordecai M. Noah. When the city's black leaders were denied an opportunity to respond to these attacks by the local papers, the only alternative was to publish their own paper.[2] Thus began *Freedom's Journal*, the first black newspaper to appear in the United States.

1. Prospectus for *Freedom's Journal*, quoted in G. James Fleming, "The Negro Press," Research Memorandum, prepared for the Myrdal Study, September 1942 (Typescript, Schomburg Collection), chap. 1, p. 3.

2. I. G. Penn, *The Afro-American Press and its Editors* (Springfield, Mass.: Willey and Co., 1891), pp. 27–28.

The particular incidents that precipitated the founding of *Freedom's Journal* were the attacks of a white racist, but the founders had more on their minds than starting a paper to answer these specific slanders. During the 1820s the program of the American Colonization Society had captured many whites who hitherto had considered themselves spokesmen for the black community. Benjamin Lundy's *Genius of Universal Emancipation* was the leading abolitionist organ of the day, and it pushed for gradual emancipation and colonization for the freed blacks. Not until William Lloyd Garrison began to publish the *Liberator* in January 1831 did a white man cease to advocate gradualism and, at the same time, demolish the assumptions of colonization.

Many historians have credited Garrison's attack on the Colonization Society for the demise of the society. What is often overlooked is that years before Garrison had begun his militant paper, the leading free blacks in the North had opposed colonizing free blacks in Africa. It was apparent that if free blacks opposed the scheme, it could never get off the ground. Black leaders in New York City, under the banner of *Freedom's Journal,* denounced the Society and declared:

> We wish to plead our own cause. Too long have others spoken for us. Too long has the public been deceived by misrepresentations in the things which concern us dearly.[3]

From first issue to last, *Freedom's Journal* stressed the negative aspects of colonization.

When the black leaders of New York met to organize a black paper, they selected Samuel Cornish and John B. Russworm to run the new venture.[4] Russworm was a native of Jamaica and the son of a white man and black woman. He received his early education in Canada and then left to attend Bowdoin College, becoming the first black man to receive a degree from a college in the United States. Cornish was born in Delaware during the

3. *Freedom's Journal,* March 16, 1827.
4. Bella Gross, "*Freedom's Journal* and the *Right's of All,*" *The Journal of Negro History* 15 (July 1932): 298.

last decade of the eighteenth century and was raised in Philadelphia and New York where he entered the ministry.[5] Initially, the paper was edited by Cornish while Russworm was the proprietor.

After the first six months of operation, Cornish left the paper and Russworm took over the editorship. During Cornish's tenure as editor, the paper flourished. Editorials were well written, and the attacks on the Colonization Society were lucid and devastating. Once Russworm assumed the responsibilities for the editorials, the paper lost much of its former crispness of style.

Cornish was extremely hostile to the Colonization Society, and from the beginning he saw it as his duty to attack and expose the society in every issue of his paper. First he concentrated on attacking the program of emigration, pointing out that even if the scheme were sound, "the principles of freedom are too rapid in their growth . . . to wait for the drizzling process of transporting two millions of people across the ocean."[6] From the attack on the idea of colonization it was only a matter of time until the men behind the society were assailed as a group of slaveholders showing an unusual concern for free blacks. "We are prepared to prove," wrote Cornish, "that the natural tendency of colonization is to retard emancipation. . . ."[7]

After Cornish ended his association with the paper in September 1827, the attacks on the Colonization Society continued, but they became less severe and less frequent until finally they ceased altogether. The only reporting about the society was done by way of allowing its supporters the opportunity to express their views in the pages of *Freedom's Journal*. Cornish had previously printed letters and articles in support of colonization, but only in order to expose the fallacies of such thinking. When Russworm's change of heart became clear to all, he was forced to resign, and with his resignation came the demise of the first black paper, two years after it had first appeared.

5. Lerone Bennet, Jr., "Founders of the Negro Press," *Ebony* (July 1964), p. 97.
6. *Freedom's Journal,* March 16, 1827.
7. *Ibid.*, June 8, 1827.

A look at this first black newspaper reveals many of the elements to be found in the black press a century later, and demonstrates the striking continuity of outlook throughout the history of the press. The peculiar institution of the South, discrimination in the North, and especially colonization were attacked relentlessly. From *Freedom's Journal,* through the *North Star,* to the Chicago *Defender,* the Back-to-Africa movement would be denounced by most leading black papers. Those advocates of emigration, whether they were white slave owners, national politicians such as Henry Clay, black nationalists such as Marcus Garvey, or white racists such as Theodore C. Bilbo, found little favor in the pages of the black press.

Besides its opposition to black nationalism and emigration, *Freedom's Journal* displayed other characteristics common to the black press of the twentieth century. Like many black papers during World War II, the black press of this period simultaneously served as a forum for militant vocal protest and advocated "good manners" among free blacks.[8] This practice of speaking to the race as men who should fight for their rights and at the same time speaking to them as if they were children can be explained by the assimilationist and middle-class outlook of the black press. It was expected that black people would have to struggle to achieve equality but equal rights alone would not be sufficient to bring acceptance of blacks into a bourgeois white society. Good manners displayed by the masses, it was hoped, would achieve this.

Cornish continued to hope for a permanent black paper to defend the race and attack emigration. In 1828 he once again took the editorship of *Freedom's Journal,* this time under a new name—*Rights of All.* The paper failed to gather enough support and he was forced to suspend publication in 1830. Six years later a new attempt was started with the *Weekly Advocate,* which also proved to be short-lived. Finally, in 1837, he made a last attempt. Cornish, backed by two other black men, Charles B. Ray and Phillip A. Bell, organized the *Colored American.* The name alone

8. For example, see *Freedom's Journal,* July 13, 1827.

indicated that Cornish was still a strong opponent of emigration. The pages of the *Colored American* continued the attacks on Colonization that had begun with *Freedom's Journal*, but by this time the tone had become much harsher. Anyone who favored such ideas was now to "be considered as a traitor to his brethren." [9] The *Colored American* lasted until 1842, a longer life than its predecessors, but not long enough to establish the black press as a permanent American institution.[10]

Between 1827 and 1847, the year the *North Star* was launched, several attempts were made to get a black paper operating on a self-sustaining basis, but they produced few results. In January 1841, for example, *Ram's Horn* appeared.[11] This attempt, lasting longer than previous efforts, came to an end in June 1848—another failure in the endeavor to establish a lasting institution operated by and for blacks. But the cause was not a lost one. A year before the demise of the *Ram's Horn*, an editor appeared on the scene who would stamp his fiery imprint deeply on black journalism and prove that the black press could be a permanent and militant institution speaking on behalf of blacks throughout the country.

The *North Star* is always associated with the career of Frederick Douglass and the anti-slavery movement of the late ante-bellum period, but too often it is forgotten that Douglass's newspaper was an important stage in the development and recognition of the black press. The paper was certainly the high point of black journalism in the pre-Civil War era in its eloquence, its duration, and the following it gathered throughout the North. Basically, the *North Star* was in the tradition of *Freedom's Journal*. Its aim was to protest against discrimination in the North and to join in the growing crusade to end slavery in the South.

9. Quoted in Fleming, chap. 1, p. 7.

10. Benjamin Quarles, *Black Abolitionists* (New York: Oxford University Press, 1969), pp. 85–86. For the most complete account of Cornish see Marlyn Dalsimer, "Samuel E. Cornish: Negro Newspaper Editor in New York City, 1827–1839." (Master's thesis, New York University, 1967).

11. Fleming, chap. 1, pp. 12–13.

There could be no other course for a black paper. Even though Douglass in many ways continued in the tradition of his journalistic predecessors, he also inaugurated a new era in black journalism.

Both *Freedom's Journal* and the *Ram's Horn* were initiated because the white press had refused to carry the black man's side in local controversies. Douglass was not faced with this dilemma. His fame was sufficient to guarantee him a hearing in the growing number of white abolitionist papers appearing in the North, and his name was usually enough to attract a large audience whenever he traveled the lecture circuit. Nevertheless, Douglass sensed that a newspaper operated by blacks would be the most effective tool in achieving his many aims.[12] Besides the obvious intentions of furthering the abolitionist cause, he saw in a black newspaper two other elements that would become cardinal principles of future black publishers. A successful press operated by black men would show whites that black people were not inferior, would make blacks "acquainted with their own latent powers, [and] by enkindling their hope of a future, and developing their moral force, [would] prove a most powerful means of removing prejudice and awakening an interest in them."[13] While directing attention to blacks, Douglass was also hoping to use the black press to impress whites. His successors continued to operate with this same approach.

Fortunately, Douglass conceived the idea of establishing a newspaper while he was in Great Britain. He discussed the possibilities with friends there who offered him both encouragement and promise of financial support. When Douglass returned to Boston in 1847 with twenty-five hundred dollars in his pocket and the *North Star* clearly established in his thoughts, he was surprised to discover how critical his white friends were of his idea of founding a new black paper.[14]

They had many objections. Douglass could aid the cause better

12. Frederick Douglass, *Life and Times of Frederick Douglass* (Hartford, Conn.: Park Publishing Co., 1882), pp. 291–92.

13. *Ibid.*, p. 291.

14. *Ibid.*, p. 294.

by speaking; the journals of the white abolitionists were sufficient; the longevity of previous black papers had left much to be desired. Finally, if so prominent a black man should prove to be a failure in the enterprise, the damage to the movement would be irreparable. It was characteristic of whites during this period, as well as later, that they believed they knew what was best for blacks. Opposition from prominent abolitionists such as Wendell Phillips and William Lloyd Garrison temporarily prompted Douglass to drop his plans to publish a paper, but he ultimately concluded that he had been ill advised.[15]

Douglass's paper was a milestone in the history of the black press. It was the first to have a black and white following of substantial size. The paper featured contributions from all over the North and Europe, and the circulation figures averaged about three thousand each week.[16] For sixteen years Douglass was to prove what he had set out to do in 1847: to show both blacks and whites that a black man was capable of publishing a newspaper of high quality and maintaining it in the face of serious and continuing hardships throughout its existence.

The most serious problem faced by the paper was financial. Douglass could barely meet operating expenses from funds received through subscriptions, and he was forced to take to the lecture circuit in order to subsidize the paper. During the first year of operation, Douglass spent half of his time away from the paper lecturing. In 1851, at the time of his ideological shift away from Garrison, he merged his paper with the *Liberty Party Paper*, and the new journal was named *Frederick Douglass' Paper*.[17] It was hoped that the combination would enable the operation to reduce expenditures and reach a wider audience. But money problems continued to plague the black paper. In 1859 a reduced size edition was put out and by mid-1860 the paper was forced to cease publication on a weekly basis. Thereafter, *Douglass' Monthly* appeared until Emancipation.

15. Philip Foner, *Frederick Douglass* (New York: The Citadel Press, 1964), p. 82.
16. Douglass, p. 297; Penn, p. 69.
17. Foner, pp. 86–91.

At the outbreak of the Civil War, black people received little assurance from federal sources that the outcome would benefit them. Official pronouncements from the Lincoln administration were careful to show that the war was being fought for the sole purpose of saving the Union. As early events indicated, it appeared that the North was doing its best to uphold slavery as much as the South. Secretary of State William H. Seward instructed United States emissaries abroad to inform the governments to which they were assigned that, despite the rebellion, "the slaves would be slaves still, and that the masters would be masters still" when the rebellion was put down.[18] As blacks in the North began offering their services to the Union Army, they were rejected.[19] Despite the many pleas to enlist the active support of blacks, the federal government's primary aim at that time was to calm the fears of the border states so that they would not follow the deep South to secession and rebellion.

Action taken by the armies of the Union offered little hope to blacks that they were about to witness a change in race relations in the United States. General George B. McClellan assured the ruling class in the South that he would keep his hands off their "property," and that should slaves attempt to rebel, he would use the Army to crush them. General Benjamin Butler also offered to put down any slave insurrection in Maryland.[20] A few commanders attempted to pursue different policies. On August 30, 1861, General John C. Frémont established martial law in Missouri and issued a proclamation freeing all the slaves in the area. But Lincoln moved swiftly to revoke the order, an act that sent Douglass into a rage of condemnation. After Lincoln voided the May 9, 1862, decree of General David Hunter outlawing slavery in Georgia, Florida, and South Carolina, *Douglass' Monthly* blasted "our rebel worshiping generals," and accused the President and his Cabinet of treason.[21]

Despite the initial hesitations and maneuverings of Lincoln,

18. Douglass, pp. 374–75.
19. *Douglass' Monthly,* May 1861.
20. Douglass, p. 375 ; *Douglass' Monthly,*. May 1861.
21. *Douglass' Monthly,* October 1861 ; Foner, p. 202.

and despite the humiliations heaped upon blacks seeking to help out, Douglass, from the first, saw that the war would mean the death sentence of the slave system. "Any attempt now," he wrote in *Douglass' Monthly* a month after the outbreak of war, "to separate freedom of the slave from the victory of the Government over slaveholding rebels and traitors . . . will be lost. The American people and the Government at Washington may refuse to recognize it for a time, but the inexorable logic of events will force it upon them in the end; that the war now being waged . . . is a war against slavery. . . ."[22]

Douglass continued to operate on this premise until the government was publicly willing to take a similar position. First in Douglass's mind was the necessity to get blacks into uniform. "We are fighting the rebels with only one hand when we should be fighting them with both." Why, he asked, are we "striking the rebels with our soft white hand when we should be striking with the iron hand of the black man." He denounced the Army for catching slaves instead of arming them.[23]

Douglass continued to use his paper to urge every black man to "get an eagle in his button, a musket on his shoulder and the star spangled banner over his head," but the black man's progress was painfully slow, and restrictions on his serving were dropped only one at a time. First, blacks were to be permitted into the Army only in a menial capacity—serving food to the white troops. Next they were allowed to perform some of the more difficult labor duties of the Army; and finally they were allowed to serve as full-fledged troops shouldering arms. But even then it was not as equals, since initially black troops were to be allowed to fight but not wear the blue uniform of regular Union soldiers.

Lincoln dealt Douglass another blow in August 1862 when he addressed a group of free blacks and urged them to support colonization.[24] A longtime foe of the idea, Douglass could not believe that at this particular time Lincoln could urge such a

22. *Douglass' Monthly,* May 1861.
23. *Ibid.,* February 1862.
24. *Ibid.,* September 1862.

position. Whereas Lincoln had expressed the belief that blacks and whites could probably not live together, Douglass was firmly convinced that this was not true.[25] By now the black editor was showing signs of despair—his editorials vehemently attacked the President and his policies as showing signs of "weakness and imbecility."[26] A shift in spirits came with the preliminary Emancipation Proclamation in September 1862. Rejecting the views of many abolitionists that it was simply an empty gesture, *Douglass' Monthly* fully supported the proclamation and the paper reversed its attitude toward Lincoln.

But the administration's willingness to employ black troops did not end Douglass's problems—in fact it created new ones for the editor. In late 1862 Governor John Andrew of Massachusetts approached the War Department to give him permission to raise two black regiments. On January 20, 1863, a War Department directive authorized this request and Andrew organized the 54th and 55th regiments.[27] Massachusetts had too few blacks to fill the ranks and Andrew was forced to begin recruiting throughout the North. In February 1863 Douglass's aid was enlisted. Douglass was not unenthusiastic and in March he published his famous call to all black men: "Men of Color to Arms." The editor related his long struggle to enlist blacks and the many discouragements he met and urged his fellow blacks not to "complain that it [his plea] was not heeded sooner." "Action! Action! not criticism is the call of the hour." "Now or Never. Liberty won by white men would lose half its luster." "They [the weak and cowardly] tell you that this is a 'white man's war'; that you will be no better off than before the war. . . ."[28] The call first appeared in *Douglass' Monthly* and was soon reprinted in Northern papers and became the most powerful piece of propaganda in recruiting blacks in the North.

Douglass toured Northern areas with significant black communities in order to raise volunteers for Andrew's regiments. He

25. The *North Star*, January 28, 1847.
26. *Douglass' Monthly*, February 1862.
27. Foner, p. 211.
28. *Douglass' Monthly*, March 1863.

was struck with the apathy of most blacks, and decided to use his paper to combat this feeling. Writing in the *Monthly* in the spring of 1863 he gave reasons why blacks should not hesitate to enlist. He told his people that there were many white racists who were horrified at the thought of arming blacks. By taking up arms, black people would establish their full rights of citizenship and gain self respect.[29]. Thus did Douglass set a precedent for black editors to follow in the next two major wars in which the United States would participate.

Once the fact of black recruitment was assured, discrimination within the Army began to raise cries of complaint from black soldiers and civilians. Douglass took this as a personal challenge since in his "Call" he had guaranteed all black enlistees fair treatment. Black troopers were paid only about half the amount whites received, which caused many to object and refuse to enlist. While Douglass opposed this unfair treatment, he still believed that the greatest issue at stake was the defeat of the South, and that black troops were vital to the North's success. Douglass spoke plainly to Northern blacks now. In an editorial he told them that they would, indeed, encounter discrimination in the ranks, but that this should not make them hesitate. "'We shall be fighting a *double battle* [emphasis added] against slavery in the South and against prejudice and proscription in the North."[30] The idea of the "Double V" used in World War II by the black press had its genesis in the pages of *Douglass' Monthly.*

Douglass was convinced that if the black man could wear the uniform of his country, he would be accepted as an equal. Once he is in that uniform, said the editor, "there is no power on earth or under the stars which can deny that he earned the right of citizenship in the United States. I say again, this is our chance, and woe betide us if we fail to embrace it."[31] Douglass's faith in white America proved to be too optimistic. But in this faith he

29. *Ibid.*, April 1863.
30. *Ibid.*, February 1863.
31. An address by Federick Douglass, printed in James W. Ford, ed., *Negroes and the National War Effort* (New York: Workers Library Publishers, Inc., April, 1942), p. 8.

was not alone, nor was it an attitude of the blacks during the Civil War era only. In 1942 black leaders were faced with a situation similar to the Civil War period. Discrimination and abuse had made blacks apathetic about the country's war aims and the leaders believed that only enthusiastic support would mean full citizenship for blacks. In trying to appeal to the masses, Frederick Douglass's Philadelphia speech was reprinted in pamphlet form and sections of the speech were widely quoted by whites and blacks in trying to bolster black morale.

Despite his paramount objective of getting blacks involved, and his paper's basic support for Lincoln after the Emancipation Proclamation, Douglass nevertheless continued to attack the administration for discriminating against blacks. Conditions in the ranks became so alarming that Douglass at one point decided to end his recruiting activities until the grievances were redressed. In the summer of 1863 he went to Washington to seek an audience with Lincoln. He told the President of his activities in recruiting blacks, and how, due to poor treatment, they were often reluctant to enlist. Out of this interview, and a later one with Secretary of War Edwin M. Stanton, came the offer of a commission for Douglass.[32] With this expectation, Douglass returned to Rochester to issue the last of his *Monthly* in August 1863. He told his readers that the paper was no longer necessary since the white dailies were now open to him and that he felt his services were needed in organizing black troops.[33]

Growth and Transitional Years

The black press entered upon a new era as the South was going down to defeat. As soon as Union troops began occupying territory in the Southern states, black newspapers began to appear. In 1862 New Orleans witnessed the appearance of *L' Union,* the first

32. Douglass, p. 386.
33. *Douglass' Monthly,* August 1863.

black newspaper published below the Mason and Dixon line.[34] *L' Union* was joined by the *Colored American*, which began publication in Augusta, Georgia, in 1865. It was, its prospectus declared, to "be devoted to the promotion of harmony and good will between white and colored people of the South. . . ."[35] The tone of the paper was manifestly conciliatory, calling for support from its "white friends," and all who were interested in harmony between the races.

L' Union and the *Colored American* were but the beginning. From the end of the Civil War until the turn of the century, black newspapers were being established at an unprecedented rate. Most of them did not last long, but enough did to indicate real progress in the field. In some years the number of new papers to appear reached over eighty. Between the years 1827 and 1862, only thirty-two black papers were initiated. From 1865 to 1900, 1,184 began operations.[36] Almost all of the papers established during this period were in the South, where most blacks lived.

Black newspapers in the post-bellum era diverged from the pattern set during the ante-bellum period by editors such as Russworm, Martin R. Delany, and Douglass. Militant black journalism seems to have diminished temporarily with the passing of *Douglass' Monthly* and the institution of slavery. Papers published after the second third of the nineteenth century were for the most part organs of the political parties hoping to capture the newly created black vote. Politicians became editors and editors in turn became office-seekers. The emphasis on racial uplift was replaced by efforts to sway voting behavior.[37] During this period black newspapers were not faced with a difficult choice between the two parties. Black papers and black people entered the Republican

34. Armisted S. Pride, "Register and History of Negro Newspapers in the United States" (Ph.D. dissertation, Northwestern University, 1950), p. 404.
35. Quoted in Penn, p. 101.
36. Pride, pp. 405, 407.
37. Frederic G. Detweiler, *The Negro Press in the United States* (Chicago: University of Chicago Press, 1922), pp. 46–47.

ranks *en masse* and seldom wavered until Franklin D. Roosevelt ushered in the New Deal in the 1930s.

Between the mid-1860s and 1880s, most papers proved to be short lived. After 1880 the press began to show more signs of stability. Many black newspapers, however, simply struggled to stay alive, never gaining much prominence. With the coming of World War I, the black press had a generation of experience behind it and was to use this and the war news to gain a mass audience. During the period between 1880 and 1917 many papers, which were to become leaders in the field during World War I and World War II, came into existence. The Philadelphia *Tribune* began publishing in 1884. This was preceded by T. Thomas Fortune's first venture, the *Roumor* in 1879 which eventually became the New York *Age* in 1888. The Baltimore *Afro-American* began as a one-man operation in 1892. These papers were in turn followed by William Monroe Trotter's Boston *Guardian* in 1901, Robert S. Abbott's Chicago *Defender* in 1905, the Pittsburgh *Courier* in 1907, the New York *Amsterdam News* in 1909, and in 1912, P. B. Young, Sr., began publication of the Norfolk *Journal and Guide*. Hundreds of others began operation during this period, but the above-named papers were the ones that would dominate the field by World War II.[38]

Most of the newspapers that began to publish immediately following the Reconstruction period remained solidly behind the Republican party, as they would until the 1930s. But the period from 1880 to 1917 was one of transition for the black press. Newspapers were published that were becoming something more than narrow partisan sheets edited by men more interested in politics than journalism. Despite a continuing large attrition rate, enough papers were holding their own to lay the foundation for the modern black press, which would emerge during World War I. But while the press was providing the groundwork for the future,

38. Fleming, chap. 2, pp. 10, 11 ; chap. 3, p. 1 ; "*The Afro:* Seaboard's Largest Weekly," *The Crisis* 45 (February 1938): 44 ; "*Amsterdam News:* Harlem's Largest Weekly," *The Crisis* 45 (April 1938): 105 ; "The Youngs of Norfolk," *Headlines and Pictures* 2 (January 1946): 16–17.

it still was aimed primarily at a small, educated, elite black audience.

The press of this period became increasingly involved in a new area outside the usual problems of black-white relations and discrimination in general. By the end of the nineteenth century black papers became the battlefields for the ideological struggles being waged among the various spokesmen for the race.

Booker T. Washington was the dominant black spokesman from 1895 to 1915. Although most blacks followed his leadership, and whites lent support to his views, there were many blacks who disputed his approach from the beginning. Washington's conciliatory Atlanta speech was attacked by many black papers initially, and only as the century drew to a close did most of them fall into line behind the Tuskegee leader.[39] Washington moved to counter his critics by various means, but one in particular is relevant to this study: the buying out or subsidizing of important black papers in order to promote the views emanating from Tuskegee. The surest way to smooth relations with a hostile press was by a generous use of money. A press with little revenue from advertising and an audience much too small to offer financial security to one aspiring to a career in journalism was extremely vulnerable to manipulation by someone controlling significant amounts of money. At this time money from white philanthropists was reaching the black community almost entirely through Washington, and he used it in developing his own image as the spokesman for his race.

Those who were in opposition to Washington eventually found little opportunity to express their views in black newspapers. These people feared that Washington's philosophy would be represented as that of the entire black leadership. Opponents of conciliation soon found that in order to mount a sustained attack on Washington, they would have to establish their own outlets. Both William Monroe Trotter and W. E. B. DuBois eventually went into the field of journalism primarily with the hope of presenting alternatives to Washington's position. Trotter, in 1901, began the

39. August Meier, *Negro Thought in America, 1880–1915* (Ann Arbor, Mich.: University of Michigan Press, 1966), p. 171.

Boston *Guardian*; and DuBois, in 1905, made his journalistic debut with the publication of the *The Moon Illustrated Weekly.*

Before these two outspoken opponents of Washington made their appearance, T. Thomas Fortune was the leading editor of this transitional period of the press. Fortune entered the field in the same way as would many future giants of the black press, beginning as a printer and eventually writing articles. Starting out in Florida working for a local newspaper, Fortune eventually journeyed North, attending Howard University for a while, working as a postal clerk and customs inspector in Delaware, and finally moving to New York. Here, in 1879, he took over the *Roumor,* a sophisticated black journal which in that year was facing serious financial difficulties.[40]

The *Roumor* was a twelve-page weekly tabloid aimed at the black intelligentsia. It emphasized, as did all black journals, racial issues, but it also published poetry and literary works, and gave much space to religious affairs. On the front page, woodcuts of famous blacks made the paper a very attractive package but at the same time a costly one. With little revenue from commercial advertising, and support coming entirely from a very select clientele, the paper was floundering.[41] When Fortune took it over in 1879, he changed the name to the New York *Globe,* and the paper, in Fortune's words, "took the leadership in most things affecting the race in New York and the nation. . . ."[42] The *Globe* served as a forum for prominent black personalities, publishing articles by such men as Frederick Douglass and Blanche K. Bruce. After Fortune's partner sold out his interest in the *Globe,* it ceased publication. Fortune then struck out on his own, starting *The Freeman,* which in 1887 became the New York *Age.*

During the 1880s, when Fortune was establishing his reputation as the leading black newspaper editor, he remained on friendly

40. Fleming, chap 2, p. 2; T. Thomas Fortune, "The New York Negro in Journalism," *New York State Commission National Negro Exposition, Official Souvenior Program,* n.p.

41. Ludlow Werner, "The New York *Age:* Lusty Veteran," *The Crisis* 5 (March 1938): 74.

42. Fortune, n.p.

terms with Booker T. Washington, even though the editor was considered somewhat of a radical at the time. The relationship had its rough spots, but was mutually beneficial, continuing until Fortune sold out his interest in the *Age* in 1907. In the early years of the friendship Fortune often aided Washington by ghost writing speeches and articles for the Southern leader. Over the years the *Age* was often to find itself short of funds and here Washington repaid the editor's past favors in the form of cash subsidies.

After the turn of the century, Washington was able to place Fred Moore on the editorial staff. Moore had previously been connected with the National Negro Business League, and before going to the *Age* had been working for Washington in trying to counter Trotter's attacks from the Boston *Guardian.* Moore, with funds supplied from Tuskegee, had bought out the *Colored American Magazine* in Boston and was using it to launch attacks on Trotter and as a vehicle for the ideas of Washington.[43] The *Age* and Washington began a formal relationship in early 1907, when the paper reorganized itself into a corporation, with Washington owning 950 of the 5,000 shares issued. This arrangement was carried out in secrecy, and Washington's shares were in the name of his secretary, Emmett J. Scott.[44] Fortune remained with the paper as editor until, in late 1907, he suffered a complete nervous breakdown and had to relinquish all of his editorial duties. He then sold out his share of the *Age* to Fred Moore (Moore obtained the necessary funds from Washington), who continued as editor and publisher until his death during World War II.

The use of the *Age* by Washington to enhance his image and spread his power was only one point where he and the black press came into contact with each other, and the use of money was only one method by which he influenced editors. Many editors agreed with the conciliatory approach of Washington and voluntarily gave

43. August Meier, "Booker T. Washington and the Negro Press: Special Reference to the *Colored American,*" *Journal of Negro History* 38 (January 1953): 68–70.

44. Emma L. Thornbrough, "More Light on Booker T. Washington and *The New York Age,*" *Journal of Negro History* 43 (January 1958): 38–39.

him wide coverage in their papers. Washington also sent out articles and advice to news-hungry local papers, which were eager to print anything written by the most prominent black man in America.

In his efforts to control the black press, Washington proved to be largely successful for many years. When the Niagara Movement was organized by black leaders opposed to the accommodationist policies of Washington, most of the black newspapers in the country either ignored it completely or gave it unenthusiastic coverage. The *Colored American Magazine*, originally taken over by Washington to counter the attacks from the militant Boston *Guardian*, soon began to use its pages to counter the equally militant attacks from the organ of the Niagara Movement, the *Voice of the Negro*.[45]

William Monroe Trotter, in 1901, organized his own paper, the Boston *Guardian*, with one thought in mind—to begin an all-out attack on Booker T. Washington. The *Guardian* was well received and sold throughout the North, due to the stinging editorials from Trotter's acerbic pen. Trotter, like DuBois, looked to an elite to lead the black people toward equality, and the paper's appeal was accordingly directed to this sector of the race. Despite the *Guardian's* success, it proved unable to limit the influence of its opponent from Tuskegee. Trotter was a successful editor and an excellent polemicist, but due to his inability to work well with others, he was never able to build a personal following or organization. As it turned out, it was Trotter's personal actions rather than his use of the *Guardian* that attracted widespread attention to the existence of a view in opposition to that of Washington.

Trotter traveled to Louisville in early 1903 to oppose Washington at a meeting of the Afro-American Council. But Fortune, the chairman of the convention, refused to give Trotter a chance to air his views. Later that year Washington appeared in Boston for a speaking engagement, and the Boston editor was able to retaliate for the treatment he had received in Louisville at the hands of Washington's allies. The turbulent Trotter, along with

45. Meier, *Journal of Negro History* 38: 68–70, 75.

some friends, went to the hall where Washington was speaking and heckled him until the Tuskegee leader was forced to retreat from the stage. Trotter and company were unceremoniously arrested and put in jail for their victory.[46] This was the first public attack on the Southern leader to receive widespread publicity in both the black and white press. Trotter claimed that the reason he instigated the "Boston Riot" was precisely because Washington controlled most of the publicity outlets in the black world and was able to suppress the views of his opposition. Thus it was clear from Trotter's own words that the primary purpose of the *Guardian*—to detract followers of Washington and to publicize an opposing viewpoint—was a failure.

Despite its failure to diminish the stature of the Tuskegee leader, the *Guardian* was able to provide a militant forum in the Age of Booker T. Washington. It did this in the face of stiff opposition and the full force of Washington's prestige and money. While the *Guardian* was unable to draw off support from Washington, the latter's efforts to counter the *Guardian* were equally unavailing. Until *The Crisis* made its appearance in 1910, the *Guardian* remained the only paper of any longevity providing an outlet to those who refused to follow the conciliatory position of Washington.

At the very moment that Trotter brought out the *Guardian*, W. E. B. DuBois was looking for an outlet for his journalistic talent. Lack of funds and available time delayed the founding of a personal vehicle for almost five years. DuBois was very conscious of the importance of a militant black press. He relates in his autobiography how the initial favorable reception of the *Guardian* had been fought by the efforts of the Tuskegee machine to build up its own favorable press. DuBois was not in "absolute opposition" to Washington at this time, but he "resented the practical buying up of the Negro press and [the] closing off [of] even mild and reasonable opposition" to the Tuskegee leader.[47] By

46. Charles W. Puttkammer, "William Monroe Trotter, 1872–1934," *Journal of Negro History* 43 (October 1958): 301.
47. W. E. B. DuBois, *The Autobiography of W. E. B. DuBois,* ed.

1904 DuBois had stepped out of this middle position between the *Guardian* and Washington. Mounting attacks on his views by the Tuskegee-controlled press forced him to respond, first, in an attack on the black press itself, published in the *Guardian,* for selling out to Washington. The final break with Washington came with the "Boston Riot" precipitated by Trotter.[48]

The incarceration of Trotter and the rest of his "rioters" infuriated DuBois even though he was not in accord with their direct action. He considered the heckling of Washington a mistake in judgment, but not a punishable crime. In the summer of 1905 DuBois contacted a few select black acquaintances and proposed a conference "to oppose firmly present methods of strangling honest criticism, to organize intelligent and honest Negroes, and to support organs of news and public opinion."[49] This was the origin of the Niagara Movement, a primary aim of which was to advocate "freedom of speech and criticism," and an "unfettered and unsubsidized press." The power of the Tuskegee machine had finally become too unbearable for those in opposition to remain silent. The Niagara Movement and its program received a not unexpected response in the black press. The New York *Age* was hostile and abusive and most of the other black papers were either hostile or indifferent.[50]

At the time DuBois sent out the call for the Niagara meeting, he had already become convinced that in order to be heard he would have to publish his own paper. In December 1905 he and two associates founded *The Moon Illustrated Weekly* in Memphis, Tennessee.[51] The *Moon* showed no interest in reaching the masses. Its circulation reached a maximum of about 300 a week and its audience was centered in Memphis and Atlanta. The weekly was never really able to get off the ground. DuBois was too occupied

Herbert Aptheker (New York: International Publishers Co., Inc., 1968), pp. 242, 247.

48. *Ibid.,* p. 248.

49. *Ibid.*

50. Francis L. Broderic, *W. E. B. DuBois ; Negro Leader in a Time of Crisis* (Stanford, Calif.: Stanford University Press, 1959), p. 79.

51. DuBois, p. 251.

with his other activities in Atlanta to give the magazine the full effort it required, and financial difficulties plagued the editors throughout its short life. When DuBois, in desperation, sought aid from white quarters, word leaked out and the New York *Age* gleefully reported the move in its editorial column.[52] Although the *Moon* had a very short life—it died before it reached its first anniversary—it proved to be a preview of what *The Crisis* would eventually become. The magazine carried stories about Africa, and about leading black Americans, it reprinted articles and editorials from the black press, and it featured militant editorials written by DuBois. The experience with the *Moon* showed that once DuBois was able to devote his full-time energies to a journal and was free from financial problems, he could develop a highly successful and militant journal presenting a view in complete opposition to the moderate tone of Washington.

When the NAACP was founded, DuBois became its Director of Publications and Research, which meant that he would edit the organization's journal. In November 1910 the first issue of *The Crisis* was published. DuBois pointed out that he had founded the magazine "over the protests of many of my associates."[53] Immediately a conflict arose over how much control the Board of Directors of the NAACP would exercise over the editorial policy of *The Crisis*. Given the personality of DuBois, and the paternalistic outlook of most of the white liberals who dominated the organization, the conflict was inevitable. The contest centered primarily around DuBois and Oswald G. Villard, Chairman of the Board of Directors. DuBois was never close to Villard, whom he considered a typical white liberal who expected the black man to manifest a humble position before the white man. The conflict reached a crisis when, in late 1913, Villard resigned his chairmanship because he was unable to control the editorial policy of *The Crisis*. DuBois's aim, of course, was to use the magazine as

52. Paul G. Partington, "*The Moon Illustrated Weekly*—The Precursor of *The Crisis*," *Journal of Negro History* 48 (July 1963): 214.

53. DuBois, p. 256.

his own personal outlet.[54] The NAACP officials believed that they had to maintain a certain degree of unity from within, and also to keep on good terms with the black press, which DuBois was attacking through *The Crisis*. The final outcome was that the magazine would represent the opinion of the editor as long as it was in general accord with the policies of the NAACP.[55]

During the early years of *The Crisis*, DuBois used the journal as a vehicle to attack Booker T. Washington. The language was never so harsh as that of Trotter's but the meaning was clear: Washington did not represent black thinking in America, and blacks were not satisfied with conditions as they existed. Not only was Washington attacked, but his "kept press" came in for similar treatment. The black press was at first suspicious of the NAACP, especially since DuBois was affiliated with it, and they responded in kind with attacks on *The Crisis* editor. The press never was able to accept DuBois, even after he left the NAACP and was a regular columnist for some of the black papers. In World War II, his "close ranks" call of 1918 was constantly used to represent the sell-out of the black leaders of an earlier generation.

It was Trotter and DuBois who bridged the gap between the old and the new. During these transitional years when the modern black press was in gestation, many papers appeared that would assume a more militant posture on civil rights, but most, in general, went along with the overall conciliatory tone of Washington. Even Washington was aware that a more militant position was required to please the black community, and he did not begin a vendetta against all who espoused a more militant outlook. His policy toward the militant black papers was one of friendship as long as a paper did not attack him personally. This can be seen best in his association with Fred Moore and T. Thomas Fortune of the *Age*, both of whom were more inclined to attack discrimination openly. DuBois and Trotter were of another type. They never hesitated to open a frontal attack on Washington and his program.

54. Elliott Rudwick, "W. E. B. DuBois in the Role of *Crisis* Editor," *Journal of Negro History* 43 (July 1958): 218.
55. DuBois, p. 261.

Their editorials were sharply critical attacks on the conciliatory approach. When Washington passed from the scene, the modern black press was making its appearance. With the death of Washington the internecine strife ended, and the black press could now direct its attack against white discrimination. The style was more militant now, and the prose was directed toward the masses.

Emergence of the Modern Black Press

The modern black press had to await two things—a more highly urbanized audience and a shift in focus from a literate elite readership to a mass appeal. Migration to the North after 1914 brought into existence the black urban masses, and Robert S. Abbott gave them a paper to read that they could understand. The ideological debates about which approach to take toward achieving equality might provide thought-provoking evenings among the elite, but front-page news of crime, brutality, and discrimination was something to which black masses swarming into urban ghettos could much better relate.

When the United States became involved as an active belligerent in World War I, black people were faced with many new problems. The military presented blacks with little hope for a chance to serve as equals. The struggle with the Army had precedents dating back to the Civil War, but this time blacks were supposed to be equal citizens of the country. Old issues reappeared once again as black leaders demanded that the Army provide for black combat troops, black officers, and an end to discrimination. The passing of Booker T. Washington and the Wilsonian rhetoric about world democracy signaled the awakening of a new black determination to gain equality. Counter forces, such as the reincarnation of the Ku Klux Klan, were simultaneously appearing, which would move to block the rising expectations of blacks.

As soon as President Wilson delivered his war message to Congress, blacks were responsive to the call of duty. The Army's response to this enthusiasm was less than encouraging. Black volunteers were not accepted with open arms, and often not at all.[56] There were in existence four black regiments created by Congress during the Civil War and black recruits were restricted to these units until the wartime draft went into effect two months after the outbreak of hostilities. The effect upon black morale was predictable, and the situation soon appeared alarming to the race leaders. There was a pervasive fear among editors and leading black men that their race would be excluded from playing any kind of significant wartime role. At the same time they were concerned with the obvious possibility that the black masses would not engage in any vigorous effort to serve where they were clearly not wanted. "Why do you want to fight for your country?" was the question on the lips of many blacks.[57] Black leaders at once found themselves fighting a two-front war: against exclusion from the war effort by whites and against a plummeting black morale.

Initially, the War Department made no provisions for blacks to train as officers. When it was announced that fourteen officers' training centers were to be organized by May 14, 1917, there was no mention of training facilities for blacks. Two alternatives presented themselves to black leaders. Either they must press for a segregated training camp for black officers, or accept a situation where blacks could not lead their own troops. Strangely enough, the strongest attempt to obtain a segregated camp was made by DuBois and the NAACP. Behind this move was a fear that the black people would not support the war if action were not taken to alleviate the situation. Deciding to "take advantage of the disadvantage," so as to prevent the "spread of disloyalty and resentment among the black masses,"[58] the militant *Crisis* editor opted for service even if it had to be on a segregated basis. Joel Spingarn approached General Leonard Wood on the matter for the NAACP and was informed that if enough college-trained black

56. John Hope Franklin, *From Slavery to Freedom* (New York: Alfred A. Knopf, 1967), p. 455.
57. DuBois, p. 265.
58. *Ibid.*, p. 266.

youths would volunteer for a segregated officers training camp, one would be established.

A Central Committee of Negro College Men was quickly organized at Howard University, which was able to gather the names of over 1,500 college graduates ready to volunteer for officer training. On May 12, 1917, the War Department released an announcement of the opening of Fort Des Moines to train black officers. Strong opposition to the segregated camp in certain black quarters appeared once the official statement was released, and DuBois had difficulty in lining up public support in favor of voluntary segregation. The response in much of the black press was hostile to the idea. Papers such as the New York *Age*, the Boston *Guardian*, the Baltimore *Afro-American* and the Cleveland *Gazette* choked over the idea.[59] Their displeasure with the Army's gesture placed the *Crisis* editor on the defensive, but he refused to back down and continued his support for the policy that he had helped sponsor.

"We are faced with a condition, not a theory," said DuBois.[60] It was either segregation or no officers, and the latter situation would be far worse. DuBois pointed out this dilemma and attacked those papers opposing his views. "If war comes," he wrote in *The Crisis*, "conscription will follow. All pretty talk about not volunteering will become entirely academic."[61] Strange talk, indeed, coming from this militant academician! DuBois warned against encouraging blacks not to volunteer for Des Moines. The choice facing blacks once conscription came would not be "between volunteering and not volunteering. The choice will be between conscription and rebellion. Can the reader conceive of the possibility of choice?" "Give us the [segregated] camp!" Spingarn, working on the same theory as most black leaders, assumed that blacks serving their country would pave the way to equality in the postwar era. He joined DuBois in promoting the officers' camp by

59. Rudwick, *Journal of Negro History* 43: 225.
60. DuBois, p. 266.
61. *The Crisis* 14 (April 1917): 271.

warning that Army officials actually desired the failure of the program, adding that if blacks opposed segregated training, they would be playing into the hands of the South.

In the early months of the war, black leaders spelled out their program. They would encourage full support for the country's war effort in the expectation that full citizenship rights would thereby be earned in payment after the war. This was not a bargaining position to be used only on condition that whites promised something in return. It was simply a hope, or honest expectation that the debt would be honored. There was also a strong feeling that if blacks allowed themselves to be excluded it would be said, once the war was over, that they deserved the status of second-class citizens. Editors and leaders saw it as their duty not to let this turn of events happen. "As Negroes we propose to fight for the right [to fight], no matter what our treatment may be. . . ."[62]

In the fall of 1917, Emmet J. Scott, secretary to the late Booker T. Washington, was appointed Special Assistant to the Secretary of War. He made his feelings about the situation quite clear, and despite his conservatism, apparently spoke for many, if not all, of the leading blacks in the country. Black people realized, he said, "that without bargaining, there must be a pledge on the part of the Negro of [his] . . . loyalty." The black man, he added, "realized that he would not be in a position to demand his rights unless he fully performed his duties as an American citizen."[63] Black people could get little comfort from their spokesmen. There appeared to be no choice open to them. Either they must accept things as they came, or their position would deteriorate.

Difficult as it was to offer the black masses so little, the leaders were faced with the problem of encouraging them to accept it. DuBois sensed an effort among certain whites to "spread disloyalty and resentment among the masses."[64] The Central

62. *Ibid.*, 16 (May 1917): 7.
63. Emmett J. Scott, *The American Negro in the World War* (Chicago: Homewood Press, 1919), p. 412.
64. DuBois, p. 266.

Committee of Negro College Men, organized to help establish the segregated officers' camp at Des Moines, did not see its job ended once the camp had been erected. Its role after this was to encourage black people to "stand by the race. If we fail, our enemies will dub us *Cowards* for all time; and we can never win our rightful place."[65] The inevitable culmination of such feeling led naturally to the "fight for the chance to fight as Negro combat units. . . ."[66]

Despite what appeared to be a universal acceptance of this point of view among black leaders, these men had to convince the white majority of their position. The South had become alarmed at the implications of training blacks to shoot at whites, and charges of disloyalty were being disseminated. Robert R. Moton, successor to Booker T. Washington at Tuskegee, became disturbed and wrote to President Wilson proclaiming the loyalty of his race: "You can count absolutely on the loyalty of the mass of Negroes. . . ."[67] The South continued its offensive, though, in trying to prevent any display of loyalty on the part of blacks.

The Universal Service Bill provided for blacks to be drafted the same as whites, but on a segregated basis. Senator James K. Vardaman told his fellow Southerners that the draft "means the millions of Negroes who come under this measure will be armed. I know of no greater menace to the South than this."[68] The white South, too, was apparently fighting a two-front war. Negro editors, by printing such statements of Southerners condemning the use of black combat troops, were hoping to use this as an incentive to arouse enthusiasm among the race. Black editors, though, never failed to emphasize that the war abroad was the paramount one for the moment. Many whites in the South made it clear that if it came to a showdown, the homefront struggle would be the primary one. During the debate over the Conscription Bill, Congressman Nicholls of South Carolina warned that "if you put a boy from Mississippi in a Negro regiment from Massachusetts, you won't

65. Quoted in Scott, p. 89.
66. *Ibid.*, p. 63.
67. Quoted in *The Crisis* 14 (May 1917): 37.
68. Quoted in *ibid.*, p. 23.

have to go to Germany to have a war. You will have it right here."[69]

Events on the homefront offered little evidence to blacks that by showing their full support in the struggle to save the world for democracy, they would share in that democracy. Lynchings increased during the war years; from 35 in 1917 they rose to 60 in 1918.[70] Southerners objected to Northern blacks being sent to the South to train, and friction within Army camps and in adjacent towns added fuel to the rising tensions. Incidents multiplied when black troops were led by unsympathetic white officers and whenever white military police met with black troops. "Internal conditions," the conservative Scott observed, "were by no means . . . conducive to loyalty and a healthy morale . . . among Negroes."[71] The tension finally erupted in riots in the summer of 1917 when East St. Louis witnessed what was probably the bloodiest racial clash in United States history. This was followed in September 1917 by the revolt of the black regiment stationed outside of Houston, Texas, against the constant mistreatment of black troops by the townspeople. The only offensive that seemed possible was either a bloody revolt or the vocal outpourings in the emerging black press of the masses. It was this lack of any acceptable alternative that gave rise to the wartime leadership of the black press.

Robert S. Abbott's Chicago *Defender* used the crisis of the homefront to elevate his paper to a position of leadership among the black people. Abbott, a Southerner by birth, moved North before the turn of the century. He spent a few years working as a printer and then in 1905 launched the *Defender*. For the next five years it remained just a small, inconspicuous black paper with Abbott serving as printer, editor, and newsboy. In 1910 Abbott hired J. Hockley Smiley, who in turn transformed the paper into a

69. Quoted in *ibid.*, 14 (August 1917): 164.

70. Jessie P. Guzman, ed., *Negro Year Book 1947: A Review of Events Affecting Negro Life, 1941–1946* (Tuskegee, Ala.: Tuskegee Institute, 1947), p. 307.

71. Scott, p. 411.

Hearst-style sheet with sensational headlines and articles. Often, if there was little that was sensational to report, Smiley would manufacture wild stories.[72] Once the war began, there was usually no need to create the news. An accurate reporting of events proved to be so sensational that the War Department became alarmed, and instead of offering solutions to the problems, moved to investigate the *Defender* for writing about them.

Coinciding with Abbott's new appeal to the masses, a large urbanized readership was coming into existence. The great migration of Southern blacks to the Northern urban areas got under way before the United States became an active participant in the war. A depression in the South in 1914–15, along with the destruction of much of the cotton crop by the boll weevil, resulted in a mobile black mass in search of work. After 1914 the flow of European immigration to the United States became limited, and Northern war industries looked southward for a new source of labor. The *Defender* began a campaign to encourage this movement North. Abbott saw the only hope for the race to be in the North. During this campaign, the *Defender* was able to raise its circulation to unprecedented heights for a black newspaper—over 200,000 by the end of the war.[73]

It is unlikely, as his biographer claims, that Abbott "single handed . . . set the great migration . . . in motion"[74] in 1917. The exodus from the South had begun in 1914 and by 1916 it had already "spread like wildfire."[75] Abbott looked to the South as an unexplored area for his new brand of militant journalism. The Chicago editor sent agents into the South to promote sales of the *Defender*, and by the end of the war at least two-thirds of the paper's sales were to be made in the South. If the *Defender* did not create the great migration, it nevertheless did all it could to encourage it. Its greatest achievement was certainly in easing the transition for those coming from the rural South to an unknown

72. Roi Ottley, *The Lonely Warrier: The Life and Times of Robert S. Abbott* (Chicago: Henry Regnery Co., 1955), pp. 72, 87, 156–57.
73. *Ibid.*, p. 139.
74. *Ibid.*, p. 160.
75. Franklin, p. 472.

urban North by publishing news of job opportunities, train schedules, and available living quarters.

The *Defender* was to become the most militant black paper during the war. Its attack upon discrimination against black troops was relentless, until pressure was brought to bear by the federal authorities. Abbott was unable to accept segregation even as a temporary necessity and refused to support DuBois's efforts to encourage blacks to volunteer for the segregated officers' camp. When the United States entered the war, the paper's cartoonist, Leslie Rogers, depicted black troops facing Germans as they were being shot in the back by white American troops. This almost resulted in a jail sentence for Abbott, but he was able to avoid arrest by buying liberty bonds and encouraging the purchase of bonds in his paper.[76] Despite his militant and outspoken objection to the mistreatment of black people, Abbott was, as his West Indian born foreign editor said, "almost pathetically loyal to the American system of government, clutching desperately to the hope that America might some day extend democratic practices . . . to her darker citizens."[77]

Other papers, less outspoken than the *Defender*, also refused to remain silent. All denounced the mistreatment of black troops, but none was able to offer any solution except to hope that white America would be shamed into putting a stop to such abuses. The Washington *Bee* summed up the desperation of the more moderate papers:

> The Negro is willing today to take up arms and defend the American President and defend the American flag; he stands ready to uphold the aims of the President; he stands ready to defend his country . . . against the cruel and unjust oppression. His mother, sister, brother, and children are being burned at the stake and yet the American flag is his emblem and which he stands ready to defend.[78]

76. Fleming, chap. 3, p. 12.
77. Metz T. P. Lochard, "Robert S. Abbott—Race Leader," *Phylon* 8 (Second Quarter 1947): 127.
78. Quoted in *The Crisis* 14 (May 1917): 23.

Due primarily to fortuitous circumstances, the war and the increasing sensationalism of the black press happened to coincide. This led some in the federal government to suspect a move by outside forces hoping to encourage disloyalty among the black population. George Creel, Chairman of the Committee on Public Information, suspected enemy agents of being the cause of the black press's complaints, and sent out "public information" circulars proclaiming that "they [German agents] have thousands of propagandists among the Negroes, exciting them with stories of impossible atrocities committed against the colored people."[79] It was this feeling among those in Washington that led to the call by E. J. Scott for a conference of black editors in the capital in June 1918.

When Scott went to Washington as an advisor on race matters for the War Department, it was primarily to do something about the poor morale of the black community. Shortly after taking up his duties he began to conduct a systematic program through his connections with Creel's Committee on Public Information and the black press to reassure blacks and to instill a higher level of enthusiasm among them for the war effort.[80] Scott himself followed Creel's line in saying that it was the fear of German provocateurs that prompted the conference call, but the discussions show that the meeting was an attempt to have the black press eliminate its discrimination articles and emphasize the more universal goals of the war.[81]

The resolutions adopted by the thirty-one editors attending the conference summarize the role of the wartime black press as those editors themselves saw it. First they reaffirmed that the struggle against the Kaiser and his allies was paramount; then they pledged the loyalty of all black people. Finally the editors proclaimed that "we wish to use our every endeavor to keep all of these 12,000,000 people at the highest pitch, not simply of passive loyalty, but of active and self sacrificing participation in the

79. Quoted in *ibid.*, 16 (May 1918): 24.
80. Scott, p. 65.
81. *Ibid.*, p. 347.

war."[82] Scott appeared satisfied with the results of the conference. After the war, he said of the black press that it had maintained the morale of blacks and stimulated their patriotism. "Our editors were conservative on all current questions, at no sacrifice of courage and absolute frankness in the upholding of principles."[83] Also at this conference was the Assistant Secretary of the Navy, Franklin D. Roosevelt. When he occupied the White House during World War II, and Cabinet members, War Department officials, and others were calling for a crackdown on the black press, he remained calm and took no action. Surely his experience from this conference must have influenced him.

Before the black editors met in Washington, the Justice Department had been in contact with DuBois about his militant editorials in *The Crisis*. In June 1918 the NAACP Board of Directors cautioned the volatile editor to show more optimism in his editorials. In that month's issue of *The Crisis*, a more encouraging editorial appeared, which signaled a shifting editorial emphasis. DuBois called on blacks to "have courage and determination," and said that "out of this war will rise too, an American Negro with the right to vote and the right to work and the right to live without insult."[84] In July, shortly after returning from the conference of editors in Washington, DuBois wrote his "Close Ranks" editorial calling for a moratorium on protest and asking that his race "forget our special grievances and close our ranks . . . with our own white fellow citizens. . . ."[85]

DuBois's call to "close ranks" was not well received by many of the major black papers. He had never been on friendly terms with the press and had in the past openly attacked many papers in his editorial writings. But aside from this opportunity for personal revenge, black papers could not forgo printing articles exposing discrimination. These papers were offering the only outlet for the frustrations of the blacks. To accept discrimination was

82. *The Crisis* 16 (August 1918): 163.
83. Scott, pp. 361–62.
84. *The Crisis* 16 (June 1918): 60.
85. *Ibid.*, 16 (July 1918): 11.

difficult enough, but to accept it without protest was asking too much. Besides, the black press was then building up a huge circulation by exposing the contradictions of the country's pronounced war aims abroad and its racial policies at home. It was apparent that, despite the black press's acceptance of the war against Germany, they would refuse to relent in the struggle at home.

The new approach taken by DuBois put him on the defensive for the rest of the war. (His position would return to plague him in World War II.) Word leaked out that in June DuBois had been approached by the War Department and offered a captaincy. Charges of selling out were immediately leveled at the editor. DuBois attempted to justify his negotiations with the War Department by saying that his acceptance of the offer would have meant a decrease in his income. He also claimed that the "Close Ranks" editorial had been written two weeks prior to the War Department's offer and was not part of any deal. Then, giving his own exegesis of the editorial, he said that its position was what "in practice the Negroes of America have already done during the war and have been advised to do by every responsible editor and leader."[86] "Was there a single leader," he asked, "who advised rebellion and disloyalty? Certainly not. Then *somebody* forgot his special grievance 'and fought for his' country. . . .*The Crisis* says, *first* your Country, *then* your Rights."[87]

DuBois was correct when he wrote that no editor had advised rebellion or draft evasion. But he was far from accurate when he stated that grievances had been forgotten when blacks fought to serve the country as equals. The modern black press was built upon the exposé of discrimination during the war. Overwhelmingly the black press was behind the war effort and for full black participation, but not many of the larger papers approved of DuBois's attempt to quiet protest on the domestic front. G. James Fleming, who did research on the black press for the Myrdal study, says that most papers were for "close ranks" during the

86. *Ibid.*, 16 (September 1918): 216.
87. *Ibid.*, p. 217.

war.[88] This can not be considered an accurate picture of the wartime press. For over a year, the press had caused Washington concern because it had refused to be silent. This was the reason for calling the editors to a Washington conference. For the duration of the war, only three months after the conference, DuBois had to defend his position from attacks from black newspapers.

The hope of gaining equality in America by fighting Germans proved to be illusory. Throughout the preparedness program, the war, and finally in the postwar period, white America made little effort to alter its racial practices. Instead of winning praise for service under almost insurmountable obstacles, blacks were forced to defend themselves against charges of rapine and of cowardice under fire in Europe. The press, in 1918, at the height of wartime hysteria, could not have opposed the war or it would have been suppressed. Its failing was that it showed too much faith in an American society that offered blacks so little evidence of reciprocity.

88. Fleming, chap. 3, p. 12.

2
The Black Press: Criticism and Recognition

The Black Press on the Eve of World War II

With the outbreak of World War II in Europe, the black press was firmly established as a mass medium and forum for expression of the black people. When Franklin D. Roosevelt entered office in the depths of the Depression, there were about 150 black papers that claimed an average weekly circulation of 600,000.[1] This figure is at best a close approximation, since before the war most black newspapers were not members of the Audit Bureau of Circulation (A.B.C.). The six papers that did belong to the A.B.C. had a total circulation of 132,000 per week. Of the five leading papers—the Chicago *Defender*, the Pittsburgh *Courier*, the Norfolk *Journal and Guide*, the New York *Amsterdam News* and the Baltimore *Afro-American*—only the last three were members of the A.B.C. With the circulation of the *Defender*[2] and the *Courier* added to the six papers belonging to the A.B.C., the total would have been about

1. P. B. Young, "The Extent and Quality of the Negro Press," *The Southern Workman* 62 (August 1933): 324.
2. Ottley, *The Lonely Warrier,* p. 298.

250,000 for eight of the 150 papers reporting circulation figures. Thus about 5 percent of the newspapers represented slightly over 40 percent of the total circulation of the black press.

When the Department of Commerce reports for 1940 were published, they showed that the black press had more than doubled its 1933 circulation to a total of 1,276,000.[3] This increase indicated a growing acceptance of the medium by the black population both as a vehicle to express the feelings of blacks toward American society and as a means of obtaining information not found in the white press or on the radio.

Of 143 black papers in 32 states and the District of Columbia during World War II, 86 were in the Southern and Border States, 18 were in the Northeast, 7 in the Far West, and 33 in the Midwest.[4] Eighteen papers, about 12 percent, at one time during the war period reached a circulation of over 20,000 a week. (This figure includes all editions of a particular newspaper as one paper. For example, *The Afro-American* had two editions in Baltimore, one National Edition, one edition printed in Washington, one in Philadelphia, and one in New Jersey.) Of these 18 papers, only 5 ever achieved a circulation of over 50,000 during the war. These five papers, the "Big Five," represented a total average weekly circulation in 1944 of 740,282. In 1943 the total average weekly circulation of all papers was reported at 1,643,311. Thus less than 3.5 percent of the black newspapers represented over 46 percent of the total circulation. The trend toward consolidation, evident after the war, had actually begun during the 1930s and 1940s.[5]

3. *National Negro Printer and Publisher* 2 (August 1940): 2. This figure is for the 155 papers, of a total of 210 that reported circulation.

4. *PEP: Negro Publisher, Editor and Printer* 1 (June 1944): 55–58.

5. U.S. Department of Commerce, Bureau of the Census, *Negro Newspapers and Periodicals in the United States: Negro Statistical Bulletin No. 1* (Washington, D.C.: August 26, 1946). These figures cannot be completely accurate. Not all papers belonged to the A.B.C., and many just made statements of circulation. There were also shifts in circulation figures at various times. These calculations are intended to show that the black press, although consisting at times of over 200 papers, meant in reality about 18 to 20 papers of importance, including the "Big Five" as the most important.

When one moves from quantitative analysis to a value analysis of the press, certain questions must be raised that can not be definitively resolved. Who read the black press during the war and how did the readers respond? Did the press reflect the thinking of the editors or aim to be an accurate reflection of the black community? Only tentative conclusions can be drawn about these questions, but they tend to show that the press, while aiming to play a leadership role vis-à-vis the black people, printed news and editorials that found favor with the majority of black people.

An important characteristic of the black press during the six-year period from 1939–1945 was the paucity of advertising it carried. Except for a few New York papers that did get more ads than the rest, most of the ads were for skin creams and lucky charms, ads many papers were reluctant, but forced to accept as a means of needed revenue.[6] Newspapers, therefore, were almost completely dependent upon circulation sales for revenue. This situation produced problems. A business group, dependent upon its reading public for revenue, was at the same time trying to mold public opinion in its role as a race leader.[7] Thus the press had to balance its business interests—with the dominant need here to please the public—with its efforts to shape public opinion in the struggle for racial justice.

The most effective test of acceptance that can be tabulated is circulation figures. A circulation of 1,265,000 in 1940 rose to 1,643,311 in 1943 and up to 1,808,060 by June 1945.[8] The black population in the 1940 Census reached just short of 13,000,000. Unlike the daily paper that is discarded at the end of each day,

6. New York *Amsterdam News,* June 24, 1944; P. L. Prattis, "Racial Segregation and Negro Journalism," *Phylon 8* (December 1947): 310.

7. Ted Poston, "The Negro Press," *The Reporter* 1 (December 6, 1949): 16; Pittsburgh *Courier,* March 4, 1944; St. Clair Drake and Horace Cayton, *Black Metropolis* (New York: Harcourt, Brace & Co., 1945), pp. 398, 401; Walter White, *A Man Called White* (New York: The Viking Press, 1948), p. 209: Ernest Johnson, "The Washington News Beat," Phylon 7 (Second Quarter 1946): 126, 129.

8. John H. Burma, "An Analysis of the Present Negro Press," *Social Forces* 26 (December 1947): 172.

the black weeklies tended to be held longer and passed around more.[9] The circulation figures cited above represent only a bare minimum of those reading the black papers. One observer has estimated that during the war from three-and-one-half to six million blacks read the papers each week, with one-third of the urban black families subscribing to a black paper each week. In their thorough study of the Chicago black belt, Cayton and Drake concluded that the Chicago *Defender*, with a circulation of 40,000 within the city on the eve of World War II, was read by at least 100,000 persons and discussed by nearly everyone. During the war, the Office of War Information (OWI), an agency very much aware of the black press, estimated that four million black people read black newspapers each week.[10]

Widespread coverage of the black soldier's role in the war effort was the most effective means of stimulating sales. Readers expressed their approval of the new emphasis being placed primarily on the activities and problems of the black servicemen, and were also in favor of the papers featuring more regularly syndicated columnists.[11] The black editors appeared to possess an intuitive awareness of just what their readers desired. During the war much of the crime news, a regularly emphasized feature of the peacetime press, was eliminated to make space for news of black troops and their role in the services. Columnists were appearing in the major papers in ever-increasing numbers, representing a range of interests and philosophies unequaled by most white papers. The Pittsburgh *Courier* carried up to ten columnists each week, and in late 1942 the *Defender* added five regular columnists to its editorial page.

Critics of the black press have usually concentrated on its sensationalism, gossip columns, and skin cream advertisements.

9. Consuelo C. Young, "A Study of Reader Attitudes toward the Negro Press" *Social Forces* 26 (December 1947) 4.

10. Burma, *Social Forces* 26: 172; Poston, *The Reporter* 1: 15; Drake and Cayton, *Black Metropolis*, p. 400.

11. Consuelo Young, *Social Forces* 26: 5; J. A. Baynton and A. Bell, "An Explorative Study of the Role of the Negro Press," *Journal of Negro Education* 20 (Winter 1951): 10–11.

Seldom do they mention the most vigorous feature of the black press—the editorial and columnists' page. As a forum for all shades of opinion, the black feature page was unequaled by most white journals during World War II. Columnists, ranging from the most conservative to the most militant, were placed side by side on the same page, and often a running disagreement took place between two or more of these writers, with the editor also taking sides on the issue in point. From the most cynical of writers, George S. Schuyler, one could then turn to E. J. Scott's column, which offered the reader a blind faith in the United States.

Unlike the white dailies, the black press featured columnists who were quite often not professional journalists by occupation. College professors such as Gordon B. Hancock and Arthur P. Davis, and race leaders such as W. E. B. DuBois and Walter White, Executive Secretary of the NAACP, appeared regularly. C. C. Spaulding and M. S. Stuart were leading business figures who often contributed columns. Labor leaders were given ample coverage: Layle Lane of the Workers Defense League, and active in the New York City Teachers Union, had a weekly column, as did Ferdinand Smith of the National Maritime Union. Politicians were not without their opportunity to be heard, either. Adam C. Powell, Jr., continued to write a column while he was a New York City Councilman and also wrote for a period after he went to Congress. Arthur P. Mitchell, while the lone black man in Congress, appeared occasionally in the columnist page of the *Journal and Guide*. If a black man had achieved any degree of success he was able to express his point of view in the pages of the black press.

This variety of views was not the only different thing about the feature page; there was also a large cross section of different races and nationalities represented. The *Courier* had two white columnists, an Indian, and a Chinese columnist. White columnists appeared regularly in the *Age*, the *Defender*, the California *Eagle*, the Savannah *Tribune*, and other black papers. These columnists usually specialized in a particular area. Komur Goshal wrote about India's problems and Lin Liang-mo about Chiang Kai-shek's struggle against the Japanese. Ted Le Berthen discussed race relations for a while and then shifted to promoting Catholicism in his columns. Rose Wilder Lane, appearing in many black papers, can be described only as a passionate advocate of the capitalistic system and an ardent foe of communism.

Besides each paper's regular columnists, the Associated Negro Press (ANP), the largest of the black news services, supplied both the larger and smaller papers with syndicated columnists. Kelly Miller, until his death in June 1940, E. J. Scott, and William Pickens were regular writers for the ANP. The columnists were important to the success of the papers, for the readers focused more attention on the feature page than on the other sections.[12] Of the Big Five, *The Afro-American* had the fewest columnists, but the *Afro* was usually considered the paper with the best news reporting.

The leading five papers had at least forty columnists who appeared with regular frequency during the war. Along with the regular columnists, columns appeared from time to time written by individuals well known in their respective fields. If a person of some prominence had something to present to the public, the usual procedure was to give him a column rather than send out a reporter to interview him. When A. Philip Randolph began his March on Washington Movement (MOWM), he was given space in most of the papers to present his program. The *Courier*, which was bitterly hostile to Randolph and his movement throughout the war, gave him column space to call for a march on the capital before many other black papers even gave the story news coverage.[13]

In his attack on the black columnists, published twelve years after the war, E. Franklin Frazier said that they were products of Southern segregated schools and severely restricted intellectually by this isolation within the segregated black world.[14] Moreover,

12. Consuelo Young, *Social Forces* 26: 3.
13. Pittsburgh *Courier*, January 25, 1941.
14. E. Franklin Frazier, *Black Bourgeoisie* (Glencoe, Ill.: The Free Press, 1957), p. 192.

he added, they revealed little knowledge of the economic and social forces operating in the modern world. But the columnists who wrote during World War II, with the exception of a few, most notably in the Southern press and the ANP, in no way fitted into this pattern.

The overwhelming majority of columnists during the war were the antithesis of the isolated Southern black. Men such as W. E. B. DuBois, Adam C. Powell, Jr., Carl Murphy, Earl Brown, Horace Cayton, Arthur P. Davis, and Roy Wilkins were educated in the leading universities throughout the North. Even F. D. Patterson and Gordon B. Hancock, whose written views closely fit that pattern described by Frazier, were holders of graduate degrees from Cornell and Harvard Universities respectively. Others were not touched by the Southern system because either they were not born in the United States or they spent many years abroad. Ferdinand Smith and J. A. Rogers were both natives of the West Indies, and the latter had spent many years in Europe gathering material for his historical works on the black race. Max Yergan also spent years in Europe and Africa doing field work for the YMCA before returning to the United States to teach at the City College of New York and write columns for the *People's Voice*.[15]

Of the forty writers regularly appearing in the Big Five, only a handful conformed to Frazier's characterization. Kelly Miller, E. J. Scott, M. S. Stuart, and F. D. Patterson are the few who come closest to conforming to Frazier's stereotype. But it should be noted that Patterson and Stuart both appeared as regular columnists for the *Courier*, the paper that critics often accused of being the most "radical" of the black press.[16]

15. Thomas Yenser, ed., *Who's Who in Colored America*, 1941–1944 (Brooklyn: Who's Who in Colored America Corp. 1944), pp. 479, 455, 454, 445, 227, 62, 169; G. James Fleming and Christian E. Burckel, eds., *Who's Who in Colored America* (Yonkers, N.Y.: Christian E. Burckel and Associates, 1950), pp. 95, 127, 423; Schomburg Verticale Files, alphabetical listings; Roy Hill, *Who's Who in the America Negro Press* (Dallas, Texas: Royal Publishing Co., 1960), pp. 23, 25–31, 35; Henry F. Winslow, "George Schuyler: Fainting Traveler," *Midwest Journal* 5 (Summer 1953): 24–44.

16. For example, see Westbrook Pegler, *New York World Telegram*, April 28, 1942.

As the war progressed, more and more black writers appeared in liberal white journals and the race question was beginning to be discussed more frequently in these publications by whites too.[17] A few of these journals even published editions devoted entirely to the black man in America. But generally, the black press during this period remained the black man's major forum for every ideological viewpoint, from conservatives such as F. D. Patterson, to the liberal Walter White, to socialist Layle Lane, and to Max Yergan, a member of the Communist party. It was true that the writers all presented a world view based on their experience as black men in America. But they were not restricted products of a Southern segregated system nor were they limited in outlook to just commenting on the American race problem.

Developments during the national defense period and the first years of United States involvement in the war imposed changes on the structure of the black press as an institution within the black world. When the defense program began, all the papers started to focus attention on a few basic policies of the government. Along with the defense program the government was initiating, a new rhetoric was emanating from administration officials, which black papers eagerly seized upon and applied to the black man within his own country. When the Four Freedoms and the Atlantic Charter were proclaimed by Roosevelt and Churchill, the black press demanded that they be applied to all oppressed people, not just to Nazi-occupied Europe. This included blacks in the United States and Africa, and the Indians seeking freedom from British imperial control.

Not only were external forces creating a unity of approach but internal factors brought into being a situation whereby a more unified theme could be assumed by all of the papers. The leadership within the black newspaper world was undergoing a change beginning in 1940. By 1943 most of the great black press lords had either died or retired from active participation in their papers.

17. *The New Republic* carried 10 articles on Negroes in 1940 and 63 in 1943, with 6 on the black press ; *The Nation* carried 18 articles in 1940 and 46 in 1943.

Robert L. Vann and Robert S. Abbott, the two giants of the modern black press, died in 1940, and within a few years Harry Smith, publisher of the Cleveland *Gazette,* and Fred Moore, of the New York *Age,* passed away. P. B. Young, Sr., of the *Journal and Guide,* left active newspaper work when appointed to the President's Committee on Fair Employment Practices, and E. Washington Rhodes, of the Philadelphia *Tribune,* relinquished his duties as editor in the spring of 1942. The *Amsterdam News* had been purchased in 1936 by C. V. Powell, a leading business figure, to be used not as a forum for racial progress, but to help promote the business interests of the Powell-Savory Corporation.[18]

Up until the 1940s, each black paper had been associated with a leading black individual. *The Crisis* and the Boston *Guardian* during the first quarter of the twentieth century had always brought to mind DuBois and Trotter. The *Courier* and *Defender* meant Vann and Abbott to their readers. Each issue of the Cleveland *Gazette* reprinted the Illinois Riot Act, which its publisher Harry Smith had introduced while serving in the state legislature. Many papers were used as vehicles to further the ambitions of their publishers. Vann's was one of the first big papers to switch to Franklin D. Roosevelt. After backing him in 1932, Vann received a position in the Justice Department as a reward, becoming one of the early members of the Black Cabinet. Abbott's prestige was so high during World War I that it earned him a position on the Chicago Race Commission established to investigate the Chicago riots of 1919.

Between World War I and World War II there was little unity of approach within the black press, except that each exposed discrimination directed against the black race. Each paper went the way of its individual publisher. Abbott's *Defender* started the

18. *National Negro Printer and Publisher* 3 (March 1942): 8; "The Youngs of Norfolk," *Headlines and Pictures* 2 (January 1946): 19; Thelma Berlack-Boozer, "*Amsterdam News:* Harlem's Largest Weekly," *The Crisis* 45 (April 1938): 105; James H. Brewer, "Robert Lee Vann, Democrat or Republican: An Exponent of Loose Leaf Politics," *The Negro History Bulletin* 21 (February 1958): 102; Cleveland *Gazette,* December 13, 1941.

program to help convince blacks in the South that they should emigrate North during World War I. At the same time that many papers were attacking racism in the United States, DuBois, who had been in the forefront of this attack, did an abrupt about-face and called for a moratorium on protest for the rest of the war—to the dismay of many of the other black papers.

By 1940 the papers were beginning to act in a more singular fashion on the central issues. During the war years certain issues were approached in as unified a manner as could be expected of any of the mass media. Few voices preached for a moratorium on protest. The issue of segregation was handled according to regional demands, but all made clear they were dissatisfied with it. Black papers did not generally press for an immediate end to segregation, but a beginning was called for in the movement toward integration.[19] The one general exception to this new-found unity was during the 1944 national elections, when the press divided along political lines.

The signal for this solidarity was the organization of the National Negro Publishing Association (NNPA). For three days in February 1940, twenty-eight publishers and executives representing twenty-one papers met in Chicago to form the NNPA and elected John Sengstacke, nephew of Robert Abbott, president of the association.[20] The primary purpose of the formation of the NNPA was to deal with the general problems of publishing black papers, and particularly with the problem of obtaining national advertising for the papers. But at the annual meetings held during the war, the publishers formulated policies to be followed by the press during the war crisis. Each meeting reiterated the black press's full support of the war policies of F.D.R. and loyalty to the United States.[21]

By World War II the black press had built up its position as one of the leading black industries, and had a following perhaps

19. At the December 8, 1941, meeting of the black editors and Army officials, Claude A. Barnett, director of the ANP asked the Army to experiment with one volunteer integrated unit.

20. *National Negro Printer and Publisher* 1 (March 1940): 8.

21. Chicago *Defender,* June 13, 1942; California *Eagle,* June 11, 1942; *The Afro-American,* June 13, 1942.

second only to the black church. Gunnar Myrdal has characterized the press during this period as "the greatest single power in the Negro race." [22] This vast following was due to the fact that the press was in many cases one of the few, if not the only, outlets for black emotions in a milieu of racial discrimination and accommodating leadership. The press often served "as a safety-valve for the boiling Negro protest," [23] and increasingly functioned in this capacity as the ideological crusade against Nazi racial theory was conducted by a country all too willing to ignore its own racist convictions.

The protest within the black press had always been directed toward all forms of discrimination and acts of violence against black individuals. Often the newspapers, especially in the North, aimed their attacks at the South, with such persons as Theodore Bilbo, John Rankin, and Eugene Talmadge being especially frequent targets. Although the federal government always had its share of attention, the focus of the press centered increasingly on the national administration in 1940 with the beginning of wartime preparations. Now the press began to emphasize more and more the federal government's relation to Jim Crow in America. Many black writers were convinced that if a war broke out, the black man's position would be frozen in the status quo, and they sought to achieve certain aims vis-à-vis the military role of blacks before a war started.

The rhetoric of the Allied leaders—the proclamation of the Four Freedoms, the Atlantic Charter, and the attacks on the Nazi race theories—was adopted by the black press and applied to the condition of blacks within the democracies. Here in the United States, the emphasis was not just to end discrimination, but also to achieve freedom. The press began a "Double V" program calling for victory at home as well as abroad. Most papers did not believe full black equality would come during the war or in the immediate postwar years; they still saw a long struggle ahead.

22. Gunner Myrdal, *An American Dilemma,* 1st paperback ed. (New York: McGraw-Hill, 1964), 2: 924.
23. *Ibid.,* 2: 910.

The call for black freedom here was to embarrass the white liberals into recognizing the paradox of fighting racism abroad while it remained secure at home, and was also aimed at building up the morale of the black people. Before these results were achieved, the black press did receive attention, but from unexpected quarters. The Southern white liberals were, unlike their Northern counterparts, very much aware of the black press. These people began to fear the reaction of the black people to the "Double V" programs of the black press. It was this segment, not the black press, that was to raise the specter of a black revolution.

The Black Press under Attack

There is little doubt that the black press hoped at least to make inroads during the war against the restrictions operating against them, but it was never entirely on the offensive. The growing military structure spread federally sanctioned Jim Crow throughout the North and West, areas long held "free" of the stigma.[24] Also, when "Dr. New Deal" became "Dr. Win-the-War," he gathered Southern support by dropping many of the New Deal agencies that were considered of great benefit to the blacks. The war against fascism abroad appeared as if it would be won only by increasing the power of the fascist elements at home.

Also at this time, many of the old mainstays of the Black Cabinet began dropping out of government service, and liberal white Southerners such as Jonathan Daniels were drafted by F.D.R. as "racial advisers."[25] The black press viewed this as the final capitulation of the administration to the Southern forces, and pointed out that the liberal white Southerner left much to be desired.

The reaction of the black press to the increasing signs of discrimination and growing tensions in the black community caused

24. Pittsburgh *Courier,* May 30, 1942.
25. W. E. B. DuBois, "A Chronicle of Race Relations," *Phylon* 3 (Second Quarter 1942): 217.

many whites to believe that the black press had launched an all-out attack against the Southern caste system and was taking advantage of the emergency situation to pressure F.D.R. into implementing a racial revolution. Since many of the attacks of the press were aimed at the liberal white Southerners, and since they constituted most of that small group of whites familiar with the black press, they responded by denouncing the press as inflammatory, irresponsible, and radical. This attack was picked up by conservatives in the South and North, along with some white Northern liberals and moderate blacks who became alarmed that the black press was destroying the morale of the race and its enthusiasm for the war. At the same time, the federal government began to take an interest in the black press.[26]

The first attack on the black press by a Southern white was not noticed by many of the Northern black papers. Only the *Journal and Guide* and *The Crisis* commented on the Richmond *Times-Dispatch* editorial "The Negroes and the War," written by editor Virginius Dabney on April 26, 1942. Dabney was a liberal Southern white, long considered by many blacks both North and South as a friend in good standing. Dabney had become alarmed about the continuing incidents taking place in Southern cities adjacent to Army posts housing black troops. He correctly characterized these incidents as "race riots" and pinpointed the conflict as between black troops and white military and civilian police (something the black press continuously pointed out). Then he wrote that the "prevailing assumption is that these bloody encounters" were instigated primarily by such publications as *The Crisis,* the *Courier,* the *Amsterdam News* and the NAACP.[27] Dabney appeared to be warning the press that certain people—but not he—were growing alarmed at the outpourings from the black press. He was making a plea to the Southern blacks not to push too fast and to abjure the tactics of the radicals from the North.

26. *Journal and Guide,* April 25, 1942; May 23, 1942; California *Eagle* May 28, 1942.
27. Quoted in *The Crisis* 49 (June 1942): 183; see also the *Journal and Guide,* May 9, 1942.

He pointed out the dangers of polarizing the extremes—the Northern black agitators and the Southern white Negrophobes.[28]

This warning was generally unnoticed or ignored in the Northern black press, but papers in the South reacted. In an editorial printed before the Richmond *Times-Dispatch* editorial by Dabney, the *Journal and Guide* scoffed at reports of concern within the government over the black press:

> We are no bolder now in our demands . . . than we were prior to the first world war, and during the two decades which elapsed between 1918 and 1939. . . . We are on the spot. Our people cry out in anguish: This is no time to stick to a middle of the road policy; help us get some of the blessings of Democracy here at home first before you jump on the free the other peoples' bandwagon.[29]

In less than three months after this editorial appeared, the *Journal and Guide* adopted a more cautious position. After the attacks on the black press by Dabney, Westbrook Pegler, Mark Ethridge, and others, the *Journal and Guide* blamed "some organizations and a few of our newspapers in the metropolitan centers" for increasing tensions. Even so, this criticism was not directed against the demands made by these newspapers, but the way in which it was done. The militants' approach, the paper's editor believed, was "creating the impressions that they are engaged in an all-out effort to integrate Negroes into the intimate social life of the American white people. . . ." [30] Clearly the *Journal and Guide* did not believe that the Northern black press was pushing for any immediate end to segregation in the South.

The *Journal and Guide,* as well as other Southern black papers, had enjoyed a long-standing friendly relationship with Dabney and other white liberals in the South. Together they had worked to make the system of separate but equal more equitable to blacks. The black press in the South had no desire to jeopardize this

28. *Journal and Guide,* August 15, 1942.
29. *Ibid.,* April 25, 1942.
30. *Ibid.,* July 4, 1942.

association. P. B. Young, Sr., editor of the *Journal and Guide,* took the lead in calling for the Durham Conference—a meeting of a group of leading Southern blacks—to discuss the increasing tensions, and this led eventually to the formation of the Southern Regional Council. The Savannah *Tribune,* apparently sensing the pressures, discontinued after April 1942 its policy of reprinting militant editorials from the Northern papers such as the *Defender, Amsterdam News,* and New York *Age.* If the white South was successful in intimidating the Southern black press, it was only to cause further problems for the white liberals in the area.

What the Southern white liberals seemed to fear most was that Southern blacks, under heavy barrage from the Northern black press, would assume a more militant position.[31] Ralph McGill, publisher of the Atlanta *Constitution* and a leading white liberal, expressed his concern about this. Placing the blame squarely on the white South, he said that Southern whites made it impossible for the Southern black papers "to enjoy the constitutional guarantee of freedom of the press." [32] This allowed the radical press from the North to dominate the Southern black readership. McGill realized that some outlet was in fact essential for the suppressed emotions of the black people. He wanted a controlled militancy of the Southern black press in order to undercut the sales of the more militant Northern papers in the area.

In the North, the initial attack against the black press came from unexpected quarters. Two days after Dabney opened up the question of the black press in the *Times-Dispatch,* Westbrook Pegler blasted the black papers.[33] Pegler's attack was unexpected, since he had not been one to concern himself with black people in the past. Admittedly Pegler was not a regular follower of the black press. He made it clear that he had familiarized himself with the subject by picking up copies of two papers. Reference to the fact that they were "standard reading among the colored men in the

31. James Boyd, "Strategy for Negroes." *The Nation* 156 (June 26, 1943): 884.

32. Quoted in the Savannah *Tribune,* February 4, 1943.

33. *New York World Telegram,* April 28, 1942.

armed forces" was parallel to Dabney's editorial placing blame on these papers for all the problems of black soldiers stationed in the South. Pegler was probably just looking for material for a few columns, but he opened a Pandora's box and for the next year the black press became a heated subject of controversy both in the North and in the South.

Pegler's critique of the black press fell into two sections. First he attacked the sensationalism of its headlines, the gossip columns, and the skin cream and magic charm ads. Next he condemned the editorials and the columnists. If the purpose was to smear the press, this was an easy way to do it. Then he compared the papers he had read (the *Defender* and the *Courier*), which "agitate violently," to Father Coughlin's weekly paper. Pegler was paradoxically trying to smear what was possibly one of the strongest anti-fascist groups in the country by associating it with the right-wing Detroit priest. His attack on the "mediocrity" of the writers was hardly fair since even Pegler could have found from the large cross section of columnists in these papers some whose views were similar to his own. Unfortunately, most white people did not read the black press; indeed, they were unaware that it even existed.[34] If their only contact with it was through Pegler's article, the damage could be great.

The response to Pegler from the black press was not unexpected and he answered it a few months later with another article, defending the white press as being "scrupulously fair and sympathetic" to the black population. "Our white press is friendly to the Negro," said Pegler.[35] The use of this term actually substantiated the long-time complaint of black leaders that the daily press was a "white" press. Later Pegler unexpectedly shifted his position when he wrote about the dirty deal the black soldier was getting and said that the "spiritual violence" he had suffered from the black press had opened his eyes to the "awful conditions" of those "fellow Americans." He added:

34. Myrdal 2: 908; Frank Mott's standard text on *American Journalism* published in 1941 does not even mention a black press.
35. *New York World Telegram*, June 17, 1942.

> If I were a Negro I would live in constant fury. . . . I would not be a sub-American, a sub-human being, and in docile patience forever yield my rightful aspiration to be a man.[36]

No black paper would have put it differently. However, Pegler had not been truly converted. After the outbreak of riots in the North in 1943, he placed responsibility for the bloodshed on the black press.

Many black writers believed that the Dabney and Pegler articles were just the opening guns of an all-out attack on them. Marjorie McKenzie spoke of the "question in government councils of how Negro morale for the war is to be improved." [37] She was aware of the low morale among the black population, and feared that the black press could be singled out as the cause, rather than the reflection of the situation. Joel A. Rogers said that it was true, as Pegler had claimed, that the black press was exploiting the war effort. But, he said, its technique was to do so in a positive manner by working "to integrate the Negro into the war effort." Then he added that the black press "softens agitation," and "it is an alloy in racial discontent, because unlike Pegler it records the good as well as the bad in race relations." [38]

Also writing in the *Courier,* George S. Schuyler, one of the most caustic critics of United States racial patterns, worried about the possibility of a government clamp-down on the press. Speaking obviously to whites, he warned that "Negro leaders and editors cautioned their people to use organized protest and . . . the courts. . . . Who will do this if these spokesmen are squelched?" [39] Later Schuyler added, "I can tell these 'gentlemen' that if it were not for the Negro newspapers and Negro leadership generally, there would be more interracial violence and bloodshed. . . . The masses of Negroes are far more ready to fight and die than their leaders and spokesmen." Most black newsmen openly acknowledged this "safety valve" function of the black press.

36. *Ibid.,* July 16, 1942.
37. Marjorie McKenzie, Pittsburgh *Courier,* May 9, 1942.
38. J. A. Rogers, Pittsburgh *Courier,* May 16, 1942.
39. George S. Schuyler, Pittsburgh *Courier,* May 23, 1942; June 27, 1942.

William O. Walker, publisher of the Cleveland *Call and Post* and at this time president of the NNPA, warned the black press to be alert and to prepare for the worst. He reported that "the F.B.I. has frightened all the Negro editors of the Southland." [40] Most of the editors were concerned and took the opportunity once again to make clear their support for the war aims of the administration. Often, though, the greatest reaction to the possible censorship of the black press was one of surprise, since the thrust of the "Double V" effort aimed at getting blacks into all phases of the war program. "The Negro has no desire whatever to hinder the war effort," and on the contrary had offered himself to the Army, Navy, and all branches and was turned down or discriminated against. "As for the Negro press, its position is clear if it is to justify its existence." [41] Walter White challenged those attacking the press to show where it had ever been disloyal or made statements "that the Japanese were provoked into this war." He also pointed out that the black press had never claimed it was not a black man's war and added that "that colored press has urged loyal support for the war effort." [42]

As Pegler was entering the battle and then retreating, Mark Ethridge, Southern white liberal and publisher of the *Courier Journal* and the Louisville *Times* cast his eye on the black press. At this time, Ethridge was a member of the Fair Employment Practices Committee (FEPC), which was holding its first hearing in the South. He was aware of the white South's attitude toward the Committee and sought to allay its fears by focusing attention on the black press as the culprit rather than the FEPC. In a long introductory speech before the hearing proceeded, Ethridge assured his Southern audience that the Committee would not alter the South's caste system. Like his counterparts in the liberal South, Dabney and McGill, he focused attention on the press. "Those Negro newspaper editors who demand 'all or nothing . . .' are

40. Quoted in Chicago *Defender,* May 30, 1942.
41. Julius J. Adams, New York *Amsterdam News,* July 4, 1942.
42. Reprint of Walter White letter to *World Telegram* in *The Afro-American,* May 9, 1942.

playing into the hands of the white demagogues."[43] Once again, the liberal whites in the South feared that an all-out attack on the segregation system was being launched by Northern black leaders. The specter of Southern demagogues was more than likely raised to help keep the Southern blacks in line. This speech was intended for Southern ears, but the black press had always taken a keen interest in the FEPC hearings,[44] and Ethridge's comments were broadcast through the North.

Black papers in the South did not attack Ethridge, and the *Journal and Guide* actually defended him, commenting that "Mr. Ethridge . . . has been and we believe still is, a friend of the Negro. . . ."[45] The editor also suggested that Ethridge might have been speaking for the President at Birmingham. Even in the North his speech was not attacked by all. The *Amsterdam News* editorialized that Ethridge was regarded as a liberal of the "New South," and had been of great help in easing tensions in the South.[46] But generally, Ethridge was excoriated by the Northern black press.[47]

By the end of 1942 the attack on the black press became national in scope. Articles appeared in the *Virginia Quarterly Review, The Atlantic Monthly,* and the *Saturday Review of Literature* which took the press to task. The *Saturday Review* article was quickly reprinted in the *Reader's Digest* in January 1943, a magazine with one of the largest national circulations in the country. The entire nation was now made aware of the existence of a militant black press.

The articles appearing in the *Virginia Quarterly Review* and *The Atlantic Monthly* were continuations of warnings and attacks carried on previously by two leading liberal Southern newspapermen. Both Virginius Dabney and John Temple Graves of the

43. Committee on Fair Employment Practice, "Seventh Hearing," Birmingham, Ala., June 18, 1942 (Typescript, Schomburg Collection), p. 18. Hereafter cited as FEPC "Seventh Hearing," Birmingham.

44. Louis Ruchames, *Race, Jobs and Politics: The Story of FEPC* (New York: Columbia University Press, 1953), p. 24.

45. *Journal and Guide,* July 4, 1942.

46. New York *Amsterdam News,* July 18, 1942.

47. Chicago *Defender,* July 25, 1942; August 1, 1942.

Birmingham Age Herald had been concerned about the increasing vocal militancy of the black population for months. Both had criticized Northern blacks and the Northern black press in their local newspapers. Now the positions of these men were given a national airing. Neither one was aimed primarily at the black press, but as always the implications were clear: "Northern radicals" had to the South become synonymous with the NAACP and the black press.

No new approach was offered. Northern agitators were giving impetus to Southern negrophobes, Mrs. Eleanor Roosevelt and Northern black leaders were giving Southerners such as Eugene Talmadge an opportunity to open a new racist attack and stir up the mass of white people, and so on.[48] Graves clearly implicated the black press when he charged that "while their country is making supreme war abroad . . . they have invited their followers to think in terms of a Double V-for-Victory. . . ."[49] The South, he said, "as sure as science . . . [is] unwavering in . . . [its] determination not to have race segregation abolished."[50] Southern liberals understood this situation and to keep peace were trying to hold back the extremists of both sides. Actually, the only alternative left open to blacks was the status quo.

Graves did admit that blacks were in need of some sort of federal aid, and that their position had been deteriorating since the initial stage of the National Defense program. Southern liberals, he said, were pleased with the progress of the FEPC. (At this time, the FEPC was not even functioning. The President had transferred it to the War Manpower Commission in July 1942 and it had done almost nothing since that time.) But then, as the black leadership and press showed a tendency to use the war "for breaking down the whole structure of Southern race relations," the liberal South was forced on the defensive.[51] Graves made a concerted effort to separate the Northern and Southern black leaders, saying that the

48. John Temple Graves, "The Southern Negro and the War Crisis," "*The Virginia Quarterly Review* 18 (Autumn 1942): 500.
49. *Ibid.*, p. 501.
50. *Ibid.*, p. 504.
51. *Ibid.*, p. 509.

latter faced a dilemma. This dilemma was at the heart of the fear among Southern liberals—that is, would the Southern black leaders end their alliance with liberal whites and come under the sway of the militant Northern black voices. Graves believed that any move of this sort would be the beginning of an all-out assault on segregation. As far as he was concerned, "segregation in the South is not going to be eliminated. That is a fact to be faced, but it does not preclude a constant improvement on the Negro's side of Jim Crow." [52]

Dabney was more apocalyptic in his view of the race problem. For months he had been surveying the scene with alarm. Although he was aware of the problem facing the black press in the midst of the wartime rhetoric and saw racial tension a natural by-product, Dabney could offer no solution for the problem facing the rising expectations of blacks other than having white papers use "Mr." and "Mrs." when referring to black people, and capitalizing the word "Negro." [53] In the summer of 1942 Dabney began talking of the "explosion" about to take place due to the black press, which was "demanding a complete and immediate revolution in race relations in America." [54] At this time he left the black leaders with a clear warning that if this continued, the white liberal friend of the black man could not be responsible for the consequences.

By the end of 1942 Dabney was ready to announce to all that the expected explosion was imminent. In a survey written for *The Atlantic Monthly,* Dabney launched an all-out attack on the black press, and once again the explosion was about to be triggered due to the "extremist Negro leaders and Negro Newspapers . . . [who were] demanding an overnight revolution in race relations." "The radical element of the Negro press both North and South, is stirring up interracial hate" to an alarming extent.[55] Dabney, while

52. *Ibid.,* p. 516.
53. Virginius Dabney, "Newspapers and the Negro," *The Quill* 31 (November-December 1943): 3, 14.
54. Virginius Dabney, "Press and Morale," *Saturday Review of Literature* 25 (July 4, 1942): 25.
55. Virginius Dabney, "Nearer and Nearer the Precipice," *The Atlantic Monthly* 171 (January 1943): 94, 96.

constantly expressing fears of racial violence, was in fact printing an alarmist and inflammatory article that could only add to the growing tensions.

Dabney claimed that if whites were to read the black press, riots would break out.[56] But it was apparent that if he believed this, he would not spend so much of his time publicizing the black press on the local and national level. While attacking the "wild statements" of the black papers, he himself wrote of rumors spreading in the South that "all the ice picks and switch blades . . . were being bought up by Negroes, with a view to a general massacre of whites. . . ."[57] In trying to show the irresponsibility of the press, he pointed to the *Courier's* upbraiding of A. Philip Randolph for calling off the March on Washington. Dabney, an avid reader of the black press, could not have been unaware that the *Courier* was extremely hostile to Randolph and the MOWM and only attacked Randolph after the march was canceled to show that he had never really been sincere or had had a movement. In closing, Dabney observed that segregation imposed an obligation on whites to make "absolutely equal facilities for the two races" and called for the "disturbing elements" on both sides of the color line to be "muzzled for the duration."[58]

Just as the essence of the black press was its function of protesting segregation, the Southern white liberal based his position on making segregation work in an equitable manner. He too was caught in the middle, needing a following of moderate blacks willing to work within the dual system. If these Southern black leaders listened to the more vocal elements of the North, some liberals in the South feared that their own position would become untenable. The warnings from these quarters were directed mostly to the moderate black leaders in the South rather than to the militant leaders from the North. The Durham Conference and the Richmond Conference seemed to indicate that white and black

56. *Ibid.*, p. 91.
57. *Ibid.*, p. 94.
58. *Ibid.*, p. 100.

moderates in the South had begun to unite to keep the black capital in the South.[59]

What Dabney must have known was that the black press, both Northern and Southern, was just as fearful of riots and violence as he was. But the papers knew what the masses were thinking and realized that the situation was explosive. The Northern black press sought to supply an outlet for this frustration by the use of militant protest, which would act as a catharsis. Layle Lane, in taking exception to Dabney, explained this function quite clearly. "What he [Dabney] doesn't seem to recognize is that there is more dynamite in trying to restrain these tensions than in directing them into constructive channels." [60]

The final blast against the press came from the most unexpected quarters—a Northern black man in the employ of a Northern white liberal organization, the Council For Democracy (CFD). The CFD was organized in 1940 at the instigation of Time-Life publisher Henry Luce, who contributed the initial funds to establish the group.[61] Its purpose was to stimulate enthusiasm among the people for F.D.R.'s defense buildup. C. D. Jackson of the Time-Life publications took a leave of absence to organize the Council. He became its first president and Raymond Gram Swing was appointed Chairman of the Board. Just before the attack on Pearl Harbor, Jackson returned to his Time-Life duties and Ernest Angell, a Wall Street lawyer, became president of the Council. The Council was well represented by international business concerns such as United Fruit Company, Bache and Company, Lehman Corporation, General Electric, General Foods, and others. Also represented were many Southern liberals such as Virginius

59. Gordon B. Hancock, educator, and columnist for the *Journal and Guide* along with the Guide's publisher P. B. Young, played a leading role in organizing the Durham Conference of Southern black leaders which was the first step toward the organization of the Southern Regional Council. Hancock, a conservative, also feared the militant action of blacks in the North and said: "It makes a world of difference . . . whether the capital of the Negro race is in New York or in Atlanta." See *New York Times*, December 5, 1943.

60. Layle Lane, New York *Age*, February 6, 1943.

61. Interview with Ernest Angell, October 1, 1969.

Dabney and Herbert Agar of the Louisville *Courier-Journal.* On the original Board of Directors representing over one hundred people, only one black man, A. Philip Randolph, was present.[62] (By 1941 Randolph had become a strong advocate of all-out aid to Great Britain.) By 1943 Walter White was also affiliated with the Council.

The CFD continued to function after Pearl Harbor in order to promote unity and morale among the people. It sponsored rallies, radio broadcasts, and pamphlets calling for support of F.D.R.'s war aims.[63] Before December 7, 1941, the CFD was one of the few white groups to turn its attention to the black man's role in the defense program. In one pamphlet, *The Negro and Defense,* it portrayed the problems facing the black community, but took no position for better treatment of the race. When it appeared, the CFD did not show any alarm at the course the black press and its leaders had chosen to gain equality in the defense program. At the time the pamphlet was circulated, the press was much more violent in its denunciation of discrimination than it was after the outbreak of war. The pamphlet affirmed that blacks were not happy with the Jim Crow Army since it implied an "assertion of group inferiority." [64] But it stated that those most opposed to the situation realized that segregation had to be accepted for the present, and only fought to keep the black units from being degraded to a menial status. This was a cogent analysis of the position of the black press in 1941. In 1942 the position of the press was the same; however, the CFD no longer perceived it in the same manner.

In December 1942 the *Saturday Review* printed an article by Warren H. Brown, Director of Negro Relations for the CFD, entitled "A Negro Looks at the Negro Press." The following month, the *Reader's Digest* reprinted the article under the title "A Negro Warns the Negro Press." This was the most devastating of all

62. "Memorandum to the Board of Directors of the Council for Democracy," November 15, 1940. New York Public Library.

63. Council for Democracy, *Brief Statement of Aims and Activities,* pp. 1–2.

64. Council for Democracy, *The Negro and Defense: A Test of Democracy,* p. 25.

the attacks on the press and black writers felt they had been betrayed by a black "quisling." Brown portrayed himself as a black man who represented and knew what other black people wanted. He implied that most blacks were satisfied with the progress being made in race relations and alleged that the incendiary black press was capable of embittering the black masses.[65] Brown said that these newspapers "are Negro first and American second," and they used incidents to breed ill will among the races.[66] Brown further implied that blacks who violated the racial rules of the South were at fault for any harm that befell them. Finally, he predicted racial clashes and told of some already taking place, which were not "wholly due to white prejudice. They are also due to an irresponsible Negro leadership. . . ."[67] Brown's attack was hardly new, but the source of the attack was.

Brown was one of the first Ph.D.'s to come out of the New School for Social Research, his dissertation being on "The Negro Press and Social Change, 1860–1880." Before obtaining his degree he worked with the New York City Department of Public Welfare and was affiliated with the *Amsterdam News* as an assistant editor. He had also been employed by the Chicago *Defender* as a reporter for a short period. There is some indication that his relations with the black press had not been so good as they could have been. He was dismissed from the *Defender* and he apparently had had trouble selling articles to the New York City black press.[68]

Why the article was written is difficult to determine. The CFD was aware of the continuing attacks on the black press, especially since its Board of Directors consisted of liberal Southerners who had been engaged in the attacks on the press. The CFD believed its function was to unify the country; hence it could have mis-

65. Warren H. Brown, "A Negro Looks at the Negro Press," *Saturday Review of Literature* 25 (December 19, 1942): 5.
66. *Ibid.*
67. *Ibid.*, p. 6
68. *The Afro-American*, June 7, 1941 ; New York *Amsterdam News*, December 26, 1942; Harry McAlpin, Chicago *Defender*, January 16, 1943.

understood the situation and allowed Brown to write the article in hope of putting a damper on the black press.

There is a possibility that the administration was indirectly involved. The CFD was a strong supporter of F.D.R.'s policies before the war and continued backing him after Pearl Harbor. Walter White, also an ardent supporter of F.D.R., was by this time associated with the CFD. Throughout 1942 there was pressure on F.D.R. to indict some black editors for sedition in order to curb the entire press,[69] but he had refused to take such drastic action. White was aware of this and had tried to warn the press during the early part of the year.[70] Later in the year, before the Brown article appeared, F.D.R. had discussed with White the possibility of quieting the black press.[71] Finally, Eleanor Roosevelt praised the Brown article in her *New York World Telegram* column on January 6, 1943, as being a fair and constructive piece of writing.[72]

About the only certainty in the entire affair is that Brown's article was written entirely by himself, and not carefully screened by any member of the Council.[73] Why the attack was so severe is not difficult to understand, in light of Brown's previous relations with the black press and his own personality. Brown was ambitious, and placed great importance on acquiring the title of Director of Negro Relations in the CFD. There was no provision for such a title, but after working for the Council for a while, Brown badgered Angell to create the position and place him in it.[74] As the *Amsterdam News* observed, "the biggest enemy the Negro has is the strange character who is always hanging around white people who have organizations trying to get them to organize a Negro division; a colored section; a black this, a black that." [75]

69. Richard M. Dalfiume, *Desegregation in the U.S. Armed Forces: Fighting on Two Fronts, 1939–1953* (Columbia, Mo.: University of Missouri Press, 1969), p. 124.
70. California *Eagle,* May 28, 1942.
71. White, p. 207.
72. Her remarks are quoted in New York *Age,* January 23, 1943.
73. Interview with Ernest Angell, October 1, 1969.
74. *Ibid.*
75. New York *Amsterdam News,* December 26, 1942.

The reaction from the black press was devastating. Brown was ruined as far as his career in the civil rights movement was concerned. Except for the Savannah *Tribune* and a columnist here and there, he was denounced as a quisling, a traitor, and an Uncle Tom. The *Defender* started a Bandannas for Brown club. Others compared him to John Rankin.[76] Brown was not unaffected personally by this response. He avoided interviews as much as possible, and when finally cornered, he refused to give out much information, except that he was very contrite and would try to atone for his past blunder.[77]

The black press, aware of its readers' approval, in no way softened its tone as a result of these attacks. Black papers were never really so militant as charged, and many editors believed that the press was much calmer than black readers would like it to be. When Northern white editors awoke to the existence of a black press and began to read the editorials and columns after the storm had broken, they were amazed to note the moderation of the writers. If the black publishers needed any additional encouragement, they got it in February 1943 when the *Negro Digest*'s poll queried its readers about how they felt concerning the black press. The response was overwhelmingly in favor of a continuation of the press's militant policy.[78] Actually, many of those questioned were of the opinion that the black press had toned down the temper of its writings because of fear of censorship.

Acceptance

Reaction to the attacks from the black press was, as expected, loud and defensive. But support for the press began to come from other quarters. Now the liberal white press began to defend the black press and became more aware of the paradox of a demo-

76. Savannah *Tribune,* January 24, 1943 ; J. A. Rogers, Pittsburgh *Courier,* January 2, 1943 ; Arthur P. Davis, *Journal and Guide,* January 2, 1943.

77. New York *Age,* January 30, 1943 ; February 6, 1943.

78. "Negro Digest Poll," *Negro Digest* 1 (February 1943): 54.

cratic America continuing its racial proscriptions while fighting Hitler. The *New Republic,* for the first time since the war began, carried articles on the black press—six in 1943 alone. Editor Thomas Sancton, a white liberal born in the South, gave the most reasoned defense of the black press. He noted the many positive features of the press and saw that one of the great benefits was that it was trying desperately to stimulate the morale of black people. Sancton was one of the few whites to observe this.[79] He was also aware that whites misunderstood the style of the black press. "When a white man first reads a Negro newspaper," he commented, "it is like getting hit with a bucket of cold water in the face." [80] He praised the quality of the editorials and columns and correctly observed that, unlike the more subtle white columns, the black ones were more open and frank—thus the shock to white sensibilities.

Sancton was aware of the conservative aspects of the black press, which all white critics ignored. He showed that papers such as the *Defender* and the *Courier*—two of the "radical" papers—carried continuing articles lecturing black people on their behavior, manners, loud clothes, and loud talk.[81] Sancton viewed the MOWM as a genuine revolutionary movement, and made his readers aware of the fact that the militant Pittsburgh *Courier,* the black paper with the largest circulation, had opposed the movement and was extremely hostile to Randolph. Finally, he said that the black press was not taking advantage of the war, and was simply continuing its time-honored policies.[82]

Others from the white community came to the defense of the black press. *The Nation* featured an article on the press by the black writer Horace Cayton, and even the *Harvard Guardian* took notice of the black press and came to its defense.[83] In 1944 Oswald

79. Thomas Sancton, "The Negro Press," *The New Republic* 108 (April 19, 1943): 558; editorial 108 (February 8, 1943): 176.

80. Editorial, *The New Republic* 108 (April 26, 1943): 559.

81. *Ibid.*

82. *Ibid.,* 108 (February 8, 1943): 176.

83. Horace R. Cayton, "The Negro's Challenge," *The Nation* 151 (July 2, 1943): 10–12; Samuel Perry, "In Defense of the Negro Press," *Harvard Guardian* 7 (December 1942): 15–19.

G. Villard wrote a critical book on the modern press and reserved complete praise for just one segment—the black press. "It uses little or no restraint in discussing the refusal of this government to grant our Negroes not only their constitutional privileges, but full equality in the army and navy. . . . These militant newspapers are both the creators of the suddenly developed Negro sense of solidarity and themselves an index of developing race consciousness. . . ."[84] Lucius C. Harper, managing editor and columnist for the Chicago *Defender,* in commenting on Villard's account of the black press, said that it would come as a shock to many blacks who believed that the press was "ultra-conservative."[85]

What started out as an all-out attack on the black press ended up with different and unexpected results. The press had been consistent in its desire to enlist white support to aid blacks in the struggle for equality. Once the attacks began, the black press received much-needed publicity—more than it had been able to gather in previous years. In mid-1942 *Time* magazine wrote a small piece about the NNPA meeting that was dripping with ridicule and scorn. The article attacked publisher Adam C. Powell, Jr., for advocating "complete world equality of Negroes and whites."[86] By 1943 whites were discovering that there was a "Double V" campaign being waged by blacks within their midsts that was being led by a militantly vocal black press.

After the hostile response to the Brown article from the black press and black leaders, the CFD, an organization established to bring unity to the support of the war program, decided to mend its own fences with the black community and sent out a call for a conference to discuss the problems facing the black press. Brown had suggested to Angell the calling of a conference to help the black press get more advertisements, and Angell was quick to accept. But the CFD was still favorable to the idea of a more subdued black press. When it sent the invitations to the confer-

84. Oswald G. Villard, *The Disappearing Daily* (New York: Alfred A. Knopf, 1944), p. 24.
85. Lucius C. Harper, Chicago *Defender,* July 15, 1944.
86. "Negro Publishers," *Time* 39 (June 15, 1942): 70–71.

ence, the original invitations scheduled only white speakers on the program. George Schuyler spoke for many newsmen when he let loose a blistering attack on the CFD for this slight, saying that it "strikes a new low in presumption and condescension." "It looks as if having failed to club the Negro press into line, these people now propose to lure it with carrots. Incidentally, not a single Negro is scheduled to speak." [87] Then he expressed surprise at the sudden interest of the CFD in trying to get more advertising for the black press. Schuyler had his doubts, but he, like many others in the field, went to the conference once the agenda was hastily revised to include black participants as well as a black audience.

The conference, as far as whites were concerned, still had as its main function the aiding of the black press in gaining access for it to the national advertisers. (The entire second session dealt with this problem.) Many white participants, though, came with the intention of putting a damper on the outspokenness of the press. William E. Haskell of the New York *Herald-Tribune* believed the primary object of the meeting was "to set in motion a moderating of thinking and writing to . . . [the] aim" of educating whites about the race problem. He also expressed the view that newspapers were "no place for violent crusading. . . ." [88] However, the conference turned out very differently from what the organizers had anticipated. White participants discovered that the "radical" black press was not so radical, and they were assured that black newsmen were not anxious to start a revolution on the homefront.

E. Washington Rhodes helped put to rest the fears of a radical black press with the following comments:

> It would surprise and startle the majority of white Americans if they knew what the so-called mass of Negroes is thinking. The mass of Negroes is more radical than P. B. Young and those of us who publish Negro newspapers. I wish I could tell

87. George S. Schuyler, Pittsburgh *Courier,* April 24, 1943.

88. Quoted in Council for Democracy, "Negro Press Conference," May 7–8, 1943 (Typescript, Schomburg Collection), 1: 7, 26.

> you what I do feel about certain things. Anyone would say that a lot of Negroes are saying that they should not participate in this war. I haven't seen anything about Negro papers saying that they shouldn't. The Negro Press argued that Negroes were Americans and that they should participate in the war.[89]

Leon Washington of the Los Angeles *Sentinel* agreed with Rhodes. He said "we are not radical; we somewhat tone down the words of our people—who would be more radical than we, as Negro newspaper editors are." [90] And P. B. Young commented on the "irresistible upsurge among the Negroes that some of us older ones have to push down on occasion, so to speak." [91] The black press, these editors claimed, was united in its wartime approach. It opposed black resistance to the war effort, and it wanted "absolute and unadulterated equality. . . ." [92]

White novelist Pearl Buck and Saville Davis, Assistant Managing Editor of the *Christian Science Monitor*, generally confirmed these facts to the conference. Buck said that she was an ardent advocate of fighting on all fronts at once and favored the "Double V" program. The way to fight the homefront battle was to educate whites about the race issue.[93] Davis admitted that he had finally read some of the black papers at the conference and found that the black press recognized that there was a "revolution in our social life . . . coming to the fore," and that these papers "appear to recognize their responsibility for controlling that revolution and making sure it does not divide and lead directly to war. . . ." [94] Thus assured, the conference had little more to do but discuss advertising and future coverage of blacks in the white media.

The efforts to tone down the black press did not come entirely from unofficial sources. The Army, unlike the rest of white America, had been acutely aware of the existence of a militant black press. Long before the United States entered World War II,

89. Quoted in *ibid.*, 1: 41–43.
90. Quoted in *ibid.*, 1: 123.
91. Quoted in *ibid.*, 2: 333.
92. *Ibid.*, 1: 45, 82; 2: 330–32.
93. *Ibid.*, 1: 15.
94. Quoted in *ibid.*, 1: 66.

the Army had become seriously concerned about the discrimination articles and accounts of incidents involving black troops that were being printed on the front pages of black newspapers. Finally, General George C. Marshall felt compelled to call the editors to Washington for a conference to try to appease the black press. This conference met on December 8, 1941, the day after the bombing of Pearl Harbor. Marshall, therefore, could devote only a few minutes to the editors, and the remainder of the meeting was conducted by his aides. What followed incensed rather than appeased the editors. All the suggestions that the editors offered to alleviate some of the problems were turned down. Even Brigadier General Benjamin O. Davis, the first black man to achieve this rank, criticized the press for sowing discontent among black troops.[95] It was ironical that Davis, who had achieved his rank largely due to the protest of the black press, was now in a position to demand that the press show more restraint.

By 1942 G–2 (Army Intelligence) was discussing the possibility of controlling the access of black papers to Army posts. Some Army posts began to confiscate the papers as they came through the camp post office. Eventually, all official acts of suppression instituted by local commanders were countermanded by Army G–2. This was done not because the actions were a violation of freedom of the press, but because proscription "would only serve to supply ammunition for agitation to colored papers."[96] Despite the official G–2 condemnation of restrictions of black papers on Army camps, individual actions of control continued. Soldiers were often unable to get black papers in post libraries and post exchanges. At times, certain Northern papers considered too radical were prohibited from being circulated on the base.[97] However, with certain exceptions, there seems to have been no serious,

95. Chicago *Defender,* December 13, 1941.

96. Quoted in Ulysses Lee, *United States Army in World War II. Special Studies. The Employment of Negro Troops* (Washington, D.C.: Office of the Chief of Military History, 1966), p. 384.

97. *Ibid.,* pp. 384–85 ; *People's Voice,* July 31, 1943 ; PEP 1 (December 1943): 15.

overt suppression of the black press during the war period by official Army sources.

The War Department was less interested in denying the black press exposure in Army camps than it was in supplying these papers with favorable articles about black troops. In late 1941 Under Secretary of War Robert P. Patterson expressed the opinion that the press was using racial incidents to promote social gains. The Bureau of Public Relations was cognizant of the problem of unfavorable publicity and decided to take a positive approach. A program was instituted to feed information to black papers about the troops, and the Bureau became an information center for black reporters seeking news. The Army also sent representatives to the annual NNPA meetings to present the Army's point of view. Quite often these men were sent to the NNPA meetings to try to get the press to avoid stories exposing serious discrimination.[98] In the summer of 1942 a special section within the Bureau of public relations, eventually officered by black men, was organized to handle news of black troops. The Army's program, by 1944, had proved to be fairly successful. More and more positive stories of black troops were appearing in the press, and though black papers continued to expose cases of discrimination, they apparently did not reveal all they knew about the incidents involving black troops that were taking place in Army camps.[99]

The draft presented problems to many black papers, especially the smaller ones, and at times was used as a means of intimidation by local officials. Some newspapers wrote about a campaign to draft enough editors to cripple the effectiveness of the press,[100] but except for a few obvious incidents there appeared to be no general move by Selective Service officials in this direction. Many papers were affected by the draft. Since the average number of workers on a black paper was five persons, a loss of only one represented a large proportion of the total staff. The California

98. *PEP* 1 (July 1943): 1.

99. *A Monthly Summary of Events and Trends in Race Relations* 1 (January 1944): 22. Hereafter cited as *Monthly Summary.*

100. *PEP* 1 (December 1943): 17.

Eagle gave eight men to the Army, including its managing editor John Kinloch.[101] Other papers also lost their key personnel through the draft, but the larger papers were not affected, nor did they appear concerned about any concerted effort to draft their staff as a means of stifling the press. One incident in Albany, Georgia, did appear to be an attempt by the local draft board to silence a black newspaper. A. D. Searles of the *Southwest Georgian* had been classified as 3–A for the first year of the war. On February 6, 1943, he wrote an article exposing a lynching in Newton, Georgia. Within one week he was reclassified 1–A and shortly thereafter inducted. His paper soon folded.[102]

By the summer of 1943, after sustaining a year of attacks, and with racial violence erupting in cities throughout the country, the black press began to receive official recognition as an institution representing a responsible and effective communications channel to the black population. Representatives of the Navy and Army Departments attended the NNPA annual meeting in July. The NNPA's executive committee held conferences with Vice-President Henry Wallace, Attorney General Francis Biddle, Paul McNutt of the War Manpower Commission (WMC) and officials of the War Production Board, Selective Service, and the OWI in order to take steps to increase black people's knowledge of "what we are fighting for." The OWI was called upon to make effective use of its facilities to present the black man's role in the war so as to augment "the effectiveness of the Negro's contribution to the government's efforts." [103] At the conclusion of these meetings, the OWI announced the appointment of a committee of black editors to advise it on matters relating to the black public; it included John Sengstacke of the *Defender* and Howard Murphy of *The Afro-American*.

During 1944 these efforts produced many results. The War Department's Bureau of Public Information set up a special

101. Charlotta A. Bass, California *Eagle*, December 2, 1943.
102. Schomburg Vertical Files: Newspapers 1.
103. *PEP* 1 (July 1943): 4; (September 1943): 1; *Journal and Guide*, July 24, 1943; November 1, 1943; New York *Amsterdam News*, September 4, 1943.

European bureau staffed with black officers to follow black troops on the continent and to serve as a clearing house for news going to black reporters. The Navy, considered the strongest bastion of military segregation, hosted a group of black newspapermen at the Great Lakes Naval Station for two days, and most of those attending were impressed with the steps the Navy was taking.[104] The culmination of official recognition came with the historic first meeting of black newspapermen and the President. Thirteen representatives of the black press met with F.D.R. on February 5, 1944, and presented a twenty-one point program stating wartime and postwar aims. The editors pledged "wholeheartedly and unreservedly" their support of the war effort and maintained their right to "fight for every right guaranteed by the Constitution."[105] The one concrete achievement of this meeting was the appointment of the first black correspondent, Harry McAlpin, to the White House. Not until 1947 did Congress open its news galleries to black men.

Within two months after F.D.R. died, his successor invited representatives of the black press to the White House once again. Most of the black papers in the Democratic ranks had been upset by the party's rejection of Wallace in 1944 as the vice-presidential candidate, and had doubts about Harry Truman. The Republican papers had even carried articles claiming that Truman had been a member of the Klan and an avowed racist.[106] The meeting, however, appeared to have pleased the editors, especially since Truman promised his full support for a permanent FEPC and fair play for the black man.

Sensing the changing attitudes toward the black press, Southern white liberals sought new means to bring their influence to bear. In early 1945 they helped to establish the Wendell Willkie Awards, which consisted of cash stipends to be presented each year to outstanding black journalists. Many of the more militant

104. *People's Voice,* March 4, 1944; Adam C. Powell, Jr., "A Big Stride Forward," *Spotlight* 2 (April 1944): 3.
105. *Journal and Guide,* February 12, 1944.
106. Pittsburgh *Courier,* October 21, 1944.

journals of the North recognized the awards as another attempt to control the black press. Dan Gardiner, writing in the *Amsterdam News,* observed that only two blacks were on the awards committee, which was dominated by Southern liberals (Dabney, McGill, Douglas S. Freeman, and Ethridge) who had spearheaded the attack on the black press two years earlier.[107] Gardiner proved to be correct. The committee presented the first Willkie award to the editor of the Los Angeles *Tribune.* This individual had, in the preceding year, joined Westbrook Pegler in denouncing the black press, and had characterized most of the reporting in the press as "nauseating." [108]

Last to come around to the realization that the black press was neither revolutionary nor an institution to be sneered at was Time-Life publications. Just before the war ended, *Fortune* conducted a survey of the black press. Although the survey dealt with the front pages only, it reflected an accurate statistical analysis of the emphasis of the black press. The study revealed that despite the government's restrictions on black participation, the black press considered the war effort as a joint venture of blacks and whites. Rather than being the negative force many had feared it was during the war, the survey concluded that stories portraying favorable black-white relations outnumbered purely protest articles by two-to-one. Most of the black papers agreed with the *Fortune* survey, and were pleased to bury the notion of an "inflammatory press" once and for all.[109]

As the war was drawing to a close, the black press achieved the status it had long sought; public recognition of its leadership role in creating amicable race relations, and its right to continue unrelenting protest against the black man's subordinate role in America. Perhaps the reason whites no longer considered the black press dangerous was that the papers themselves never sug-

107. New York *Amsterdam News,* January 27, 1945.

108. Guzman, *Negro Year Book,* p. 393 ; Roy Wilkins, New York *Amsterdam News,* April 22, 1944.

109. "Fortune Press Analysis: Negroes," *Fortune* 18 (Spring 1945): 235–38. This survey covered the first page of four issues of the leading 25 papers. See also Chicago *Defender* May 5, 1945.

gested revolutionary methods.[110] Most were either conservative or New Deal in their political outlook, and those few on the Left became the most ardent supporters of Roosevelt's wartime leadership. Throughout the war, and under the most trying of conditions, the press had encouraged full support for the struggle abroad.

110. Doxey Wilkerson, "The Negro Press Today," *Journal of Negro Education* 14 (Fall 1947): 576.

3
The Role of the Wartime Black Press

Remember that the Negro Press had to sell their readers the idea that, despite the injustices which they suffered, they must give all to their country.[1]

The Homefront Crisis

As the United States was shifting from mobilization into a state of actual belligerency, those concerned with the black man's role were forced to focus their attention on what they considered an alarming situation: the apathy toward the war and the deteriorating state of black morale. From 1941 until well into 1943, black morale was a leading topic of conversation among black leaders, the black press, and concerned whites. In 1942 liberal Southern whites were becoming uneasy about the outpourings of protest from the black press. Many perceptive officials in the administration were more concerned with the lack of any positive response to the war aims from the black masses.[2]

1. E. Washington Rhodes, "The Negro Press Takes up its Burden," *The Brown American* 6 (Spring-Summer 1942): 10.

2. Malcolm S. MacLean to Marvin H. McIntyre, November 20,

A major role of the wartime black press—and in this it reflected the thinking of most black leaders—was to elevate the morale of the race and channel the hostility of blacks into a positive attitude about their role in the war. To do this, the war aims of the country were combined with the aspirations of blacks at home in a double struggle: the "Double V"—victory at home and abroad. The struggle for equality at home would continue, but the press would emphasize its connection with the worldwide struggle against the Axis. In so doing it combined the struggle within—with which blacks displayed a heightened sense of awareness—with the struggle abroad. By combining the two objectives, the black press hoped to bolster morale and enlist the masses' full support for the country's war aims.

The often-stated position of the black press during World War II was that blacks were "Americans" first and "Negroes" second. The papers almost unanimously agreed that the future status of blacks in the country largely depended upon their serving as equals in the armed forces. Experience had taught blacks that if they did not protest, they would be relegated to a menial role in the armed forces, to work in the labor battalions. Under this assumption, the black press had to engage in its own double struggle of resisting the degrading status of blacks in the services, and encouraging blacks to "fight for the right to fight." Platitudes and promises would no longer suffice in arousing the disgruntled masses and any call to "close ranks" for the duration would have been ignored. Black people rejected the political naiveté of World War I, when propaganda manufactured by George Creel's machine could arouse patriotic enthusiasm.

During World War I blacks were emerging from a generation of accommodation. The immediate postwar period was a time when various movements within the black community stimulated racial consciousness. The Association for the Study of Negro Life and History, organized in 1915, began to reveal the role of blacks in the nation's past. In Harlem, the 1920s witnessed the birth of

1942, OF 93; Elmer Davis to Stephen Early, September 5, 1942, PPF 6943, Franklin D. Roosevelt Library.

the "New Negro" movement, which was a stimulant to a growing racial consciousness and fostered group identification at least among the intellectuals and literati. Marcus Garvey's Back-to-Africa movement, which attracted the largest mass following among the race in the nation's history, aroused a pride in the color black. During the Depression, this growing group identity led to more aggressive action on the part of black masses led by younger and more activist-oriented leaders. Protest movements increased. Black groups organized "don't-buy-where-you-can't-work" movements in the Northern cities, and black workers took a more active role in labor's organizing drives. Growing Northern black communities created bases for political activity and blacks were able to send a black representative to Congress in 1928 to be joined by Adam C. Powell, Jr., in 1944.[3]

Thus, when World War II broke out in Europe, black attitudes were different from those of 1914. The new generation was not raised under the accommodating guidance of Booker T. Washington, and the older generation had not forgotten the unfulfilled expectations and broken promises of World War I.[4] No leader could remain a leader and counsel his followers on the benefits of patience. In the midst of the Depression, which continued for blacks despite the defense build-up, few black spokesmen could tell their people how much progress they had made, and that conditions were improving. If the black masses were to be led at all during the war, and if blind outbursts of rage were to be avoided, then the tone of black leadership had to be militant and demanding. Or as A. Philip Randolph often said, "The leadership would have to catch up with the followship."

Even before the outbreak of hostilities in Europe, many observers noted an indifference in the black community about the possibility of a European war and American involvement. George Schuyler predicted that if America went to war, blacks would be

3. Horace R. Cayton, "Negro Morale," *Opportunity* 19 (December 1941): 371–75; see also Arnold M. Rose, *The Negro's Morale* (Minneapolis: University of Minnesota Press, 1949).

4. Kelly Miller, New York *Age*, September 23, 1939; J. A. Rogers, Pittsburgh *Courier*, May 13, 1940.

indifferent, but would go through the motions of intense loyalty.[5] He was only partially correct. As it turned out, many blacks were not even going through the motions. *The Afro-American,* concerned about black apathy during the defense buildup in 1940, assailed *Time* magazine for printing an article dealing with discrimination in the Army, and said such publicity would "encourage the colored population to become slackers and fifth columnists." [6] Indifference toward the war, as America was increasingly being drawn into it, worried many black writers. Horace Cayton, in the spring of 1941, discussed the low morale among blacks and how most of the race despised Great Britain as much as Germany. He warned that blacks were more sophisticated than they had been during the last war and would not be held back or bouyed up by government propaganda.[7]

Talk of the European war's being "a white man's war" was spreading and accentuating black resistance to involvement. The New York *Age,* in trying to curb this trend of thought, informed its readers that only Garveyites and Communists spoke this line and said, "we are Americans first; that we are Negroes is only incidental." [8] Just before the attack on Pearl Harbor, the editor of the Oklahoma *Black Dispatch* wrote that black leaders were doing their best to create enthusiasm for the defense program, but the "Negro masses are getting more intelligent, more restive and articulate." [9] Repeated articles in the black press telling of how blacks would remain loyal and fight should America enter the war, indicated an awareness of the hostile feeling of blacks, and probably revealed some doubt as to the black response in the eventuality of war.

There were many who perceived the European war and American defense preparations as a portent of benefits to be gained by blacks, but they soon realized that they had been too optimistic. The initial focus of the press was on obtaining for the black man

5. George S. Schuyler, Pittsburgh *Courier,* August 12, 1939.
6. *The Afro-American,* August 2, 1940.
7. Horace R. Cayton, Pittsburgh *Courier,* March 22, 1941.
8. New York *Age,* June 15, 1940.
9. Quoted in Savannah *Tribune,* September 19, 1941.

a chance to serve in the Army and get work in the expanding defense industries. The press, when defense preparations were getting underway in the country, did not overly concern itself with speculation about the possibilities of United States involvement in a European war.

In 1938 the *Courier* began to publicize the lack of opportunity for blacks to serve in the Army. For over two frustrating years the *Courier* and other black papers tried to persuade the Army to allow more blacks to enter the ranks. In 1940 Rayford W. Logan told a Senate committee that "the morale of Negro citizens regarding national defense is probably at the lowest ebb in the history of the country." [10] Just prior to the enactment of the Conscription Bill, almost all of the black press, following the *Courier's* lead, called for black proportional representation in all branches of the Army. Hoping to gather black support for both conscription and his reelection, President Roosevelt accepted the principle of proportional black representation in the Army. At the same time, however, the White House announced that the policy of segregation in the Army would continue. It was a stunning blow to black morale.[11]

Time and circumstances had altered the situation. Increasing rhetoric against fascist racism made official pronouncements of segregation less palatable. Besides, what appeared to be one victory —the opening up of all branches of the Army to blacks—inevitably led to the next challenge: segregation in the service.

Proportional representation combined with segregation created physical problems that in turn further dampened the enthusiasm of blacks for the defense program. Facilities for black units had to be erected and despite the Army's early plans to utilize blacks in all branches, it had made little effort to provide the separate areas in which blacks could be trained. Blacks were to be called by the local draft boards on a quota basis, but there were delays because of the lack of preparations to handle black draftees. The local boards began to "select" black men in 1941, but instead of in-

10. Quoted in the Pittsburgh *Courier*, May 13, 1940.
11. See chap. 4.

ducting them when their numbers were called, most were told to "stand by." Many who were selected believed that they would be inducted shortly and left their jobs, only to discover that induction delays lasted for months. These standbys, after depleting their funds, had to look for new jobs in order to provide for their day-to-day needs until their draft boards finally called them.[12]

After an initial increase in the number of blacks being called to duty in the first quarter of 1941, during the remainder of the year there was a decrease. The swing upward did not begin again until the summer of 1942. The most telling effect on blacks was when, immediately after the attack on Pearl Harbor, the War Department announced that it could not accept the full quota of blacks. At the same time that F.D.R. called for a declaration of war against Japan, 30,000 blacks were passed over in the month's draft call. Many blacks reacted to the shock of Japan's sneak attack by volunteering for the Army, but were turned down. The Selective Service system, which served as the Army's selection agency, and was not in favor of quotas, believed that this situation was "a definite threat to the patriotic enthusiasm of the Negro. . . ," which was not removed until increased draft calls began at the end of 1942.[13] Selective Service officials observed that "civilian and soldiers morale among Negroes was low during the defense era and early years of World War II." Draft boards believed that blacks were "a ready made morale problem" due to the "difficulty in reconciling day-to-day experiences with the . . . Four Freedoms." Despite the fact that all of the agencies involved in the war effort recognized the morale problems, Selective Service admitted that "no solution was seriously attempted." [14]

12. *Selective Service in Peacetime.* First Report of the Director of Selective Service, 1940–1941 (Washington, D.C.: G.P.O., 1942), pp. 254–56 ; C .A. Dykstra to Henry L. Stimson, February 14, 1941, OF 93, Franklin D. Roosevelt Library.

13. *Selective Service in Wartime.* Second Report of the Director of Selective Service, 1941–1942 (Washington, D.C.: G.P.O., 1943), pp. 281–87.

14. U.S. Selective Service System. *Special Groups.* Special Monograph No. 10, Vol. I (Washington, D.C.: G.P.O., 1953): 51, 56, 190. Hereafter cited as Selective Service: *Special Groups.*

At first only the Army reversed its policy of restricted use of black troops and promised full participation. The Air Corps and Navy were harder to budge. In 1939 the Schwartz Amendment to Public Law Number 18 set aside funds for the training of black aviators. The Army interpreted the amendment to mean that it should lend equipment to a private school certified by the Civil Aeronautic Authority: that is, a nonmilitary training program.[15] When, after repeated inquiries about "Negro aviation" proved fruitless, the NAACP brought suit on behalf of Yancy Williams to enter the Corps, the Army hastily established a segregated training center at Tuskegee to train thirty-three pilots. This liberal "experiment" by the Army came at a time when the service had called for the training of 30,000 pilots as quickly as possible.

The Navy proved to be the most obstinate foe. This branch of the service had ceased accepting black seamen completely after World War I. Only in the early 1930s did it reverse this policy and begin to accept blacks for duty in the messmen's branch of the service. The Navy maintained this position until June 1942, when a change of policy was to take place on a small scale, to permit some blacks to be accepted outside of messmen service. Not until March 1943 did Navy policy conform to the Army plan of accepting blacks up to ten percent of its manpower. In June 1942 the Marines finally broke their one-hundred-and-sixty-seven-year-old tradition and enlisted blacks. Only when the election of 1944 was approaching and the importance of the black vote calculated were black women allowed to enter the Waves.[16] The Navy's preliminary resistance did much to hamper the efforts of the black press to arouse a martial spirit among its readers. When "Dorie" Miller, a messman on board ship at Pearl Harbor on December 7, 1941, manned an anti-aircraft gun and continued firing until he had exhausted his ammunition supply, the black press discovered

15. Lee, pp. 56–57.

16. Dennis D. Nelson, *The Integration of the Negro into the U.S. Navy* (New York: Farrar, Straus & Young, 1951), pp. 14, 17; John W. Davis, "The Negro in the U.S. Navy, Marine Corps, and Coast Guard," *Journal of Negro Education* 12 (Summer 1943): 348.

the incident and had to prod the service for twelve weeks just to obtain the young man's name.[17]

The pattern of discrimination in the armed forces offered black people little evidence of any fundamental change from World War I policies. Charles H. Houston, an NAACP counsel who was active in the early days of the program to include blacks in all branches of the services, observed in the summer of 1943 that the "general overall pattern is the same—segregation, compromise and hesitation" in the armed forces. The effect of this was apparent to Houston, who expressed the belief that conditions were "more tense and explosive now than in World War I." [18] Even Walter White, while claiming some improvements over the previous war, said they were "slight and may prove ephemeral. . . ." [19] The nation's armed forces, from 1939 to 1943, seemed bent on publicly committing the black man to an inferior role by standing firm on old policies and making concessions only grudgingly. Conditions were such that the Selective Service considered the fact that there were few black "Conscientious Objectors, delinquents and evaders or seditionists" as "little short of phenomenal." [20]

Some editors believed that the European war would alleviate the employment problems of blacks as it had done in the last war. This assumption would eventually prove correct but, unlike 1914, there were millions of whites unemployed and black workers were generally employed only after the supply of white labor was exhausted. Jobs for black workers did not begin to pick up rapidly until the second half of 1942, almost three years after the defense build-up had begun. In the spring of 1942 blacks represented less than three percent of all war workers.[21] Often, the shortage of

17. Doris Miller was the seaman's real name, but while the Navy was withholding his name, word leaked out that the young hero was Dorie Miller, and the name stuck.

18. Charles H. Houston, "Critical Summary: The Negro in the U.S. Armed Forces in World Wars I and II," *Journal of Negro Education* 12 (Summer 1943): 365.

19. Walter White, "Race Relations in the Armed Services of the U.S." *Ibid.*, p. 354.

20. Selective Service: *Special Groups*, 1: 51.

21. Fair Employment Practice Committee, *First Report*, July,

white workers in a locality did not mean the recruitment of blacks within the area. Many aircraft companies placed ads in out-of-town papers rather than hire local blacks. North American Aviation announced in the spring of 1941 that its policy was not to hire black workers. At this time nonwhites held only fourteen of the 11,000 skilled and semi-skilled jobs in the aircraft industry.[22]

Where blacks were traditionally employed in industries such as shipbuilding, construction, iron and steel, and meat packing, jobs were becoming available to them by early 1940. Industries that traditionally did not employ black labor remained adamant in their hiring policies. Lester Granger, Executive Secretary of the National Urban League, noted that "throughout 1940 and 1941 . . . Negro job applicants . . . [were] blocked at almost every turn." While in 1941 black unemployment dropped thirty-six percent, during the same year white unemployment was down forty-six percent. Often, WPA roles had an increase of black participants, for whites were leaving the agency to fill the defense jobs. In New York blacks on WPA rose from 14.2 percent in February 1939, to 17.6 percent in February 1942. Most of the work that did become available for black workers during 1940–41 was not in the defense industry and this caused concern and anger.[23]

It was this plight that prompted A. Philip Randolph to organize his March on Washington Movement in early 1941. Besides the obvious purpose of opening up defense jobs for blacks, Randolph explained that black leaders were becoming alarmed because "a wave of bitter resentment, disillusionment and desperation was sweeping over the Negro masses. . . ." To prevent this condition from erupting into "blind, reckless and undisciplined outbursts of emotional indignation against discrimination in defense jobs. . . ,"

1943–December, 1944 (Washington, D.C.: G.P.O., 1945), p. 65; Robert C. Weaver, *Negro Labor: A National Problem* (New York: Harcourt, Brace and Company, 1946), p. 79.

22. Lester B. Granger, "Negroes and War Production," *Survey Graphic* 31 (November 1942): 446; Federal Security Agency, Social Security Board, Bureau of Employment Security, Division of Research and Statistics, *Negro Workers and the National Defense,* pp. 1, 5–7.

23. Lester B. Granger, *Survey Graphic* 31: 469–70.

Randolph said that the "threatening situation" had to be met with "sober, sane and constructive action. . . ." [24] As an advocate of nonviolence, Randolph had sensed the explosive atmosphere within the black community and believed that only positive and resolute action could ease the pressures that were leading to violent eruptions.

Randolph's MOWM did force F.D.R. to take action, and the President issued Executive Order 8802, which established the President's Committee on Fair Employment Practices. Many black papers hailed this action as the second emancipation, but despite this "victory" defense jobs still failed to open up for blacks during the following year. Three months after F.D.R. issued the executive order banning discrimination in companies holding defense contracts, the Bureau of Employment Security surveyed defense contractors and found that blacks would not even be considered for forty-nine percent of the 282,245 job openings expected by February 1942.[25]

F.D.R. established the FEPC to get Randolph to call off his threatened march on Washington. The President did not take this action to alleviate the economic distress of unemployed blacks, nor did he have any intention of creating an agency that would force open the doors of industry to black workers. Will Alexander, long time racial advisor to F.D.R. and a member of the WMC at the time the FEPC was functioning within this commission, expressed his belief that the FEPC was "good as a propaganda agency" on the race issue, but "as far as getting anybody employed in the war industries, I don't think it did. It was set up in such a way that it couldn't." [26]

Alexander said that the country had to have war material flowing uninterruptedly out of the nation's war plants. The men

24. Quoted in the New York *Amsterdam News,* July 19, 1941.

25. Speech of Lawrence W. Cramer, Executive Secretary of the FEPC, presented at the Regional Meeting of the National Conference of Social Work, New York City, March 11, 1943 (Schomburg Collection).

26. Will W. Alexander, "The Reminiscences of Will W. Alexander," Oral History Research Office, Columbia University, 3: 693.

operating these industries were aware of this, and were able to ignore any pleas the FEPC made to hire black workers. An example of this was the Western Cartridge Company, a division of Olin Industries in East Alton, Illinois. This plant, which manufactured bullets and cartridge brass, employed 13,000 white workers and refused to hire blacks throughout the war despite the intervention of both the WMC and FEPC. Malcolm Ross, who was Chairman of the FEPC during its negotiations with Western Cartridge Company, later noted the failure of FEPC to get black workers hired. He summed up the dilemma by asking: "Who is to judge the present value of lives against the long term value of democracy?" [27]

The manner in which the FEPC was established and functioned largely confirms Alexander's opinion that it was not set up in such a way as to force industry to accept black workers. Bernard L. Gladieux, in charge of the War Organizational Section of the Budget Bureau, played a key role in drafting Executive Order 8802. Along with Wayne Coy, Liaison Officer for Emergency Management, and his assistant Joseph Rauh, Gladieux drew up the Executive Order. He later noted that "there was a big element of giving something to the Negroes to keep them quiet." Gladieux added that the President had no specific powers he could delegate to FEPC, but said "we had to pull something out of the air that made it look like his commission was going to have real standing authority." [28]

Although the FEPC order sounded fine and did get Randolph to call off his march, its ability to deal with industrial discrimination was never adequate, nor did the administration appear to want it to exercise any real power. When the White House offered the first chairmanship of the FEPC to Mark Ethridge, Stephen Early, the President's Press Secretary, told him that the office would not require him to "remain steadily on the job here," only about

27. Malcolm Ross, *All Manner of Men* (New York: Reynal and Hitchcock, 1948), pp. 49–60.

28. Bernard L. Gladieux, "The Reminiscences of Bernard L. Gladieux," Oral History Research Office, Columbia University, pp. 196, 200.

two days a week.[29] In light of this attitude from the White House in the face of the magnitude of the problem, one can only concur with Alexander that the FEPC was never intended to secure jobs for black workers.

Despite the fact that the FEPC was unable to obtain more jobs for black workers during the early phase of its operations, it was obviously a needed boost to the sagging morale of blacks. It was not an unmixed blessing, though, as the black press focused on the FEPC and revealed a cautious, hesitant committee during its first three years of operation. Black newspapers had to expend much energy during the initial years just to see that the agency would remain independent and vital.

Nevertheless, by early 1942 when Southerners began to fear a social revolution, they looked to the FEPC as one of the forward agents of the revolution. To calm their fears, Mark Ethridge, the first chairman of the Committee, addressed the first public hearing held by the FEPC in the South and assured his audience that "not even all the mechanized armies of the earth, Allied and Axis, . . . could force the Southern white people to the abandonment of the principle of social segregation."[30] Within a month, Roosevelt transferred the FEPC to the WMC, a move that the black press correctly interpreted as a way to curb the Committee and appease the South. Not until the Committee dramatically intervened in the Philadelphia Transportation Company strike of 1944 did it prove itself to the black community. Thus during the period from 1941 through 1943, the crisis period for blacks on the homefront, the FEPC did little to convince blacks that the federal government was behind their efforts to gain equal job opportunities.

To the struggle for equal treatment in the armed forces and defense industries was added the problem of providing decent housing for blacks, especially in the Northern ghettos to which blacks were moving in hopes of sharing in the new job openings. Detroit became the most volatile of all the cities in the North, with

29. Stephen Early to Mark Ethridge, July 9, 1941, 4294, Franklin D. Roosevelt Library.

30. FEPC, "Seventh Hearing," Birmingham, p. 19.

racial tremors being felt for two years before finally erupting in 1943 into the worst wartime riot. Before this major disaster, the problem of housing the influx of blacks into the city caused the first wartime riot, one that involved no fatalities and therefore received little attention in the major daily papers.

Detroit's black population had increased from 23,000 in 1917 to 150,000 in 1940. The increase from 1940 to 1943 swelled the number to a total of almost 300,000.[31] To house some of these people the Federal Housing Authority began a program that included a 200-unit housing project for blacks and whites on the border of a neighborhood separating the two races. Under pressure from local real estate agents acting through their district Congressmen, the federal government vacillated and finally certified the project as an all-white development—an anomaly since the Housing project was named after Sojourner Truth, the noted black abolitionist and underground railroad leader. Aroused blacks in Detroit organized a group to represent them in Washington and were successful in reversing the all-white policy on February 2, 1942, just in time for the opening of the housing units, which was scheduled for February 28.

White opponents of the project refused to be deterred by the change of heart in Washington and began organizing mobs to prevent the black occupants from moving into the project. As the blacks attempted to occupy the units on the designated day, they were met by over 1,000 hostile whites who prevented their entry, while the police did nothing to assist the blacks in occupying the facilities to which they were legally entitled. When fighting broke out, the police moved against the blacks rather than those who were trying to obstruct the law, and arrested over 200 blacks along with five whites.[32]

Events at Sojourner Truth Housing, coming within weeks of

31. "The Negro's War," *Fortune* 25 (June 1942): 78; Louis Martin, "Prelude to Disaster: Detroit," *Common Ground* 4 (Autumn 1943): 21.

32. Chicago *Defender,* March 7, 1942; *People's Voice,* March 7, 1942; Louis Martin, "The Truth About Sojourner Truth," *The Crisis* 49 (April 1942): 112–13; *NAACP Annual Report for 1942,* p. 22.

the disaster at Pearl Harbor, added to the depressing effect of discrimination on the morale of the black population. The federal government, after providing housing, had backed down under a small amount of pressure from hostile whites, once again demonstrating its refusal to meet its obligation toward the black minority. Most observers believed that it was the initial vacillation that encouraged the whites to try for another reversal of policy, using this time the tactics of terror and open violence.[33] They failed only because the blacks organized and refused to be intimidated. These events did not go unnoticed by the Japanese and Germans. Both countries played up the riot in their English-language broadcasts, especially the Japanese, who aimed much of their anti-American propaganda at the oppressed minority within the United States.[34]

The Detroit housing riot was just a prelude to the summer of 1943 when major riots occurred in Detroit, Harlem, Beaumont (Texas), and Los Angeles (The Zoot Suit Riots). These were the most sensational and received widespread coverage in the nation's press, but Charles Johnson revealed that there were at least 242 "major incidents" from March 1 to December 31, 1943.[35] As devastating as these riots proved to have been, racial conflict could have been far worse had not blacks, by the summer of 1943, been absorbed more fully into the armed forces and the country's industrial plants.

These, then, were the major elements that were militating against a total effort on the part of the blacks for America's war program: discrimination in the services and in employment and violence between the races. Few blacks remained unaffected by these occurrences and even white liberals in the South conceded that the problems facing blacks were actually increasing during the early war period.[36] Incidents multiplied and discrimination appeared to be spreading openly on the federal level.

33. Chicago *Defender,* March 14, 1942.
34. "The Negro's War," *Fortune* 25 (June 1942): 77.
35. *Monthly Summary* 1 (January 1944): 2.
36. Howard W. Odum, *Race and Rumours of Race: Challenge to American Crisis* (Chapel Hill: University of North Carolina Press, 1943), p. 4.

While the country was facing a worldwide crisis, blacks were experiencing a crisis on the homefront. Despite the increased income of the black sector after 1943, living conditions often became deplorable as blacks moved into highly congested urban slum areas. The dislocation created by rural blacks moving to urban industrial areas was manifested in broken families, juvenile delinquency, and general social instability. Already existing social problems, of which the race issue was a major one, were exacerbated, and the result was increased racial tension and violent racial conflict in many sections of the country. One study of the homefront during the war concluded that the war "intensified, but did not substantially modify the social problems of a peace time society." "As a result, America suffered casualties on the homefront which compared in severity with those on the battlefield," [37] Blacks made up a disproportionate share of these homefront casualties.

The bitterness of these crisis years was spread across the pages of the black press. Despite the attempt to bolster morale, each issue after Pearl Harbor brought news of added insult. In the spring of 1942 the OWI conducted a survey in Harlem, the most populous black community in the North, to determine the black man's attitude toward the war. This study concluded that "resentment at Negro discrimination is fairly widespread throughout the Negro population." [38] When those who were interviewed were asked if they were better off before the war, more responded that they were either the same or worse off than they had been. The answer to the question, "Would you be better off if America or the Axis won the war?" was especially revealing. Most believed that they would be treated either the same or better under Japanese rule. (A large majority responded that conditions would be worse under the Germans.) Most of those interviewed had few illusions

37. Francis E. Merrill, *Social Problems on the Homefront* (New York: Harper and Bros., 1948), pp. 9, 24. See also United Urban League Service Fund, *On the Same Team* (1944?).

38. Office of War Information in Collaboration with the National Opinion Reasearch Center, *The Negro Looks at the War* (Typescript: Schomburg Collection, May 19, 1942), p. 1. This survey was conducted between April 1942 and May 11, 1942.

about their position in a victorious postwar America, for only 11 percent responded in the affirmative when asked if conditions would improve for blacks if the United States won the war.[39]

The OWI was cognizant of what the black masses thought about the war even before it conducted the survey, since it is doubtful that such questions would have been presented to whites. The United States had not been very tolerant of dissent during its wars and this outspoken lack of concern about the possibility of a Japanese victory revealed not only a sense of frustration, but a high degree of militancy and tension among blacks that could have become explosive.

Not only in the North, but throughout the country black anger was mounting. From the uneducated to those in college, blacks were expressing their resentment at being asked to support the war effort while being treated as second-class citizens. In one Southern city, 150 students were queried about the war and 83 percent of them believed that under the existing conditions blacks should not be expected to fight. A black janitor in Little Rock, Arkansas, declared, "I ain't caring a damn about going to the Army because of the way they treats colored people." A black college student said he wouldn't resist if drafted, but added: "I have no interest in the kind of war they are fighting; I'd like to wage a little war on some of these white people here." Others were ready to resist. A black attorney in Chicago said "If I go, they'll have to come and get me. Why should I join a Jim Crow Army. I'm not that anxious."[40]

This feeling was perhaps most eloquently expressed by a black Philadelphian who said:

> I ain't about to give it [my life] to no country that treats folks like they do us. What really puts it in the groove is the way they keeps on treatin' us while they's still askin' us to fight. And black folks, like me ain't sayin' the things we're sayin' about the

39. *Ibid.*, appendixes III, IX.

40. Charles S. Johnson, *To Stem this Tide: A Survey of Racial Tension Areas in the United States* (Chicago: The Pilgrim Press, 1943), pp. 90–92.

war 'cause we're afraid to fight. . . . I can fight. See this partner of mine? (knife). There ain't many around that can cut cleaner. But when I knifes a damn "nigger" with this baby its because I'm fighting for somethin' I wants—yes maybe its my old lady—but I wants it. But there ain't nothin' that this war's got that I wants. You can't kick a man's behind and then tell him to go and fight for you." [41]

After the war, studies on this subject lost sight of the extent of black anger when they summed up the wartime black mood with comments such as: "Negroes on the average tended to show less enthusiasm for the war than did whites." [42]

The press was well aware of the explosive nature of black resentment and frustration. Black editors and columnists were alarmed by this situation; more so than their editorials implied. Privately they expressed great fear that blacks would not willingly offer their services to the country. Edgar T. Rouzeau wrote to President Roosevelt about "those individuals of Negro descent who falsely preach to the masses that 'This is a white man's war, nothing for the American Negro to be concerned about.' " Rouzeau assured F.D.R. that he was combating this view by his writings in the Pittsburgh *Courier*. Leon Lewis, Executive Secretary of the New Orleans Press Club, informed F.D.R. of the "general unrest among Negroes . . . growing by leaps and bounds across the country." Sensing this general mood, the Chicago *Defender* published a special Victory Edition, which was apparently designed "to help offset Negro disaffection." And William Pickens worried about the "considerable confusion in the minds of our colored citizens" after Pearl Harbor. He said many blacks believed that "these Japanese are colored people," and the war was not a black man's war.[43]

Within a few weeks after the outbreak of war, the black press,

41. *Ibid.*, p. 100.

42. David Mandelbaum, *Soldier Groups and Negro Soldiers* (Berkeley: University of California Press, 1952), p. 95.

43. Edgar T. Rouzeau to F.D.R., February 24, 1942, OF 93; Leon Lewis to F.D.R., October 2, 1942, OF 93; Elmer Davis to Stephen Early, September 5, 1942, PPF 6943; F.D.R. to John H. Sengstacke, September 1942, PPF 6943, Franklin D. Roosevelt Library; William

in response to this pervasive resentment among black citizens, began to coalesce around a position that became the underlying motif of the wartime minority press.

Those editions of the black newspapers that appeared immediately following December 7, 1941, all responded to the advent of hostilities by affirming the full support of blacks against the Axis powers. Black readers were less enthusiastic, or became so as soon as the intial shock of war receded. Many black citizens who did respond in the normal patriotic manner by rushing to their local draft center to volunteer after the Pearl Harbor attack, were soon reassured that as far as blacks were concerned it would be business as usual, that is, they were turned down because of the lack of segregated facilities.[44]

At the same time the Army was rejecting black volunteers, the press discovered that the Red Cross was refusing blood from prospective black donors. For over a month the press gave front page coverage to this Red Cross policy, while the NAACP questioned Red Cross officials to determine who was responsible. Responding to the NAACP inquiry, the Red Cross said that in refusing blood from black donors, it was "acting pursuant to the requests and instructions of the army and navy." The NAACP then contacted Navy Surgeon General Ross T. McIntyre, who denied issuing orders to the Red Cross to refuse the blood of blacks. Because of the continuing protest, a meeting was held in Washington with Norman H. Davis, President of the Red Cross; McIntyre; Army Surgeon General James Magee; and F. D. Patterson, President of Tuskegee Institute and an official of the Red Cross. The press reported that a statement was prepared saying that all blood would be accepted, but Magee refused to sign it unless the Red Cross stored the blood separately. On January 21, 1942, the Red Cross announced that it would accept and segregate blood from black donors.[45]

Pickens to Peter H. Oddgood, William Pickens Papers, Schomburg Collection.

44. New York *Age,* December 23, 1941.

45. Chicago *Defender,* December 27, 1941, January 2, 1942; February 7, 1942; Pittsburgh *Courier,* December 27, 1941; January 3, 1942.

Blacks were particularly incensed by the Red Cross policy because black physician Charles R. Drew, an authority on the preservation and storage of blood plasma, had played a leading role in developing the Red Cross blood bank system. The blood bank program grew out of experiments carried out during 1939–40 by Drew and John Scudder. In 1940 Drew became Medical Supervisor of the Blood Transfusion Association, which collected blood (from blacks and whites) for shipment to Great Britain. In 1941 Drew was appointed Director of Blood Procurement for the National Research Council, where he was in charge of collecting blood for the United States Army.[46]

Not satisfied with the Red Cross policy, many blacks refused to give blood. Randolph called on blacks to demand that the Red Cross change its policy. Others noted that the Red Cross refused to accept blood while continuing "to accept money from Negroes." The comic aspects of segregation carried to such extremes were also elicited. Whites who refused "black" blood had no aversion to injecting into their veins the blood (serum) from rabbits, horses, and other animals. Wrote one woman to columnist J. A. Rogers, "I bet the same person who would refuse a transfusion of Negro blood would gladly accept a monkey gland transplanted into his carcass to restore his manhood. . . ."[47]

Violence continued in the South during the weeks just after the outbreak of hostilities. On January 9, 1942, twelve black soldiers were shot in a riot in Alexandria, Louisiana, near camps Claiborne and Livingston. The shooting grew out of an incident in which a white police officer clubbed a black soldier on the street.[48] Two weeks later the black press reported as front page news the most vicious lynching in the South in many years. Cleo Wright had been arrested in Sikeston, Missouri, on charges of assaulting and raping a white woman. After the police took him into custody, a

46. Guzman, p. 42; Chicago *Defender,* January 31, 1942; Pittsburgh *Courier,* December 27, 1941.

47. Pittsburgh *Courier,* January 24, 1942; J. A. Rogers, Pittsburgh *Courier,* February 21, 1942.

48. Pittsburgh *Courier,* January 24, 1942.

mob of over 600 whites seized him, tied him to the back of a car, and dragged him through the black section of town at high speed. It ended when the mob poured gasoline over Wright and set him ablaze.[49]

William Hastie, the racial advisor to the Secretary of War, convened a conference of black leaders in New York City on January 10, 1942, to discuss the black citizens' role in the war. Realizing that the only way to correct the problem of black morale was first to bring to public attention the true feeling of the race, he created a stir when he confronted the leaders with the issue by calling for a vote on whether they believed that blacks were fully behind the war effort. Many of those in attendance were so upset that a vote had to be taken to determine if Hastie's question should be put to a vote; it passed 31 to 24. The vote on Hastie's question showed: 36 said blacks were not behind the war effort; 5 said they were; and 15 remained silent. Later comments revealed that those abstaining sided with the majority opinion.[50]

This was not a group of militant leaders trying to intimidate government officials into granting concessions. The mood of the masses was far more militant than that of the leaders, and it was clear that any leader taking a timid stand would have few followers. They did believe that if the government did not act to ameliorate some of the worst areas of friction, an explosion could occur. Schuyler believed that these representatives aimed "to bag concessions out of the white folks while holding the disgruntled Negro masses in check."[51] He was one of the few observers to suggest that many of the old conservatives hoped to use militant pronouncements to hold blacks in check. Schuyler insisted that should anyone risk jail in order to implement the militant rhetoric, no leader of the race would encourage it. When Winfred Lynn did

49. Chicago *Defender,* January 31, 1942.

50. *Ibid.,* January 17, 1942; Savannah *Tribune,* January 21, 1942; Roi Ottley, "A White Folks War?" *Common Ground* 2 (Spring 1942): 26; *NAACP Annual Report for 1942,* p. 12. The meeting was called by the NAACP. Granger, White, and Hastie were among those present.

51. George S. Schuyler, Pittsburgh *Courier,* January 31, 1942.

just this in refusing to enter the segregated Army, the nation's black leaders and organizations, as predicted, refused to lend active support.

Origins and Aims of the "Double V"

Black editors faced a dilemma. They supported the war against the Axis, but not in the manner in which the United States was waging it. Black papers continued to print pledges of full support and loyalty, but within a few weeks after Pearl Harbor the contradictions within America's democracy became more pronounced, and had the press ignored this, it is unlikely that it could have maintained its circulation. The *Journal and Guide* understood this. In December the editor called for a closing of ranks for the war effort, but by April 1942 he realized that this was not a tenable position and that black papers, following the wishes of their readers, were "on the spot" to "get some . . . democracy here at home first before . . . [we] jump on the free the other peoples 'bandwagon'. . . ." [52]

The press was on the spot. It had to maintain its policy of exposing and condemning discrimination within the country, but to continue to print these stories alone could further alienate the black masses. A positive approach had to be found to enable the papers to continue their protest function and at the same time convince the race that a total commitment to participate fully in the war effort was the path toward eventual equality.

Most editors and spokesmen for the race believed or hoped that the white majority would come to its senses after the war and begin to end the caste system. Lester Granger, writing in the *Amsterdam News,* expressed the view that "if Negro Americans doing their part as 100 per cent loyal Americans will back the war effort . . . there is no question that something will be done along the lines of the thinking of reasonable white Americans—

52. *Journal and Guide,* April 25, 1942.

and I believe that most white Americans are reasonable."[53] This form of thinking prevailed among a great many of the leading spokesmen of the race during the war.

The editor of the New York *Age*, believing that those who participated in World War II would run things later, said that this was why blacks "must fight for a chance to help the United Nations, segregation and Jim Crowism to the contrary notwithstanding."[54] The *Eagle*'s editor commented in its initial post-Pearl Harbor editorial that, "So long as our service remains complete and unsullied, the cry for 'total emancipation' is just inevitable."[55] Rayford Logan, in this same vein, told an audience at Greensboro, North Carolina, "If we stand back and let the white man fight this war then it will be the white man's country and he will have the right to do as he pleases." "That, it seems to us," he continued, "is the danger of extreme agitation that brings about the apathy the American Negro is showing for the war effort." He concluded, "If we lay down our arms . . . we can never claim, nor be entitled to the fruits of victory."[56]

There were some who did not agree with this assumption and tried to warn the race not to expect any postwar thanks for loyal support. Benjamin Quarles, a historian aware of the many postwar failures to accord blacks justice in the nation's history, attacked the position of black leaders looking forward to white gratitude. *The Crisis's* editor disagreed with Quarles, and responded: "We believe he has greatly undervalued the bargaining power of battlefield bravery in the struggle for advancement. . . ."[57] Menial military status along with homefront loyalty, though, was not

53. New York *Amsterdam News,* March 20, 1943.
54. New York *Age,* November 7, 1942.
55. California *Eagle,* December 11, 1941.
56. Quoted in the New York *Amsterdam News,* October 31, 1942; for similar statements, see also *Monthly Summary* 2 (May 1944): 170; Doxey Wilkerson, "Freedom through Victory in War and Peace," *What the Negro Wants,* ed. Rayford Logan (Chapel Hill: University of North Carolina Press, 1944), p. 210.
57. *The Crisis* 50 (September 1943): 268.

sufficient. "Negroes know that if they don't fight in this war like men, they won't be treated like men after the war."[58] Others expressed the view that wartime support was the "one and only basis for full enjoyment of all rights and privileges."[59]

The wartime position of the black press was determined by the belief among black editors and leaders that blacks would have to serve as equals in the armed forces in order to gain eventual equality, and by the militancy of its readers. The black press would continue to protest, and the black population had to support the war effort and fight to participate equally in combat action against the foreign enemy. These aims were not mutually exclusive; in fact they complemented each other. A double victory—one at home and one abroad—was the answer. This would channel the frustration of blacks into positive action by joining the struggle against the Axis with the struggle at home.

A double struggle was not new to World War II. Frederick Douglass had used the idea to rouse free blacks to get into the Army during the Civil War. He had the same thing in mind in 1863 as did the black editors in 1942: convince blacks that the fight against the threat to the entire nation would enhance their future position as a minority group and help bring an end to discrimination against the race. Nor was the fight for the right to fight as combat troops an innovation of the World War II leaders; DuBois had called on black people to do exactly this during World War I. Few papers discussed these facts, but rather concentrated on DuBois's call to "close ranks" and end protest during World War I, which received much of the onus for the lack of progress after that war.[60] An editorial in the *Courier* explained the need for

58. Charley Cherokee, Chicago *Defender,* February 19, 1944.

59. Earl Brown, New York *Amsterdam News,* January 8, 1944 ; *The Afro-American,* September 16, 1939. There are exceptions to this, but they are generally views expressed before December 7, 1941. See California *Eagle,* January 9, 1941, where the editor said, "volumes of martial heroism will secure no immediate freedom," and the editorial September 12, 1940, when the writer said "Afro-Americans are tired of fighting to fight."

60. Kelly Miller, New York *Age,* September 23, 1939, October 28, 1939.

the "Double V" as follows: "In World War I our leaders declared an armistice for the duration. Even W. E. B. DuBois . . . seemed to support this point of view by his speeches and in an article captioned 'Close Ranks.' "[61]

Although DuBois was attacked for his World War I "Close-Ranks" editorial, and, by implication, for the failure of blacks to make progress during the postwar period, black writers generally ignored his protest writings prior to the "Close Ranks" editorial, which were militant enough to cause the Justice Department to intervene. Moreover, they neglected to remind their readers of the extremely militant World War I editorials in the Boston *Guardian,* Chicago *Defender,* and other black papers. Actually, DuBois's "Close Ranks" editorial appeared in July 1918, only four months before the Armistice; therefore, it can hardly be credited with establishing a wartime position for blacks.

In the summer of 1941, most papers envisioned United States involvement in the war as inevitable and they were moving toward the "Double V" position. The *Defender's* editor praised a speech made by Dr. Harold M. Kingsley of the Church of the Good Shepherd, in Chicago. Kingsley had declared that fifth-column activities would make the black man's position worse. He added that blacks would have to participate fully in the eventuality of a war despite internal discrimination. "It is sound wisdom," he summarized, "that we fight both of these battles at the same time. . . . "[62] The *Defender* later added that blacks must defend "the system that hoisted us out of slavery. . . ."[63]

The Philadelphia *Tribune* had already editorialized on the same theme, saying that a homefront battle would be the "second thing" black people should consider in the eventuality of a war. "The second element . . . is not inconsistent with the fight for the security of America, it supplements the first."[64] Noted blacks were speaking along similar lines. Ralph Bunche, at a Howard University

61. Pittsburgh *Courier,* August 8, 1942.
62. Chicago *Defender,* May 31, 1941.
63. *Ibid.,* June 7, 1941.
64. Philadelphia *Tribune* editorial, reprinted in Savannah *Tribune,* September 12, 1940.

speech in early 1941, reflected on coming events and said that "we are forced to fight on two fronts," and added that only when the external war was won could the internal struggle have meaning.[65]

During the first few weeks after the attack on Pearl Harbor, the black press continued to attack discrimination, but at the same time seemed to be edging toward the adoption of a "close ranks" attitude as its wartime position. One of the *Courier's* readers, concerned with the outpouring of loyalty and total support pledges from the black press, wrote a letter to the editor cautioning the press not to forget about the problems facing blacks on the homefront. James G. Thompson, the correspondent, posed the question: "Should I sacrifice my life to live half an American?" and suggested that blacks keep victory abroad in the forefront but continue the struggle at home. "Let . . . colored Americans adopt the Double VV for a double victory. The first V for victory over our enemies from without, the second V for victory over our enemies from within." Thompson wrote that "this should not and would not lessen our efforts to bring this conflict [from without] to a successful conclusion."[66]

The next *Courier* edition had a large "Double V" printed on page one and the campaign began. Commenting on the program, Edgar T. Rouzeau, editor and manager of the New York edition of the *Courier*, emphasized, as did Thompson, that the first victory must be against the Axis, or "Black America may not emerge victorious in its war at home. Our two wars were inextricably intertwined."[67] Other papers quickly joined in the call, and the "Double V" and "fight for the right to fight" became the wartime slogans of the black press.

Most contemporary observers and later historians have misunderstood the underlying basis of the idea of a double struggle. Liberal Southerners immediately saw it as an effort to break down racial barriers. Jonathan Daniels, Southern liberal and war-

65. *The Afro-American*, February 22, 1941.
66. Pittsburgh *Courier*, January 31, 1942.
67. *Ibid.*, February 7, 1942.

time racial advisor to F.D.R., expressed anger with the idea of "two victories or none," and labeled it an attempt at extortion on the part of the black press. The Communist party in the United States visualized a program to encourage a double victory simply as a disruptive impediment in the battle against the Axis powers and at first either opposed it openly or ignored it.[68] Historians looking back on the period have offered their own judgments on the "Double V" program. Some viewed the black editors as striving to encourage black people "to improve their status while the war was going on, rather than wait patiently for the war to be over before doing so." The eminent black scholar John Hope Franklin mentions the double-victory program in his textbook and comments that the "double preoccupation must have caused both efforts to suffer." [69]

Some of these views contain at least elements of accuracy, but all miss the primary thrust of the campaign. It is true that many did see the war as an opportunity to break down barriers confronting the race. Suggestions of this sort were heard often before the United States became a belligerent, and despite fewer expressions of this belief after 1942, it is likely that those who had previously expressed these opinions still held to them. Even so, these people did not expect any social revolution to occur, since the memory of World War I was too vivid to harbor such hopes.

The fear that the "Double V" would hamper the war effort was totally unfounded. When the war was drawing to a close, the Communist party began to alter its initial view, for it realized that a militant homefront posture on the domestic race issue actually increased the efficiency of black soldiers and defense workers.[70] As

68. Jonathan Daniels, "New Patterns for Old," *Survey Graphic* 31 (November 1942): 487; Wilson Record, *Race and Radicalism* (Ithaca, N.Y.: Cornell University Press, 1964), p. 123.

69. Guzman, p. 387; Thelma T. Gorham, "The Negro Press: Past, Present and Future," *U.S. Negro World,* ed. Frank B. Sawyer (NYC: NP, 1967), p. 4; Franklin, p. 599; Roi Ottley, *"New World A-Coming": Inside Black America* (Boston: Houghton Mifflin Co., 1943), p. 268.

70. Record, p. 120.

for encouraging blacks not to forget their grievances, this was obviously an unnecessary function of the "Double V" slogan.

The papers that espoused the "Double V" idea were assimilationist and were convinced that eventual integration would never occur unless blacks played an equal part in the war effort. Therefore, the primary aim of the "Double V" was to motivate blacks to push for equal participation in the war program. But the psychological outlook of the black man in 1941–42 did not augur well for an enthusiastic struggle to participate in the armed services. If the press had remained silent about discrimination, or had called for a closing of the ranks, there conceivably could have been less enthusiasm for fighting the Axis. There was little need to encourage blacks to continue the struggle within, but a major effort was needed to get them to struggle to serve as equals in the war abroad. To identify the struggle abroad with a struggle the press pledged would continue at home, could only encourage blacks to see them both through.

If contemporary critics and later historians misunderstood the thrust of the "Double V" program—that of arousing enthusiasm for the war abroad—it was not the fault of the black press, for editors and columnists often made it quite evident. It was always apparent when one read past the headlines and between the lines, and not infrequently it came out more directly.

The California *Eagle*, before editor Charlotta Bass shifted to the Communist party line and all-out support for the war against Germany, supported the idea of a "Double V" effort, but criticized the way in which the campaign was being used. Bass was concerned that it might become the road to compromise and betrayal, because, as she observed, most of the emphasis of the press and black leaders was on the victory abroad. She was suspicious of the black leaders who spoke of a "Double V" and devoted all their energies to convincing blacks of the necessity of defeating Hitler first and the importance of proving the loyalty of blacks to the country. Calling for a relentless opposition to "every fascist vestige in America," this editor warned her readers to beware of what could be "American history's biggest sellout in the gentle raiment of loyal devotion."[71] Within a short time, the *Eagle* did an about-face in its political philosophy and with this change took up the very position on the "Double V" against which it had previously warned its readers.

What Bass had originally perceived was that by combining the battle abroad with that at home, the black press was aiming at funneling black anger against white America toward the Axis powers. In fact, she was alarmed because the "Double V" was placing so much emphasis on the external war that she feared the program would actually cause blacks to compromise with or put into abeyance the problems at home for the duration of the war. While the black press always made clear that demands for racial equality would continue, it made these demands in such a way as not to hamper the war effort.[72] A study of the black press in the immediate postwar period showed that the papers were not primarily protest organs, but essentially advocates of "positive values consistent with the ideal patterning of American culture."[73] This positive approach and the integrationist basis of the wartime press were the motivating forces behind the "Double V."

There was a new mood among the black masses, and propaganda from the government similar to that of 1917–18 was not suited to this new awareness. Believing they had been duped during World War I, both blacks and whites were highly suspicious of traditional propaganda efforts.[74] Studies of propaganda and morale made during World War II concluded that the basic premise upon which a high morale could be built was "realism." "Tenacity in the face of adversity is the most unequivocal index of high morale."[75] Thus the basis of a high morale, reality and tenacity in the face of adversity, meant that a double struggle was

71. California *Eagle*, March 26, 1942.
72. Ralph N. Davis, "The Negro Newspapers and the War," *Sociology and Social Research* 27 (March-April 1943): 373–78.
73. Maxwell R. Brooks, *The Negro Press Reexamined* (Boston: Christopher Publishing House, 1959), p. 96.
74. Bruce Smith, Harold D. Lasswell, Ralph Casey, *Propaganda, Communication and Public Opinion* (Princeton, N.J.: Princeton University Press, 1946), p. 31.
75. Kurt Lewin, "Time Perspective and Morale," *Civilian Morale,*

the most effective means to elevate a sagging morale. Many studies of morale were made after the war broke out, but the press and black leaders were using these assumptions before December 1941.

Editors of the black press realized, a full year before war came, that a major problem in the advent of a war would be "guaranteeing the maintenance of morale. . . ." At the Hampton Institute Conference on the Participation of Negroes in the National Defense, the Committee for Morale and Mental Hygiene said that "sound morale among Negroes can only be maintained by a fresh crusade to remove the inconsistencies between democratic theory and practice." The report concluded by warning the black leaders not to "conceal the facts concerning discrimination. . . ."[76] The committee studying the role of the black press concluded that it was vital for black newspapers "to do everything possible to make ourselves a powerful and effective force in maintaining the traditional loyalty of the Negro to his country. . . ."[77] By 1942 the press was convinced that to achieve these aims a "Double V" program had to be stressed.

Dr. Kenneth Clark, the prominent black psychologist, studied the problem of black morale while the war was in progress and summed up the ingredients as a combination of frustration, bitterness, hope, apathy, and indifference. Differentiating morale into three classifications, he described the first category as "Synthetic" morale, that is, stimulated by symbols and slogans as in World War I. This type of morale he labeled unstable and transitory. "Perverse" morale was described as frustration "uncanalized" and "unfocused," resulting usually in outbursts of rage and fury. "Genuine" morale, the third basic morale pattern, Clark explained, was a belief that one would die for if need be. Symbols

Second Yearbook of the Society for the Psychological Study of Social Issues (New York: Houghton, Mifflin Co., 1942), p. 51.

76. "Report of the Committee for Mental Hygiene," at the Hampton Institute Conference on the Participation of the Negro in National Defense, *Findings and Principal Addresses* (Hampton, Va., November 25, 26, 1940), p. 19.

77. "Report of the Committee for the Press," *ibid.*, p. 21.

and patriotic slogans, Clark concluded, could reinforce the latter, but could never maintain it.[78]

Propaganda techniques during World War I produced a synthetic morale—if not among the masses, then at least among the black leaders. Clark emphasised that the old slogans would not work during World War II. He was convinced that the outlook was quite different, more "reality bound" than during the previous war. There was no sign of good "fundamental morale," but neither was there any evidence of the synthetic morale of World War I. What opportunities existed to elevate the morale of the black masses remained within the prevalent feeling of militancy, which could be utilized to "galvanize [black people] for unified actions." Finally, Clark said what just about every black spokesman was aware of: "The morale of the Negro cannot be raised by asking him to be content with an inferior, Jim Crow, or unjust role in the war effort of the nation." [79]

The "Double V" was a campaign that was perfectly attuned to the "reality bound" state of mind among the black masses. Black commentators pointed this out during the war, and held that while whites might be stimulated by slogans such as the Four Freedoms and calls to stamp out fascism, "minority morale [could only be] reassured by pressure campaigns for a 'Double Victory' and for victory at home as well as abroad." "Were it not for pressure group activity . . . Negro morale might sink to a danger point." [80] As Kenneth Clark had observed, good morale meant that a person was willing to fight and die for what he believed. Black leaders did not have any illusions about black masses wanting to fight and die to free the captive nations by crushing the European fascists. They realized that blacks were more willing to struggle against fascism at home. If the two struggles could be

78. Kenneth B. Clark, "Morale on the Homefront: World Wars I and II," *Journal of Negro Education* 12 (Summer 1943): 418.

79. Kenneth B. Clark, "Morale Among Negroes," *Civilian Morale*, p. 247.

80. Roscoe Lewis, "The Role of Pressure Groups in Maintaining Morale among Negroes," *Journal of Negro Education* 12 (Summer 1943): 472–73.

united, then, it was hoped, full support for the war effort could be obtained.

Black writers placed both struggles before their readers as equally vital. "If we fight the two wars . . . we can win them both. If we try to fight either one alone, we can lose them both."[81] Every effort was made to show that black leaders would not sell out those serving in the struggle abroad. "You fight the [foreign] enemy," wrote *The Afro-American*'s editor, and "let civilians keep up the battle for full citizenship on the home front."[82] This position of the press was not an easy one to assume. The bi-racial system in the United States showed few signs of easing, and many black youths expressed anger with the press for insisting that blacks be allowed to die for the country.

Apparently, many were surprised to find the black press calling for their all-out support of the war effort. In January 1942 J. A. Rogers commented that those in the press who were calling for 100 percent black participation (he was one of them) were likely to find themselves unpopular among many of their readers. He quoted from the letter of one hostile critic, and said that it seemed to reflect what a large sector of the black masses was thinking. The letter said:

> So called intelligent race leaders are yapping all out for victory. I ask what victory? The white man feeds his jive to the race leaders and they take up the yapping and feed it to the ignorant masses. . . . Each week when I read how the whites do the race it cements me against them and their war.

Adding that he had thought black writers would keep hammering away when the war came, he concluded: "Well, you're doing that but not in the way I thought you would."[83]

This feeling persisted throughout the war. Ollie Stewart, a reporter for *The Afro-American* who had visited many Army

81. Quoted in a full-page statement in *The Brown American* 4 (Spring-Summer 1942): 2.
82. *The Afro-American,* June 26, 1943.
83. J. A. Rogers, Pittsburgh *Courier,* January 24, 1942.

camps during the early defense build-up, was of the opinion that young black soldiers were ready to start the fight at home before the European war ended. He said that with some encouragement and ammunition they would head for Washington to end discrimination.[84] A black reporter returning from the Italian Theater was asked how the troops felt about the black press, and he responded that they were "mad as hell" because the press had got them into the war zone.[85] Harry McAlpin, speaking at the graduation ceremonies at Tuskegee Air Field, was forced to defend the press's fight to get black combat troops, and assured the graduates that after the war they could join together, press and citizens, to achieve another victory at home.[86]

Editors constantly spoke about the problem of "selling" the idea to the wary masses, who appeared to be displaying much sales resistance. E. Washington Rhodes did not hesitate to speak frankly about the role of the wartime black press. He believed that if the press tried to conceal the true situation it would be "absolutely useless. . . . In fact such a policy would destroy morale." Rhodes knew there was widespread talk of the war's being a "white man's war" and that blacks had no stake in the outcome. "It was," Rhodes claimed, "the Negro press which changed this attitude by insisting that Negroes are American citizens and as such had a duty to fight. . . . This has been an awful burden. Remember that the Negro press had to sell their readers the idea that, despite the injustices which they suffered, they must give all to their country."[87]

If the press had to "sell their readers" on the proposition that it was their duty to aid the country, why did the papers continue to print such vivid accounts of violence and discrimination against the blacks? Rhodes defended this function of the black press by

84. *The Afro-American,* July 25, 1942.

85. Ernest E. Johnson, "The Washington News Beat," *Phylon* 7 (Second Quarter 1946): 127; see also Simeon Booker, *Black Man's America* (Englewood Cliffs, N.J.: Prentice-Hall, Inc., 1964), pp. 153–54; Pittsburgh *Courier,* June 10, 1942.

86. Harry McAlpin, *The Afro-American,* June 2, 1945.

87. E. Washington Rhodes, "The Negro Press Takes up its Burden," *The Brown American* 7 (Spring-Summer 1942): 10.

warning that to deny the papers this right to protest would do irreparable damage to the total war effort. The press had never "suggested apathy or indifference. Not once had it stated that the price of participation *Had* to be full emancipation." The press had to protest, Rhodes believed, in order to "keep high the morale of 13 million citizens" and show whites that blacks were not happy with their second-class status.[88]

Others confirmed what Rhodes had stated. Carter B. Wesley, editor of the Houston *Informer*, admitted the difficulties in "selling the masses of Negroes the idea of being Americans" and joining enthusiastically in trying to force their services on an unwilling white majority.[89] The executive committee of the NNPA took the same position when at a meeting in Washington in the fall of 1943 it "agreed that weekly newspapers would attempt to sell their readers on two propositions: 1) That our soldiers . . . must get into this war wholeheartedly. . . . 2) That while they fight to win the war those of us left at home must continue unitedly our battle to end segregation. . . ."[90]

Black papers, then, had to "sell" their readers on the proposition that the ultimate outcome of the war was of vital importance to the race and that the part blacks played in the victory would be essential to their future status in American society. To achieve this the press had to change the black man's conceptualization of the Allied war aims by converting his apathy toward the war abroad and anger with conditions at home into enthusiasm for the foreign struggle by offering this as the best approach to future equality. A double victory was the positive approach to the problem.

The press assured black soldiers that there would be no relenting in the civil rights fight at home, and the record of these soldiers would be the "claim for recognition as full-fledged citizens" in the post war world.[91] But because white America had so often

88. *Ibid.*
89. "Negro Press Conference," 1: 127.
90. *The Afro-American,* November 20, 1943.
91. Editorial, *Negro History Bulletin* 7 (May 1944): 170.

reneged on its obligations to the minority race, the leaders at home would not sit back and wait for equality to be given, but rather they would continue the battle on this front. In order to show that a moratorium on protest would not be declared, the press promised to push for better laws and expose discrimination against the race.

Once the two-front battle was established as a necessity, the problem of actually participating as equals still remained. The "Double V" entailed a double struggle and anyone who fell back in accepting the challenge to participate in combat units instead of just labor units would only be "playing into the hands of the enemies of freedom." If a fight had to be made to get a chance to die for the country, it was necessary because those standing in the way of black soldiers were the racists at home who were "anxious to keep Negroes out of the war for fear that black men may learn to fight too successfully."[92] If blacks did not win the fight for the right to fight, then after the war the attitude of the majority race would be: "After all boy, you didn't do any of the fighting," you just stayed behind the line and drove trucks.[93]

This position meant that black papers had to encourage their readers to feel that, despite segregation, discrimination, and violence directed against blacks in the services, they must insist on serving in all branches. When Lewis Jones chose to go to jail rather than enter the segregated Army, *The Afro-American* sent one of its reporters, Michael Carter, to try to persuade him to change his decision. Jones, a graduate of Moorehouse College, remained adamant. Carter later reported in the paper his failure to sway Jones and said that by "taking this attitude Jones has divorced himself from the large section of white people who usually defend colored peoples' rights." "He also has alienated most of the colored people. . . ." Apparently the *Afro* was so certain that Jones was out of step with other blacks that Carter brought Dr. Kenneth Clark along to the interview in order to determine the

92. *Ibid.*
93. *Journal and Guide,* November 27, 1943.

young man's mental outlook. It was, said Clark, that of a normal person.[94]

This incident represents both the resentment of many black youths, and the lack of any broad consensus between the black masses and leadership on the "Double V" approach. Joining the *Afro* in condemning Jones was the editor of *PM,* John Lewis. *PM,* a liberal daily in New York City, was one of the few white newspapers in the country to take continuous note of the plight of blacks and call for racial equality. Lewis was in total accord with the "Double V" effort, and like most black editors believed victory against the Axis had top priority. In a letter responding to Lewis's editorial attacking Jones, forty Howard University students said his argument left them "strangely cold," and Jones had their complete support. "Thousands of Negro men and women will count him as much a hero as Dorie Miller or Joe Lewis. They will rank him with Frederick Douglass and A. Philip Randolph. . . ." [95] Although these Howard students realized that most blacks submitted to the draft, it was their view that most felt the same way Jones did but could not bring themselves to take such drastic action.

Other black editors took a position familiar to the *Afro*'s. The editor of the New York *Age* expressed understanding and sympathy with two youths who refused to be inducted because, as one of them put it, of the "various crimes committed against my race in the name of democracy." But understanding aside, the editor expressed relief when he said, "Fortunately for us as a group, Negroes of the same mental attitude are now but a small minority in this country." [96] An editorial in the Houston *Informer* chastised a black soldier for attempting suicide in protest against discrimination, saying it would have been more courageous to "live and make his life a challenge in spite of these discrimination." [97] J. A. Rogers commented about those blacks going to prison rather than serving

94. *The Afro-American,* November 7, 1942.
95. Open letter to John P. Lewis, October 9, 1942, Schomburg Vertical Files: World War, 1939–1945.
96. New York *Age,* May 30, 1942.
97. Quoted in *Headlines* 1 (July 1944): 39.

their country. One of them, Samuel Bayfields, went to jail for two years saying he regretted having been born in America. "Such men are very foolish. . . ," said Rogers.[98]

While some refused to be inducted and some attempted suicide, others went AWOL because of the "raw deal" given them in the Army. The editor of the *People's Voice* warned that conditions would not be changed by running away—"the Army is to fight Hitler and those of us at home will fight hitlerism at home."[99]

Just as the press discountenanced individual acts of resistance once the United States entered the war, so too did it oppose non-violent civil disobedience on the part of the black masses. This became evident as the black press began to shift away from a favorable view of A. Philip Randolph's leadership between 1941 and 1943. During the early months of 1941, as the black masses stood helpless in the face of continuing discrimination while their leaders were groping unsuccessfully for a solution, the press eagerly seized upon Randolph's march movement with a rare display of unanimity. But for the exception of the *Courier*, whose hostility always appeared to be a personal enmity against Randolph rather than his program, even the most conservative elements of the press were jumping on the bandwagon by late spring. The old leadership, with its traditional methods of inquiry and protest, had been floundering and appeared helpless when Randolph offered his daring proposal to lead 10,000 (later it grew to 100,000) blacks to Washington. After F.D.R. issued Executive Order 8802, most black newspapermen hailed Randolph as the leading black man in the country.

Randolph's MOWM proved to be so popular that many papers attributed to their own efforts the idea for a mass march on Washington. The *Amsterdam News* congratulated itself for being the first to call for an executive order and added that "soon the idea captured the imagination of leaders and a campaign started."[100] Even the staid New York *Age* gave credit for the mass march

98. J. A. Rogers, Pittsburgh *Courier*, July 4, 1942.
99. *People's Voice*, May 22, 1943.
100. New York *Amsterdam News*, June 21, 1941.

technique to its regular columnist Layle Lane (a participant on the executive committee of the MOWM). After conceiving of a mass protest, the *Age* commented, "Miss Lane, with the assistance of Mr. Randolph got busy and formed a committee . . ." to organize a march on Washington.[101] The Chicago *Defender,* while fully supporting Randolph, said, once the executive order was issued, that "the greatest single contributing factor in the whole fight . . . was the Negro press." [102]

Even in the South, the black press showed an unusual amount of enthusiasm for Randolph's movement. As early as February 1, 1941, the *Journal and Guide* carried a column written by Randolph announcing his program. Although this paper did not comment editorially on the issue for months, its silence seemed to imply approval. By June the paper threw caution to the wind and endorsed the march in its editorial columns. There appeared to be little doubt that in 1941 the black newspapers fully supported Randolph and his program.

Once the country was at war, the press began to have second thoughts about Randolph's leadership. In the summer of 1942 the *Journal and Guide* attacked the MOWM for conducting mass meetings in the Northern cities, saying no benefits would result from such action.[103] Apparently in response to Randolph's comment that he was going to continue his protest activities and didn't "give a damn what happens," the *Amsterdam News* editor wrote of the need for calm good judgment, "because of the growing response of the Negro to radical leadership. . . . They are cropping up all over with ill-planned, ill-conceived and dangerous principles which range all the way from national race riots to civil disobedience campaigns throughout the nation." [104] The *Courier,* always hostile, conducted a poll that revealed that five out of nine interviewed rejected the MOWM.[105] (A geographical breakdown of the poll showed that a majority of blacks residing in the North

101. New York *Age,* July 5, 1941.
102. Chicago *Defender,* July 5, 1941.
103. *Journal and Guide,* July 4, 1942.
104. New York *Amsterdam News,* August 1, 1942. For Randolph's comment, see the Pittsburgh *Courier,* July 11, 1942.
105. Pittsburgh *Courier,* October 17, 1942.

was still favorable.) Most papers at this time still continued to view Randolph as the leader to follow. Six months later his star began to decline.

When in early 1943 Randolph openly espoused a Gandhian program of moderate civil disobedience, which would attack on a very limited scale some aspects of segregation in the North that would not interfere with military or defense work, the press moved away. Randolph at once was on the defensive and for months he was clarifying his position and answering critics. The *Defender* allowed him to present a detailed defense of his program of civil disobedience in a series of columns, but by July 1943 even this friendly paper came out against Randolph.

In his excellent study of the MOWM, Herbert Garfinkel concludes that Randolph's movement received "a fatal blow" when the Detroit race riot occurred ten days prior to the MOWM convention that ratified civil disobedience.[106] It is true that because of the fear of subsequent riots should the black masses take direct action, many black editors openly denounced the program after the 1943 riots. But even before the riots swept the country, Randolph's approach was diverging from that of the black press, and a fear was spreading that Randolph would focus the issues away from the "Double V" program. In June 1943, before the outbreak of violence, P. L. Prattis of the *Courier* expressed his anxiety about this. Admitting that the mass protest movement would yield a harvest, he questioned only the type of harvest blacks would reap. "Is it going to be made clear to them [the masses] that the nation's fight is also their fight or are they going to become emotionally engulfed in the fight for themselves to the extent that the value of the service they are giving to the nation may be questioned." [107] Editors voiced their concern that civil disobedience would shift the focus of the "Double V" away from the war abroad to an emphasis that placed primary attention on the struggle at home.

106. Herbert Garfinkel, *When Negroes March: The MOWM in the Organizational Politics for FEPC* (Glencoe, Ill.: The Free Press, 1959), p. 144.
107. L. Prattis, Pittsburgh *Courier,* June 6, 1943.

A number of papers concentrated their opposition on Randolph's all-black policy as well as his civil disobedience program. When the MOWM was organized it was an all-black movement and no paper raised an objection. But in 1941 many viewed it as a temporary group, and blacks were receiving little notice from white liberals, who were occupied in gathering support for the President's defense program. After the outbreak of hostilities the interracial movement began to pick up, and with the race riots of 1943 it reached its height.[108] The black press, always assimilationist, would not jeopardize this movement by supporting Randolph's all-black organization.

As early as 1942 the California *Eagle* noted certain "inaccuracies" in the approach of the MOWM, among which was the all-black membership policy.[109] Writing three weeks prior to the Detroit riot, a *Defender* columnist commented that "St. Philip was our best leader until he let racism throw him. Believing 'if it ain't black it ain't no good' is just Ku Kluxism in reverse." [110] Another columnist simply called Randolph a "racist." [111] The editor of the *Defender* also took Randolph to task for his all-black policy. "We are unalterably opposed. . . ," he wrote, "to any form of separation that draws us away from the arena in which the issues of American democracy are being decided." [112] The *Courier* believed that blacks would not "get anywhere at all without the good will . . . and co-operation of the white Americans." [113] P. L. Prattis said that although blacks must follow their own minds, they had to have "the help of their white friends to hold off their white enemies." [114] The New York *Age*, which claimed credit for the march program in 1941, now voiced its opposition to the all-black policy.[115] Adam

108. *Monthly Summary* 1 (September 1943): 2. Between June 1943 and September 1943, 117 local, state, and national interracial groups were established.
109. California *Eagle*, July 30, 1942.
110. Charley Cherokee, Chicago *Defender*, May 29, 1943.
111. J. R. Badger, Chicago *Defender*, July 17, 1943.
112. Chicago *Defender*, July 10, 1943.
113. Pittsburgh *Courier*, August 14, 1943.
114. P. L. Prattis, Pittsburgh *Courier*, July 17, 1943.
115. New York *Age*, September 4, 1943.

C. Powell, Jr., was the only member of the MOWM's executive committee to oppose cancellation of the march in 1941 after the FEPC was created. By July 1943 his *People's Voice* printed its disapproval of Randolph's all-black movement, calling it "highly regrettable." Warning its readers that no minority could survive by isolating itself, the editor said that any program preaching black nationalism was "ridiculous." [116]

Black editors were not just using the all-black issue to oppose Randolph's civil disobedience program. They considered alliances with white liberal groups essential to ultimate equality. In April 1943 Roscoe Dungee, editor of the Oklahoma *Black Dispatch,* opposed the conference of Southern black leaders at Durham because it excluded whites. "Only through interracial conferences," he said, "can Negroes secure action." [117] During the 1944 election campaign William Hastie threatened to resign from the Democratic National Citizen's Political Action Committee unless F.D.R. moved toward a program espousing full racial equality. Dungee wrote to Hastie attacking the extreme protests of black leaders and their inability to compromise. Said Dungee, "I am of the opinion that the salvation of the black man is coming through combination and unity formed with other groups." [118]

The "Double V" policy was considered a long-term view, a program that would continue after the war, with white allies joining in once the victory abroad was won. An all-black movement at this time, with a large mass following and direct action policy, could destroy all hopes for the postwar period that the papers envisioned.

The wartime aim of the "Double V" press campaign was an "all out plea for national unity," and did not include "any who preached disunity." The program was not conceived as a radical approach, but rather a "middle of the road position" between the all-now-or-nothing groups and those calling for closed ranks. The *Courier*'s editor visualized it as a response to the "close ranks"

116. *People's Voice,* July 17, 1943.
117. Quoted in Pittsburgh *Courier,* April 3, 1943.
118. Quoted in Chicago *Defender,* September 30, 1944.

approach of World War I, but at the same time made it clear that the black man's patriotism was not conditional.[119]

Since the press rejected all forms of individual resistance to the Army and the draft, and since it rejected the civil disobedience program of A. Philip Randolph, how then did the "Double V" differ from "close ranks?" One can only conclude that it was an approach that sought to encourage mass support for the war aims of the country attuned to the propaganda needs of the black community. It was also a program that could, hopefully, continue after the war and prevent a reversion to a Garveyite program away from integration. Perhaps the most immediate value of the wartime press was its serving "as an outlet of the Negro's otherwise thwarted ambitions and repressed anger. . . ." [120]

119. Pittsburgh *Courier,* March 7, 1942; August 8, 1942; Horace R. Cayton, Pittsburgh *Courier,* July 25, 1942.

120. V. V. Oak, "What About the Negro Press?" *Saturday Review of Literature* 25 (March 6, 1943): 4.

4
The Black Press and the Armed Forces: The Fight for the Right to Fight

The Army is not a sociological laboratory.[1]

The Pittsburgh *Courier* and the Quota Movement

Black Americans have fought in every war in which the United States has engaged, but in each major conflict their military status created a problem for the white majority. In the war that created the new nation, the Continental Army did not accept black volunteers until the Army's manpower needs and the fear aroused by Governor Dunmore's call to all slaves to flee to the British Army caused Washington to alter his all-white policy. After this, the Continental Army accepted blacks and integrated them into the ranks along with white troops.[2]

During the Civil War Lincoln hesitated for over a year before enlisting black troops. Finally military necessity, along with in-

1. Colonel E. R. Householder to twenty black editors, December 8, 1941, quoted in Chicago *Defender*, December 13, 1941.
2. Franklin, pp. 131–38.

cessant demands of Northern black militants and white abolitionists, forced the Army to open its ranks to black volunteers. The war that ended slavery saw the institutionalization of segregated regiments, which in turn created new problems to be faced during World War I. In separate regiments black troops could easily be singled out for labor duties, and the practice of using all-white officers created problems when they were commanding all-black regiments. In 1917 many black leaders accepted segregation for the duration of the war, but they fought for black officers to lead the segregated troops.

When events suggested that a second European war was approaching in the late 1930s, black leaders began to demand that black troops should not be relegated primarily to labor battalions as they were during the previous war. This raised the question of the combat effectiveness of black troops. After World War I, Army officials studied the combat ability of black soldiers. Although most black soldiers had served in labor battalions, two infantry divisions—the 92nd and 93rd—did see combat action; and it was around these two divisions that the discussion centered. Testimony came almost entirely from white officers who had commanded the troops of these two divisions, and the findings concluded that black combat troops were ineffectual unless under the close supervision of white officers. This led to the continued acceptance of segregation and a policy of concentrating black soldiers in labor divisions.[3]

Between 1922 and 1940 the Army high command formulated various policies for the employment of black troops under war conditions. By 1940 the Army had decided to continue segregation, but to use black soldiers in all branches of the service. This policy also allowed for the use of black soldiers in combat units on the same proportional basis as whites. The Army did not make these contingency plans public until the end of 1940, and blacks, until then, believed that the Army had no new program for the com-

3. Lee, pp. 15–18 ; L. D. Reddick, "The Negro Policy of the United States Army," *Journal of Negro History* 34 (January 1949): 23–29.

plete utilization of black troops and that the policy of World War I would continue.[4]

The Pittsburgh *Courier* initiated the drive to open up all branches of the Army to blacks as early as February 1938.[5] The Army, for no apparent reason, did not reveal that its 1937 plan met all of the *Courier*'s demands. It seems reasonable to assume that the Army had no serious intention of implementing the plan, for during the war most blacks still remained in labor units, and many black combat units were ultimately converted to labor battalions without ever seeing combat.[6] Or, seeing that the demands raised in the black press were not different from its 1937 plan, the Army might have decided to hold back until the opportune time. That time appeared to be in October 1940, during F.D.R.'s third bid for the presidency.

Thus, because the Army had not revealed its plans for the proportional employment of blacks in all branches of the service, the initial thrust of black protest in the press was aimed at just this—the opening up of all areas of the Army on a percentage basis according to the number of black people in the total population. The *Courier* disclosed that at the end of 1939 there were only 4,451 black enlisted men and five officers in the service compared to 229,636 white enlisted men and 1,359 white officers.[7] Besides the immediate aim of using the Army to alleviate black unemployment, the eventuality of being drawn into the European war meant that blacks had to achieve equal status quickly, since it would be too late once the country was at war.

In April 1940 the *Courier* stepped up its efforts to break down the exclusionary policies of the armed services. Each edition of the paper carried front page articles, often headline stories, and the editorial page offered comments on the military situation. The *Courier's* program was in effect a threefold approach: publicizing the lack of opportunity in the armed services, educating its readers

4. Lee, pp. 48, 76.
5. Pittsburgh *Courier,* February 19, 1938.
6. Selective Service: *Special Groups*, 1: 4.
7. Pittsburgh *Courier,* May 4, 1940.

about the approaches they could take to break down these barriers, and the initiation of a lobbying committee in Washington. Readers were urged to flood their congressional representatives with letters demanding an end to "military taxation without representation," and when the *Courier's* committee appeared before Congress, they were urged to encourage their congressmen to support its proposals. While conceding that few blacks were able to vote, the *Courier* pointed out that the coming election would be closer than the 1936 Roosevelt landslide, and blacks who were able to vote were situated in key states that would help decide the coming election. Finally, the *Courier* called on its readers to organize local committees to prepare for holding mass meetings to protest against the exclusion of blacks from the military and industrial defense program.[8]

On April 27 the *Courier* announced the organization of a committee to appear before the Senate Subcommittee on Military Appropriations. Attorney Charles Houston headed the eleven-man delegation, which included representatives of various fraternities, American Legion posts, the YMCA, the Elks, Negro Reserve Officers, the Washington Chamber of Commerce, and The Association for the Study of Negro Life and History. Nine of the delegates were World War I combat officers. Howard University professor Rayford W. Logan, representing the Alpha Phi Alpha fraternity, acted as spokesman for the group. He told the Senators that there were no black commissioned officers in combat units, no black flying cadets, and no black Reserve Officers serving in the Army despite the recently enacted Thomason Act, which allowed 650 officers to be drawn from colleges to train with regular Army troops. In order to bring blacks into the services, Logan requested that the 1941 Military Establishment Bill be amended "in such a way as to provide a general 10-percent strength for Negro enlisted men and officers in the Regular Army."[9]

8. Pittsburgh *Courier,* April 27, 1940; May 18, 1940; May 25, 1940; December 7, 1940.

9. United States Congress, Senate. *Hearings before the Subcommittee of the Committee on Appropriations on H. R. 9209, Appropria-*

Although he asked for the establishment of black quotas, Logan expressed his disapproval of "the continuation of separate Negro units. We deplore segregation in any form, especially when it is practiced by the Federal Government. But in accepting these separate units which are forced upon us, we do so only in hope that these units will be commanded by Negro officers." In conclusion, Logan said to the Senators:

> There are three prevailing attitudes among the Negro citizens of this country. One is that Negroes should be integrated into all branches of the Military Establishment without regard to race or color. A second attitude holds that since Negroes are the victims of many forms of oppression and discrimination, comparable to those which this Government has condemned in foreign countries, they should refrain from any participation in the armed forces of the United States. The third attitude, represented by members of this committee, while deploring this segregation, this oppression and this discrimination, insists that Negroes be given the opportunity to exercise their rights.[10]

The *Courier* publicized the committee's activities and supported its position on black quotas. Said the editor, "If the United States Government has thoroughly adopted the psychology of the unreconstructed South and is not committed to a separate but equal' system of bi-racialism (as seems to be the case), then we demand that we receive this equality, even though separate." [11] The Senate, however, took no action on the *Courier* committee's request. The committee then announced that it would continue to work in Congress and also take its demands to the War and Navy Departments and the President. Also, it was preparing to appear before the platform committees of both parties' nominating conventions to request that they include provisions in their platforms for black participation in the armed services.

On June 3, the *Courier* committee announced that it was re-

tions for the Military Establishment for the Fiscal Year Ending June 30, 1941. 76th Cong., 3rd Sess., p. 366.

10. *Ibid.*, pp. 367, 375.

11. Pittsburgh *Courier*, May 25, 1940.

organizing itself as a permanent, independent group to be known as The Committee on Participation of Negroes in the National Defense Program (CPNNDP). The new committee, headed by Rayford W. Logan, intended to act as a "watch dog for the race" in the entire defense build-up program, both military and industrial. Although it was no longer directed by the *Courier,* this paper remained closely associated with the committée's activities. Louis Lautier, a *Courier* reporter, was the committee's Secretary, and the committee received financial support and worked with the paper until it ceased to function in the summer of 1941.[12]

The committee's initial efforts were directed toward getting Congress to insert a nondiscrimination clause in one of the many defense measures under consideration that would compel the Army to establish black quotas in all of its service branches. On June 7, Louis Lautier, working through William J. Thomkins, Recorder of Deeds for the District of Columbia, contacted Senator Sherman Minton and persuaded him to get a clause inserted into the Bill to Expedite the Strengthening of National Defense that read: "No one shall be excluded from enlistment in any branch of the Military Establishment on account of race, creed or color." The House conferees, however, objected to the amendment and it was deleted. The *Courier* then wired 65 congressmen in an attempt to have the clause reinserted, but no action was taken.[13]

The CPNNDP then turned its attention to the political parties, which were preparing to nominate their presidential candidates for the November elections. The Republicans openly courted black voters for the first time in years. Wendell Willkie attacked the exclusionist policies of the armed services, and promised to give everyone a chance to serve in the military should he win the election. He also said that if he won the election, blacks would receive their share of political appointments. Senator Robert Taft,

12. Pittsburgh *Courier,* June 8, 1940; William G. Nunn to Rayford Logan, July 10, 1941; July 24, 1941; Logan to Nunn July 12, 1941; July 21, 1941, Committe on Participation of Negroes in the National Defense Program Papers, Moorland-Spingarn Collection, Howard University Library. Hereafter cited as CPNNDP Papers.

13. Pittsburgh *Courier,* June 22, 1940.

another Republican presidential hopeful, spoke out in favor of "proportionate representation of the Negro in our Government," in industry, and in the armed services.[14] Logan appeared before the Republican platform committee, while Houston and Vann appealed to the Democrats for approval of their program. The Republicans came out with much the stronger platform, calling for a square deal for Negroes and an end to the barriers preventing blacks from entering the armed services. The Democrats emphasized past performance.[15]

In August Logan was again in Capitol Hill, this time before the House Committee on Military Affairs (May Committee), which was conducting hearings on the Burke-Wadsworth Selective Service Bill. Again the CPNNDP attempted to open up all branches of the Army to black soldiers. In spite of the Army's unannounced 1937 plan to include blacks in all branches in proportion to their percentage of the total population, the authorized increase of enlisted personnel scheduled to go into effect after August 15, 1940, called for only an additional 3,395 blacks. The authorized increase for whites was just under 145,000. Logan, therefore, asked the House to insert a nondiscrimination clause in the proposed Conscription Bill so that blacks would be assured of a proportional share of service positions. Houston appeared along with Logan as a special representative of the *Courier* and supported Logan's request.[16]

In seeking the nondiscrimination clause, Logan and the *Courier* were not opening an assault on segregation. They believed that it was unrealistic to attack segregation during a world crisis. When the war in Europe began, Logan advocated a colored division commanded from "top to bottom by colored officers." He said that there was "not going to be any mixing of colored and white troops in the American army," and the choice facing blacks was between "colored troops commanded by colored officers and

14. *Ibid.*, July 8, 1940; July 29, 1940.
15. Pittsburgh *Courier,* June 29, 1940; July 6, 1940; July 13, 1940.
16. U.S. Congress, House of Representatives, *Hearing Before the Committee on Military Affairs on H.R. 10132 Selective Compulsory Military Training and Service.* 76th Cong., 3rd Sess., pp. 585–87.

colored troops commanded by white officers."[17] The *Courier*, of course, had always conducted its campaign under this assumption. Other black papers adopted the same position. *The Afro-American*, as early as October 1939, said, "We are not going to have that [integration] in the next war. . . . But if we must have colored units we can insist upon colored officers, and our present attack should be centered on this point."[18]

Their position differed little from that of DuBois in 1917. This "realistic" approach of accepting segregation and asking only to have black officers lead black troops was not, in fact, realistic at all, since the Army seemed to have been as opposed to black commanding officers as it was to integration. Besides, even if the Army did make concessions to Logan's request, there would not have been time to train sufficient numbers of black officers for high command positions. In 1940 there were only five black officers, of whom one was nearing retirement age and three were chaplains. The most Logan could have expected was more junior grade officers, which, as the previous war had shown, did not solve many problems. Actually, discrimination against black junior officers often added to the bitterness and frustration of the black troops.

The open acceptance of segregation and the call for black quotas was the cause of a rift between the *Courier* and the CPNNDP on the one hand and the NAACP on the other. As far as the NAACP was concerned, the quota approach was the antithesis of its own integrationist philosophy, and one that would only lend support to white segregationists. An incident that occurred in the early stages of the defense build-up clearly illustrates the NAACP's hostility toward the quota movement. Executive

17. Rayford Logan, New York *Amsterdam News*, September 23, 1939.

18. *The Afro-American*, October 7, 1939. The New York *Age* suggested that the race leaders quit "quibbling over what camps the Negroes will be trained in, [and] insist that we be given a proportional number of trainees in all branches of the service." New York *Age*, July 27, 1940. See also Savannah *Tribune*, May 30, 1940, for a call for proportional representation in the armed services.

Secretary Walter White, in a letter to Secretary of War Harry Woodring, protested the barring of black trainees from the Army Air Corps. Responding to White, Woodring commented:

> Following a well established principle that the races should not be mixed within organizations, a principle endorsed by your own people, it is necessary to set up specific units to which colored personnel may be assigned.[19]

Woodring concluded that since no all-black air units existed at that time, the Army could not accept black volunteers for this service branch. White, angered by this reply, believed that it was "one of the results of the *Courier*'s campaign for Negro units in the armed forces. . . ."[20]

Although White was antagonistic to the quota approach from its inception, his association did not confront the movement, which was picking up support in the black press. Nor did the NAACP publicly engage in any large-scale effort of its own to attack the Army's practice of limiting black participation prior to the introduction of the Selective Service Bill in mid-1940.[21] So aloof did the NAACP appear, that by early 1940 some members began to express their concern about the growing disenchantment with the association in the black community due to the NAACP's apparent inaction.

The reason for the NAACP's refusal to openly oppose the quota movement between 1938 and 1940 can only be surmised. A

19. Harry H. Woodring to Walter White, December 12, 1938, NAACP Papers, Library of Congress.

20. Walter White to Daisy E. Lampkin, December 14, 1938, NAACP Papers.

21. During 1939 *The Crisis* carried several articles dealing with discrimination in the defense program, but the association's legal and lobbying activities remained focused on the issues of the anti-poll tax and anti-lynch bills. See *NAACP 30th Annual Report for 1939* (New York, 1939); NAACP, *Let's Be Honest About Democracy* (New York, 1939). First mention of NAACP activity in the defense program appears in the *NAACP Bulletin,* which was first published in December 1940 to deal with the subject of the black community and national defense.

strong possibility is the association's realization that the black press and the black community were not averse to a quota approach. The leading proponents of quotas, the *Courier* and the CPNNDP, were so confident of public support that they never hesitated to point out the NAACP's refusal to cooperate in the quota drive. When the original *Courier* committee appeared before Congress, the paper emphasized that Houston, who was a special counsel for the NAACP, would represent the *Courier* and not the NAACP. The *Courier* noted that "it is understood that Mr. White does not want his organization introduced into the fight at the present time because of that organization's 'idealism of no segregation,' as against the *Courier*'s policy of the 'practicality of separate divisions.' " The CPNNDP was also openly annoyed with the NAACP. Logan said that the reason he became active in the struggle with the Army was the "profound slumbers" of the NAACP during the early phase of the fight for equal treatment in the national defense program. He also revealed that the NAACP had refused several offers from his group to join forces with every black civil rights group in the struggle.[22]

It would be impossible to gauge black public opinion during this period regarding the issue of quotas. However, some indication of public opinion was apparent at a mass rally held in Harlem in October 1940 sponsored by the Citizens Non-Partisan Committee for Equal Rights in Defense. Frank Reeves, a confidant of Walter White and one who was hostile to the quota movement, attended the rally and reported his rather discouraging observations to White. The rally drew from four to six thousand people "from all levels of the economic scale and of all ages and political philosophies." Reeves said that Charles Houston and Adam Clayton Powell, Jr., drew the most spirited responses from the audience. Houston had demanded the establishment of an air corps training center for blacks, while Powell's comments "were the most dynamic and enthusiastically received remarks made. There was an

22. Pittsburgh *Courier,* April 27, 1940; Address delivered by Rayford W. Logan to the American Teachers Association, West Virginia State College, Summer 1941 (Typescript), CPNNDP Papers.

obvious bitterness on his part and a spoken tendency to discredit the NAACP." The NAACP, unrepresented on the speaker's platform, sent a telegram that when read to the audience "stimulated no spontaneous reaction as did some of the others." [23]

Another reason for the seemingly "profound slumbers" of the NAACP was that it had no positive program to present to the black community other than its opposition to segregation. This problem became acute by the spring of 1940, when several of the association's officials were faced by people who questioned the NAACP's ability to develop programs geared to meet existing needs. In May 1940 Roy Wilkins, Assistant Executive Secretary, touched on this issue in a memorandum to White. He said that he was often met with the question: "What is the NAACP doing about the Negro in the defense program?" He was also impressed by the general public feeling that either the NAACP had no agenda to deal with the defense program, or that its approach was no longer suitable. Wilkins suggested the following approaches that the association could espouse as those which might gain a "popular response":

1) Oppose entrance of America into the war and the sending of troops abroad.
2) Oppose repeal of the Johnson Act.
3) Insist that any defense program must include the lifting of restrictions against Negroes in all branches of the Army and Navy.[24]

The first two suggestions were obviously too drastic for White, who held decidedly pro-Allies sympathies. The third one, since it did not raise the question of integration, might have appeared too similar to the demand for quotas. There is no record of White's response to these suggestions, but for the next few months the association continued to offer little direction in the battle for

23. Frank D. Reeves to Walter White, October 29, 1940, NAACP Papers.
24. Roy Wilkins to Walter White, September 16, 1940, NAACP Papers.

equality in the defense program. The NAACP was faced with a dilemma. The quota movement had the support of a large segment of the black press and seemed to have the ear of the black masses, so the association could not become openly hostile. And if it launched a vigorous integration program, it would have to meet the quota forces head on. The policy, for the time being, remained in a state of uncertainty.

This lack of central direction created confusion within the ranks of the NAACP. Various local branches began acting on their own initiative until the national office was forced to face the issue. On August 8, 1940, the Buffalo branch came out against the pending Conscription Bill, legislation that the national office favored with the proper anti-discrimination clause included.[25] Thurgood Marshall, alarmed by this lack of central command, urged White to elaborate an official NAACP policy on conscription. He also observed that if the association did not publicly make its position on quotas quite clear, "some of our branches might endorse the question of segregated units in the armed forces." [26]

As the Burke-Wadsworth Bill was moving into its final stages in Congress, the NAACP became active in the move to get an anti-discrimination clause inserted into the bill. An August 8, the association sent a circular telegram to 72 senators describing the exclusion of black volunteers from the current armed forces build-up, and requested the inclusion of a clause in the draft law "to guarantee to Negroes the right to serve in every branch of the armed forces without discrimination because of race or color." [27] This telegram did not raise the subject of integration, but concentrated on opening up all branches of the services to blacks—a goal the quota forces had long sought. Since it was Senator Robert Wagner who, after receiving the NAACP's telegram, introduced the anti-discrimination clause in the Senate, his comments during the debate are revealing. When asked by Senator Overton if the

25. Buffalo *Evening News*, August 28, 1940, in NAACP Papers.

26. Thurgood Marshall to Walter White, September 12, 1940, NAACP Papers.

27. Copy of a circular telegram sent to senators from Walter White, August 8, 1940, NAACP Papers.

clause would establish "mixed units," Wagner replied that "it had nothing to do with that." And when prodded by Senator Ellender if he believed that there should be mixed units in the Army, Wagner answered in the negative. Much of the opposition to the Wagner amendment focused on the implication that the amendment would force the Army to set up all-black units in every branch.[28]

It is likely that the NAACP at this time became convinced that integration could not be achieved during the world crisis, and was willing to settle temporarily for the *Courier*-CPNNDP program without publicly stating it. The association made no public comment on Wagner's position on mixed units, and was pleased with the Senate's adoption of his anti-discrimination amendment. The only disappointment expressed by the NAACP was that the Wagner amendment included only black volunteers and not black draftees. The NAACP moved to close this loophole in the House, still avoiding the integration issue.[29]

The similarity of the NAACP's position at this time with that of the quota advocates becomes evident with the association's reaction to the Fish amendment to the House version of the Burke-Wadsworth Bill. On September 3, the NAACP sent a circular telegram to several House members asking for support of the Wagner amendment with the addition of a provision to cover blacks who were conscripted as well as those volunteering. On September 6, the House passed an amendment sponsored by Congressman Hamilton Fish that included both black volunteers and draftees in its anti-discrimination provisions.[30] The following day White got in touch with Wilkins and suggested that he send out a special story to thirty or forty black newspapers so that they

28. United States *Congressional Record,* Senate, 76th Cong., 3rd Sess., August 26, 1940, No. 156, pp. 16625–31.

29. Copy of a circular telegram sent to Congressmen from Walter White, September 3, 1940, NAACP Papers. Privately, White maintained his firm opposition to segregation, and expressed this conviction to Wagner. See Walter White to Robert F. Wagner, September 18, 1940, NAACP Papers.

30. Pittsburgh *Courier,* September 14, 1940.

would know the "the NAACP was responsible" for the Fish amendment. That same day the association's *Press Service* sent out a special release taking credit for the amendment.[31]

This amendment, which the NAACP hailed as an important advance and for which it claimed credit, was actually introduced by Fish at the request of the CPNNDP. On September 4 Rayford Logan, Louis Lautier, and two other men met with Fish, handed him a draft of an anti-discrimination clause, and told him where they wanted it inserted in the bill. After the House incorporated the Fish amendment, the CPNNDP continued its activities on behalf of the bill until it became law with the Fish amendment included. This amendment, for which the NAACP claimed credit, was directed toward the establishing of black quotas in the Army.[32]

There was no uniform approach in the black press to the Selective Service Bill. Some favored it with the safeguards called for by the CPNNDP, and others denounced it as the first step toward a dictatorship. At the same time, many believed that the bill would be an opportunity to force the Army to open its door to blacks. There was also the expectation that conscription would lessen the severity of unemployment for the black population. Political affiliation had little effect on a paper's position on conscription.

The *Defender,* in the Democratic ranks, viewed conscription as a potential weapon to silence the black press, and said that the draft would not solve the problems facing blacks. This paper did make a point of opposing the draft because of the Army's segregation policy, but its editor emphasized that this was not the primary reason for its opposition. Its great fear was that conscription "would silence our militant voices" against lynching, poll tax, and discrimination.[33] The *Defender* had almost come to grief with the Justice Department during World War I and this apparently was the basis for its opposition to the draft in 1940. When the bill was

31. Walter White to Roy Wilkins, September 7, 1940, NAACP Papers; *Press Service of The National Association for the Advancement of Colored People,* September 7, 1940.

32. Statement by Rayford W. Logan (Typescript), CPNNDP Papers; Pittsburgh *Courier,* September 14, 1940; September 28, 1940.

33. Chicago *Defender,* August 31, 1941.

signed by F.D.R., the *Defender* boasted that it was the only Negro paper to oppose the bill from the beginning.[34]

In early 1940 *The Afro-American*, a paper that would support Republican candidates in 1940 and 1944, began to attack Roosevelt for not adequately building up the defenses of the United States. In June the editor wrote, "We can't afford to be rhetorical in the present situation" and said that everything else should be dropped except for the issue of defense preparations.[35] The *Afro*, in early 1940, emphasized the issue of defense in its totality and not so much the role of the black soldier. The editor was fully behind the Conscription Bill and denounced those who opposed quotas, thereby lending support to the CPNNDP. At one point, this paper blamed slackers, Communists, and labor unions for obstructing the passage of the Conscription Bill, and called for a limitation on free speech when it went beyond acceptable limits in opposing defense preparations. Once the Draft Bill became law, the *Afro* announced its support for Wendell Willkie, and denounced F.D.R. for permitting a Jim Crow Army.[36]

On September 16, 1940, F.D.R. signed the Conscription Bill. The *Courier* appeared pleased with the law and boasted of its role in obtaining the nondiscrimination clause. The paper reviewed its part in the long endeavour to get the clause inserted, and said that in 1939 every indication pointed to an Army that would restrict blacks to labor battalions. It was, the paper wrote, the *Courier* and its committee headed by Logan that prevented this. Nothing was said about segregation at this time, despite the fact that the *Courier* realized that the Army would remain segregated. The *Courier* had, on September 7, printed excerpts from the debate on Senator Wagner's amendment that showed that the Senate was not trying to provide for integrated Army units. One week after the Selective Service Act was enacted, the *Courier* announced that it was winning its battle against the Army because the War Department revealed that, with conscription, the Army would bring

34. *Ibid.*, September 21, 1940.
35. *The Afro-American*, June 1, 1940; May 25, 1940.
36. *Ibid.*, August 17, 1940; September 4, 1940; October 19, 1940.

blacks into the service up to their relative proportion of the population, and would create new all-black units.[37]

On October 9 the White House released a policy statement concerning black troops. This seven-point statement was the first time the War Department's program was made public, but as Ulysses Lee has shown, it was basically identical to the War Department's earlier contingency plans. The first six points of the statement granted all that the *Courier* and CPNNDP were fighting for—proportional representation in all branches of the Army and black commissioned officers. The seventh point was what all had accepted as inevitable before October 9: "The policy of the War Department is not to intermingle colored and white enlisted personnel in the same regimental organizations." [38]

The official White House sanction of segregation in the Army changed everything. It became a national insult to black citizens, and black papers reflected their indignation on every fron page.[39] But it could not have been an unexpected policy. The fact that Roosevelt had remained silent until this time—a few weeks before the election—and then released the statement from the White House rather than from the War Department, seems to indicate that he thought the policy would be acceptable. Had he believed otherwise, it is unlikely that he would have released the statement before the election while his opponent was making a strong bid for black votes. As one astute administration official commented, the blunder was in saying anything at all about segregation. "It was," he said, "not necessary to publicize the fact because it had already been accepted as part of the Army procedure." [40]

37. Pittsburgh *Courier*, September 7, 1940; September 21, 1940; September 28, 1940.

38. Robert P. Patterson to Franklin D. Roosevelt, October 8, 1940; Stephen Early to Robert P. Patterson, October 9, 1940, OF 93, Franklin D. Roosevelt Library. The October 9 statement can also be found in *The Crisis* 47 (November 1940): 35.

39. See for example, *The Afro-American*, November 2, 1940; Chicago *Defender*, October 26, 1940; letter from Eugene K. Jones to Franklin D. Roosevelt, reprinted in National Urban League, *The Negro and National Defense* (New York, n.d.), p. 9.

40. Wayne Coy to Oscar Ewing, October 17, 1940, Wayne Coy Correspondence, Franklin D. Roosevelt Library.

The October 9 statement was the first official notice of the Army's program for the use of black troops, and it seemed to be the satisfactory culmination of a three-year struggle inaugurated by the Pittsburgh *Courier*. The *Courier* responded by calling the White House statement "alarming."[41] When White House Press Secretary Stephen Early released the October 9 statement, he implied that Walter White, A. Philip Randolph, and T. Arnold Hill, at a September 27 meeting with the President, had approved of the proposed policy statement on black troops. These three black leaders quickly denied their complicity and released a memorandum they had presented to President Roosevelt at their meeting showing that they had called for complete integration in the armed forces.[42] These men, commented the *Courier*, were for complete integration, and, in favoring this position, "they were merely supporting the Pittsburgh *Courier*'s campaign."[43] The *Courier* took its first step in retreat away from its quota program.

During the following weeks the Courier began to attack those blacks urging the race to accept segregation as "better than nothing." "We must stop asking for more segregation, even if there is a prospect of having complete Negro units in every branch of the service; and we must start fighting segregation sincerely. . . ."[44] Finally, in an editorial entitled "Let's Make Up Our Minds," the paper appeared to accept responsibility for its own role in the past, which called for the acceptance of segregation:

> For years we have trumpeted the *Principle* of *'No Segregation'* but accepted the *Practice* of segregation, and we can scarcely now blame the government if it is giving us what our actions indicated we wanted. While claiming to be opposed to segregation, we have also adopted the principle of racial proportionalism in the hope that the segregation we got would be so good that

41. Pittsburgh *Courier*, October 19, 1940.
42. Stephen Early to Walter White, October, 18, 1940; October 25, 1940; White to Early, October 21, 1940, OF 93, Franklin D. Roosevelt Library.
43. Pittsburgh *Courier*, October 19, 1940.
44. *Ibid.*, December 28, 1940.

> it would equal whatever the other citizens got. The current campaign for equal opportunity in the national defense is an illustration of this evasive and indefinite policy. We did not launch our campaign on the high ground of equal opportunity and no segregation whatever, but asked for Negro units in all armed services. A minority, of course, took the highest position.[45]

The *Courier* continued to denounce racial proportionalism throughout World War II. As the war was nearing a conclusion, the paper stated that blacks had accepted the segregated draft only because they did not want to impede the war effort; but they would never accept a segregated peacetime draft.[46]

Without knowledge of the Army's contingency plans, the black press had been forced to fight for all that it thought it could realistically achieve: blacks in all branches of the Army and black officers, within a segregated framework. Once this had been accomplished, though, the *Courier* and the rest of the black press cut loose from their long-held position and launched an all-out verbal assault upon segregation in the armed forces. The *Courier* had elevated its circulation figures to the highest level of all the black papers by 1940. Its policy was one of continuous demands and outspoken militancy, and this was not an unimportant factor in increasing circulation. Had the Army revealed its 1937 plan to utilize blacks in all the service branches, it appears likely that the *Courier* would have inaugurated a protest movement to abolish segregation in the Army at that time.

The October 9 White House statement did, at least temporarily, bring praise from some papers. The *Amsterdam News* was excited about the granting of a full quota to black soldiers and expressed thanks to Robert Vann, publisher of the *Courier*, for his consistent efforts to bring this to fruition.[47] The *Journal and Guide* praised Roosevelt for opening up all branches of the Army to blacks; "and what is more," wrote the editor, "the Administration intends to . . . establish colored combat units upon the basis of our per-

45. *Ibid.*, February 1, 1941.
46. *Ibid.*, June 6, 1943; August 26, 1944.
47. New York *Amsterdam News*, October 12, 1940.

centage of the population."[48] The Savannah *Tribune* said that for the present, segregation was in "vogue," and the granting of black combat divisions was a practical victory for black people.[49]

A consistent foe of conscription and all forms of segregation, the *Defender* observed the similarity of approach taken in 1940 to that of 1917. "We have asked for a Negro Division, a Negro this and a Negro that, without an intelligent awareness of the defeatism incurred by such a pleading." The *Defender* placed the blame not on F.D.R., whom the paper supported, but rather on "confused leadership."[50] Commenting on the dilemma facing the black citizen because of a Jim Crow draft, the editor of the California *Eagle* said that since it was law, Negroes would accept it—but without enthusiasm. It was better under any circumstances for the Negro to serve, wrote this editor, "in order that America might know and applaud his courage."[51]

The outcome of this early struggle with the Army was the reemergence of the NAACP to its previous position of prestige in the black press. The association was not publicly active in the quota campaign that preceded the enactment of conscription. It did take an active role in getting Senator Wagner to sponsor an anti-discrimination clause to the Selective Service Bill, but refrained from joining the CPNNDP and *Courier* because of their open acceptance of segregation. By late October the *Courier* was writing favorably of the NAACP's actions in fighting the Jim Crow Army.[52] The NAACP was able to assume the scepter of leadership once again by late 1940. At the war's end the general view within the black press was that the NAACP had led the fight for racial equality during the war. Adam Clayton Powell, Jr., who five years earlier had received applause for his denunciation of the NAACP, now called Walter White "the nation's Number One Negro."[53]

48. *Journal and Guide,* September 21, 1940.
49. Savannah *Tribune,* October 24, 1940.
50. Chicago *Defender,* October 26, 1940.
51. California *Eagle,* September 12, 1940.
52. Pittsburgh *Courier,* October 26, 1940.
53. Adam C. Powell, Jr. *Marching Blacks* (New York: Dial Press, 1945), p. 143.

Draft Resistance

Of all the means to counter the segregated Army, opposition to the draft would have been the most direct and the most drastic. After there had been repeated physical attacks on Southern-based black troops, an angry George Schuyler said, "Why not be radically honest and advise Negroes to refuse military service except under democratic circumstances."[54] Few newspapermen were as outspoken as Schuyler. Once the country was at war, such a position would not have been tolerated and, as has been shown in chapter 3, the press discouraged the few individual acts of resistance after Pearl Harbor. But between September 16, 1940, and December 7, 1941, an opportunity to organize draft resistance to the segregated Army did exist. The press did not encourage such a program, but when a few individual acts of defiance occurred, some papers offered what can only be termed passive support.

Shortly after the release of the War Department's official policy, the *Defender* printed a small news item on page five about St. Clair Drake's advocacy that blacks register as Conscientious Objectors in order to break down army Jim Crow.[55] A few months later, when Ernest Calloway, Educational Director of the United Transport Workers of America (Redcaps), said that he would refuse to enter the segregated Army if drafted, the *Defender*, on page one, headlined the news: "Balks Call to Arms; Cites J.C."[56] Later, Calloway's statement was printed in the paper with the editorial comment that many blacks felt the same way, but were "perhaps too timid to register their sentiments with similar vigor and sentiment."[57] The following week Drake, Calloway, and three other resisters had their pictures on page one of the paper.

This was the limit of the *Defender*'s open opposition to the segregated draft. Other papers were not so outspoken. The *Journal and Guide* printed Calloway's moving statement on page eight

54. George S. Schuyler, Pittsburgh *Courier*, September 13, 1941.
55. Chicago *Defender*, October 26, 1940.
56. *Ibid*., January 11, 1941.
57. *Ibid*., January 18, 1941.

with no editorial comment. By the spring of 1941 war seemed to be approaching and the "fight for the right to fight" and "Double V" programs were gathering momentum as the basic wartime approach to be followed by the press. Also, much of the news in the spring of 1941 was drawn toward the MOWM. Part of the problem involved in opposing the segregated draft was that, despite the pledge to allot blacks a proportional quota in the service, this condition was not being met in 1941. Therefore, the press, while attacking segregated units, was at the same time calling on the Army to comply with the black quota. The contradiction was obvious; papers could not attack draft quotas and at the same time attack the Army for ignoring the quotas.

DuBois clarified the issue as few others in the press would when he wrote that Negroes on the one hand denounced the government for its discrimination (quotas) in the defense program, and on the other hand black leaders were anxious to show their eagerness to fight for the country. "If you love your country," he wrote, "suffer for it! don't bargain. If you hate it for rape and insult and slavery, say so, don't lie." This was written in 1940. After Germany attacked Russia in June 1941, DuBois did not believe that there was any longer a choice for blacks—Hitler had to be defeated.[58]

Probably the most outspoken press attack on the segregated draft was an editorial in *The Afro-American* in May 1941 entitled: "Should More of Us be Unwilling to Fight?" Relating how blacks could serve only as messmen in the Navy and how the Army offered only Jim Crow units, the editor revealed that only the Conscientious Objector camps were operated on an integrated basis. Concluding that only those blacks who refused to fight for the country received equal treatment, the editor commented: "Moral—More of us should be unwilling to fight. Patriotism does not pay."[59]

This was an exception. The *Afro* was not prepared to mount

58. W. E. B. DuBois, New York *Amsterdam News,* December 21, 1940; July 12, 1941.

59. *The Afro-American,* May 31, 1941.

an attack on the draft when it had been one of the most internationalist black papers during 1940–41. Shortly after this editorial, the same editor commended Randolph for canceling the Washington march, despite the failure to achieve one of its stated aims—the abolition of segregated Army units. At this time the *Afro* said that the country's defense was the primary issue.[60]

It was not until six months after Pearl Harbor that the only major legal test of the segregated Army was initiated. In June 1942 Winfred Lynn, a gardener in Jamaica, Long Island, was classified 1-A by his local draft board. Lynn wrote his draft board:

> Gentlemen: I am in receipt of my draft-reclassification notice. Please be informed that I am ready to serve in any unit of the armed forces of my country which is not segregated by race. Unless I am assured that I can serve in a mixed regiment and that I will not be compelled to serve in a unit undemocratically selected as a Negro group, I will refuse to report for induction.[61]

Lynn's brother Conrad, who was a lawyer, decided to test the segregated Army under Section 4 (a) of the Draft Act (the Wagner anti-discrimination clause).

Winfred Lynn was ordered to report for induction on September 18, but refused to appear. The Army and Selective Service officials were anxious to avoid the legal contest and tried to persuade Lynn to withdraw his opposition. He refused, and the F.B.I. arrested him. Conrad Lynn then sought his brother's release by a writ of habeas corpus on grounds that the quota system was illegal. On December 4, the case was brought before Judge Mortimer Byers in the New York City Court.

Before December 4, Conrad Lynn, a legal counsel for the local Jamaica branch of the NAACP, sought help from the national office. The NAACP refused to aid him, and in fact did all they

60. *Ibid.*, July 1, 1941.
61. Dwight MacDonald, "Winfred Lynn vs. Jim Crow," *Negro Digest* 1 (April 1943): 55 ; *The Story of Jim Crow,* leaflet published by the National Citizens Committee for Winifred Lynn (New York, n.d.), in Schomburg Vertical Files: Lynn Case.

could to discourage him from carrying the case through the courts.[62] William Hastie, Civilian Aide to the Secretary of War, informed Lynn that the NAACP had agreed to Roosevelt's request not to test the draft law during the war. Lynn refused to be deterred and went to the American Civil Liberties Union (ACLU) to seek aid. On behalf of the NAACP, Thurgood Marshal intervened with the ACLU and asked that organization not to accept the case. Since at that time the ACLU had a working arrangement with the NAACP whereby it would defer to the NAACP in cases where blacks were involved, they reluctantly informed Lynn that they could not accept his case. Lynn then sought aid from the Worker's Defense League, to which A. Philip Randolph belonged, and was turned down there too.[63]

In 1956 Conrad Lynn met with Eleanor Roosevelt at an NAACP dinner and she confirmed that a bargain had been struck in 1940 between Walter White and F.D.R. The debate over the Draft Bill was then taking place in the midst of an election and Willkie was making a strong appeal to black voters. At the same time, Hamilton Fish, Republican Congressman from New York, was supporting an anti-discrimination clause in the House sponsored by the *Courier*, a Republican paper. F.D.R. finally agreed to support the Wagner amendment, sponsored by the NAACP, if that organization agreed not to test the Draft Act in the event of a war. When Lynn first brought suit against the draft, F.D.R. actually believed that Walter White had broken his promise.

As F.D.R. must soon have discovered, the NAACP kept its part of the bargain and did nothing to aid Lynn. Conrad Lynn, in fact, was dismissed from the local branch of the NAACP on the ground that his court test of the draft was unpatriotic. *The Crisis* had little to say about the case as it went through the courts and not until the war was drawing to a close and the Supreme Court

62. Conrad Lynn, "Autobiography" (unpublished manuscript), p. 124.

63. Interview with Conrad Lynn, October 16, 1969. Unless otherwise cited, information in the following paragraphs is from this interview.

had once refused to hear the case did the NAACP step in to file a brief *amicus curiae* on behalf of Lynn in his appeal to the court for a writ of *certiorari* to reconsider the case.[64]

At the last minute before their first appearance in court, Arthur Garfield Hayes, of the ACLU, contacted Conrad Lynn and offered his services as an individual lawyer, unaffiliated with the ACLU. On December 4, 1942, Judge Byers informed Lynn that he would not consider his writ, because the defendant did not allow himself to be inducted and therefore no discrimination was involved.[65] Conrad Lynn and Hayes persuaded Winfred to submit to induction so they could further test the case. As soon as the criminal charge against Lynn was determined *nolle prosequi,* Conrad was able to obtain a writ of habeas corpus issued to the commanding officer of Camp Upton, New York, where Winfred Lynn was stationed, asking for his release.[66] This writ became the basis of the legal test for the following two years.

Conrad Lynn's original brief was based on the illegality of the draft quota for blacks (whites were called by number and blacks by quota), but he extended it in a brilliant attack on federally sanctioned segregation. Lynn showed that the courts had never interfered with state-imposed segregation, and had taken no stand on federal segregation. Using the Fifth Amendment, Lynn said that the federal government was obligated to protect Winfred Lynn "in the status he enjoys as a citizen of New York State," [67] where segregation laws were not in force. Lynn's brief also implied that segregation in and of itself was discrimination, and in so doing anticipated by more than a decade the NAACP's legal brief in the 1954 *Brown* v. *Board of Education* case.

The case reached the Supreme Court in May 1944 and the court denied the writ on the grounds that the case was then "moot," because Lynn had been shipped overseas and was no

64. *NAACP Annual Report for 1947,* p. 64.

65. Lynn, "Autobiography," p. 125 ; Lynn's brief presented before the U.S. District Court, December 12, 1942, reprinted in *Politics* 1 (February 1944): 24.

66. Lynn's brief, *Politics* 1 (February 1944): 26.

67. *Ibid.*

longer in the hands of the original respondent. A petition for a rehearing of the case was denied in January 1945.[68]

Black papers followed the case through the courts, but the initiative for publicizing the case came primarily from the Lynn Committee, which was organized for the purpose of gathering support for Lynn. (This committee eventually extended its services to other blacks involved in military discrimination cases.) The *Defender*, which in 1941 gave front-page coverage to those refusing the draft, printed Lynn's letter of refusal on page seven.[69] The reportage was generally in news articles, with editorial comment limited.[70] Some columnists followed the case and their comments did help clarify the proceedings, but this coverage was limited.[71]

Selective Service officials believed that had the case been tried on its merits, the quota system could have been found illegal.[72] Therefore, the press did not make a major issue out of a case that had a potential for a successful outcome. Why they allowed such an opportunity to slip by is unclear, but as Conrad Lynn pointed out, when Judge Campbell dismissed the writ against Winfred's commanding officer, he did so because he believed that if he granted the writ, it would lead to a movement on the part of other black soldiers to be released from the Army.[73] The "Double V" program, with its emphasis on the war abroad and black participation, did not allow for a mass black exodus from the armed forces.

Perhaps it was the NAACP's opposition to the case that led to the lack of sustained publicity in the press. Black papers relied heavily on the NAACP's news information services, especially in matters involving legal cases, and *The Crisis*, the NAACP *Annual*

68. Dwight MacDonald, "Supreme Court's New Moot Suit," *The Nation* 159 (July 1, 1944): 13–14; Selective Service: *Special Groups*, 1: 50.

69. Chicago *Defender*, December 5, 1942.

70. E.g., see *The Afro-American*, January 2, 1943; March 6, 1943; *People's Voice*, January 1, 1944.

71. Horace Cayton, Pittsburgh *Courier*, March 4, 1944; Charley Cherokee, Chicago *Defender*, June 17, 1944.

72. Selective Service: *Special Groups*, 1: 50.

73. Lynn, "Autobiography," p. 127.

Reports and the NAACP *Bulletin* did not publicize the Lynn case. Only Layle Lane, the militant columnist for the New York *Age*, noted this lack of enthusiasm on the part of the NAACP. When the Supreme Court finally rejected Lynn's case, she denounced Walter White for refusing to handle it. The NAACP, she insisted, should have used its influence to arouse Americans to the hypocisy of a segregated Army.[74]

The Wartime Black Cabinet

After the White House released the October 9 policy statement, the first step in assuring equal treatment for black troops was to get black officials appointed to strategic advisory positions within the military establishment. This was not a difficult task. A precedent had been established during World War I, when the Secretary of War appointed E. J. Scott to assist him on racial matters. F.D.R. had established the principle of appointing black advisors to the New Deal agencies, and by 1940 the "Black Cabinet" had become a permanent fixture in Washington.

When it appeared certain that Congress would enact the Conscription Bill, the *Courier* once again took the lead. This paper began printing editorials warning blacks that they had to get ready "to bring pressure to bear" on the government in order to protect the troops. The *Courier* encouraged blacks to organize defense committees in each community, and demanded the appointment of blacks to important positions in the War Department and Selective Service Administration.[75]

F.D.R. moved swiftly to recoup some of his lost popularity within the black community after the furor created by the October 9 statement. During the final weeks of the election campaign he appointed William Hastie, Dean of the Howard University Law School, as Civilian Aide on Negro Affairs to the Secretary of War. Campbell C. Johnson received a similar appointment with the

74. Layle Lane, New York *Age*, March 17, 1945.
75. Pittsburgh *Courier*, August 3, 1940; September 28, 1940.

Selective Service Administration as special advisor to Director Clarence Dykstra. At the same time the Army promoted Colonel B. O. Davis, Sr., to the rank of Brigadier General. The Davis promotion was the occasion of relief and satisfaction in the black press. There was a strong fear that the Army would pass over Colonel Davis as it had done during World War I when Colonel Charles Young was retired just before his time for promotion came.

Most black papers recognized the proximity of these appointments to the day of election and realized that F.D.R. was thinking about the black vote. But this did indicate that the black vote would no longer be taken for granted, and could be used as leverage in seeking advancement for the race. During the 1944 election this fact was further substantiated. Black papers received more campaign ads than in 1940, and F.D.R. used the occasion to open the doors of the Navy and Coast Guard to black women. The latter action was something the black press had been demanding for years.

The response to the 1940 appointments was generally favorable, with Democratic papers praising the President and Republican papers denouncing him for not doing more. *The Afro-American* called the Davis promotion merely a sop, and considered it part of Roosevelt's new "appeasement" policy, since what blacks really wanted was an end to segregation.[76] Democratic papers were jubilant and often made exaggerated claims for F.D.R.'s actions. Roy Wilkins, writing in the *Amsterdam News,* claimed that Roosevelt had to force the Davis promotion and Hastie appointment upon the Army. Wilkins also reported that F.D.R. had never even seen the October 9 policy statement, implying thereby that he was not responsible for the segregation policy of the Army.[77]

The Davis appointment turned out to be a disappointment to many papers during the war. The black press had become dis-

76. *The Afro-American,* November 2, 1940.

77. Roy Wilkins, New York *Amsterdam News,* November 2, 1940. F.D.R. did read the policy statement and initialed it "O.K." See Stephen Early to Robert P. Patterson, October 9, 1940, OF 93, Franklin D. Roosevelt Library.

illusioned with the Black Cabinet by 1940. These racial advisers were almost universally considered tools of the administration to be used as "buffers between the white people and the colored people." [78] Davis appeared to fit into this category of acting as a spokesman for the Army to ease tensions, rather than speaking out strongly against racial discrimination within the service. The Army often sent Davis to investigate racial clashes, and his reports were not forceful enough for the black press. His public comments about black morale usually painted a picture more congenial to Army publicity desires than the realities of the situation as the black press perceived it.[79]

The press felt otherwise about Hastie. After working for over two years to effect changes of approach within the War Department, he was frustrated at almost every turn, and eventually ignored in the decision-making process concerning black troops.[80] In January 1943 he resigned his position, and rather than silently fade away, he used the occasion to dramatize the discriminatory policy of the Army. Hastie wrote a series of articles denouncing the Army's policy toward blacks, which appeared in most of the major black papers.[81] For this outspoken action Hastie received the universal acclaim of the black press, a distinction few members of the Black Cabinet ever received.

The Navy

During the inter-war years the Navy, unlike the Army, did not formulate any overall policy to utilize black seamen in all branches of the service. The Navy Department refused to adopt a policy of

78. Philadelphia *Tribune,* quoted in Savannah *Tribune,* July 31, 1941 ; Oklahoma *Black Despatch,* quoted in *The Crisis* 48 (September 1941): 209 ; Lucius Harper, Chicago *Defender,* October 18, 1941.

79. George Schuyler, Pittsburgh *Courier,* December 12, 1942 ; Chicago *Defender,* May 25, 1944 ; August 19, 1944.

80. Lee, p. 146.

81. These articles were summarized in a pamphlet written by Hastie entitled *On Clipped Wings* (NAACP, 1943).

accepting blacks on a proportional basis until almost a year and a half after the war began. Nevertheless, this service branch never received so much attention from the black press as the Army, since the Army had tenfold the number of blacks as the Navy during the War.

During the Revolutionary War, the War of 1812, the Civil War, and the Spanish American War, black seamen served on integrated ships, but remained restricted to the enlisted man's ranks. This policy continued during World War I, but blacks were finding themselves more and more limited to messmen duty, and de facto segregation was becoming more pronounced. The Navy, in 1920, officially ended the practice of integrating crews. Two years later blacks were no longer eligible to volunteer for the messmen service, as the Navy found men of Philippine origin more suitable. Not until 1932 did the Navy once again open the messmen's branch to black volunteers, and up to June 1, 1942, this was the only branch of this service in which blacks could serve.[82]

A few papers began to raise questions concerning Navy policy when the Navy Department revealed that black sailors at the end of 1939 numbered only 2,807 of a total of 116,000. No blacks were enrolled in the Naval Academy, they were excluded from service in the Marine Corps, and in the Coast Guard they could serve only in the kitchen.[83] In June 1940 Dennis Vallen, President of the San Diego (California) Race Relations Society, wrote to the Secretary of the Navy challenging that service's rigid segregation policy. The reply from the Bureau of Navigation was as follows:

> After many years of experience of not enlisting men of the colored race for any branch of the naval service except for the messmen branch, . . . [this policy] was adopted to meet the best interest of general ship efficiency.[84]

82. Nelson, pp. 1–11; Pittsburgh *Courier,* November 16, 1940; L. D. Reddick. "The Negro in the Navy During World War II," *Journal of Negro History* 32 (April 1947): 203.

83. *Journal and Guide,* January 6, 1940; Pittsburgh *Courier,* February 24, 1940; May 11, 1940.

84. Quoted in Chicago *Defender,* August 10, 1940.

While spearheading the campaign for proportional representation in the Army, the *Courier* did not neglect the Navy. Naval officials did not particularly like the *Courier*, which was apparently widely read by black seamen, and these readers informed the *Courier* that the paper had been barred on many ships. One subscriber wrote to the *Courier* that because he received his copies of the paper unwrapped, he was caused much embarrassment. In the fall of 1940 the *Courier* became directly involved in the case of 15 black messmen discharged from the Navy. These men, aboard the U.S.S. *Philadelphia* in the Pacific, wrote to the *Courier* to publicize their discontent with the Navy's racial policy.[85] When the commanding officer discovered this, he had the 15 men draw up statements explaining their reasons for signing the letter, and then placed them under confinement and ordered their court martial. He charged them with attempting to "lessen the respect due to . . . [their] commanding officers." (Articles of War, subparagraph 7 of Article 8).[86] The men managed to send off another letter to the *Courier* revealing their plight. When this paper publicized the arrests, the court martial was canceled. The men were then sent back to the United States and discharged; 13 received Undesirable Discharges and 2 received Bad Conduct Discharges.[87]

After the Navy discharged these black seamen, the *Courier* continued to work on their case. Executive editor P. L. Prattis was able to arrange for a personal interview with Admiral C. W. Nimitz to ask for a reconsideration of the discharges, but his efforts proved fruitless.[88] Still undeterred, the *Courier* maintained an interest in the case until the Bureau of Navigation informed the paper in March 1941 that the case was closed. The Navy maintained that the letter sent to the *Courier* brought discredit upon the service and "spread discontent among Negro mess at-

85. Letter to the editor, Pittsburgh *Courier*, November 12, 1940.
86. Pittsburgh *Courier*, December 7, 1940.
87. *Ibid.*, November 2, 1940; November 9, 1940; November 16, 1940; November 23, 1940; December 28, 1940; California *Eagle*, November 28, 1940; Chicago *Defender*, November 23, 1940.
88. Pittsburgh *Courier*, December 7, 1940.

tendents." The Bureau added that the Navy's policy of restricting blacks to the messmen's branch was in the best interests of ship efficiency, and:

> Experience in former years has shown clearly that men of the colored race, if enlisted in the seamen branch and promoted to the position of petty officer, cannot maintain discipline among the members of the white race.[89]

The dismissal of the 15 from the Navy did not inhibit other black messmen from writing letters of complaint to the black press but instead, according to the *Courier*, seemed to have encouraged these men to express their discontent with the Navy's racial policy. The *Courier* reported that letters were pouring in from black sailors warning blacks not to volunteer for the Navy.[90] Six messmen from the U.S.S. *Davis* wrote to the *Courier* disclosing indignities they had suffered. They said that due to the small size of their ship they were not placed in separate quarters. To maintain strict segregation, however, their commanding officer billeted these men in a corner of the sleeping area and placed a canvas separator between them and the white sailors. Their duties consisted largely of washing, shining officer's shoes, and serving meals. Concluding their letter, they said, "We sincerely hope that until the Negro is given other ratings that the Negro youth of America will cease to enlist in the U.S. Navy."[91]

After the attack on Pearl Harbor, the NAACP called on Secretary of the Navy Frank Knox to initiate a new policy for blacks. The Navy Department replied that there would be "no change in the Navy's policy regarding the enlistment of men of the colored race, and for the time being no change is contemplated."[92] The Navy was not under the same pressures as the Army to accept blacks since it manned the ranks entirely through volunteers and was not subject to absorbing draftees until Febru-

89. Quoted in Pittsburgh *Courier*, March 29, 1941.
90. Pittsburgh *Courier*, December 14, 1940.
91. Quoted in *ibid.*, December 7, 1940.
92. *NAACP Annual Report for 1941*, p. 12.

ary 1943.[93] On April 7, 1942, Knox announced the first change in policy concerning blacks, but not until June 1, 1942, did this policy become effective.

The April 7, 1942, policy statement offered blacks the opportunity to volunteer for duty in the general services of the reserve components of the Navy, Marine Corps, and Coast Guard. Training was to be segregated and assignments would be made to shore installations and harbor craft. The Navy considered this move strictly an experiment. Obviously it offered those calling for a new policy very little, and the black press was disillusioned with this small change.

Just about every black paper censured the new policy for its timidity of approach. The *Defender* informed its readers that "reserve" status meant that black seamen would be used only for the duration of the war. The black press had already moved away from its previous acceptance of segregated quotas after the Army policy statement of October 9, 1940; and, as the *Defender* pointed out, the new Navy policy simply accepted and extended the Army's policy of segregation.[94]

Joining in the chorus of protest, the *People's Voice* declared that the new policy was not a "noble experiment." "This is no time for timid experimentation, cautious beginning or cheap compromise."[95] This paper considered the policy a legitimization of segregation. The *Amsterdam News*, New York *Age*, and *Afro-American* all agreed; but the *Age* did consider it a step in the right direction.[96] The NAACP did not take its usual unequivocal public stand against segregation. The *Defender*, in turn, roundly denounced Walter White for the NAACP statement that the new policy was "progress toward an enlightened point of view."[97] The NAACP apparently reconsidered its initial statement, and when

93. Nelson, p. 17; Selective Services: *Special Groups*, 1: 103.
94. Chicago *Defender*, April 18, 1942.
95. *People's Voice*, April 18, 1942.
96. *The Afro-American*, March 14, 1942; New York *Age*, April 18, 1942; New York *Amsterdam News*, April 18, 1942; See also *Opportunity* 20 (May 1942): 130; *Our Fight* 1 (April 24, 1942): 1.
97. Chicago *Defender*, April 11, 1942.

The Crisis appeared in May, the new Navy policy was called "only a gesture" and an extension of the Army's policy of segregation.[98]

Only the *Courier* looked upon the new policy with some favor. Its headline read, "Knox Hasn't Said Enough," but further down the page the paper wrote that the "cracking of the door to service is a forward step," and considered the policy a victory for the *Courier's* sustained agitation. Then, shifting its position, it added that despite the gain, it was a setback for race relations in general.[99]

After the Navy relented slightly with its modification of April 1942, the black press devoted little attention to this service. Black seamen were still relatively few in number until the Navy began absorbing black draftees on a proportional basis in 1943. The absence of large numbers of black seamen precluded the racial friction that was taking place on Army bases, where the press focused its attention. With the exception of the Port Chicago mutiny,[100] it was not until 1944 that the press began to report once again on Navy policy. This time a feeling of optimism prevailed.

The Navy commissioned black officers for the first time in February 1944, a move hailed as a step toward democracy.[101] A short while later black women were finally permitted to volunteer for service in the Waves and Spars. The Navy Department also invited 29 black publishers to tour the segregated Great Lakes Naval Training Center. [102] Powell, one of the publishers visiting the center, considered the camp the "nearest approach to democracy" to be found in any of the service training camps, despite the rigid segregation.[103] In August 1944 black seamen were assigned to 25 auxiliary ships and integrated with whites. The following April blacks were considered eligible for service on all auxiliary ships,

98. *The Crisis* 49 (May 1942): 151.
99. Pittsburgh *Courier,* April 18, 1942.
100. See chapter 5.
101. Chicago *Defender,* March 25, 1944; Pittsburgh *Courier,* March 4, 1944.
102. *Journal and Guide,* January 29, 1944; Chicago *Defender,* March 18, 1944.
103. Adam C. Powell, Jr., "A Big Stride Forward," *Spotlight* 2 (April 1944): 33.

and the Navy ordered all boat-training facilities to integrate. By February 1946 the Navy opened up the general service to all blacks.[104]

Unlike the Army, the Navy Department never appointed a black advisor to work with the service on racial matters. As the war was drawing to a close, the Navy asked Lester Granger to tour its training bases and prepare a report on racial policies. His report was optimistic and full of praise for the recently instituted changes put into effect by the service. Many black papers remained skeptical of the report and believed that Granger had been used by the Navy. But they all agreed that the Navy had taken steps to limit or end segregation in training facilities and on board ship.[105] Papers remained hostile to the Navy at this time because of the military trials at Guam and Port Chicago, but its new policies were still considered a great advance.

The Navy's plans to democratize the service by integrating black seamen and using them for general ship duty were not put into effect for years. At the end of 1945, only 5 percent of black seamen were in general service, while 95 percent remained in the messmen branch.[106] When the war ended, there were only 54 black commissioned officers serving in the Navy compared to 7,767 in the Army.[107] Officially, the new Navy policies of 1944–45 were more advanced than the Army's racial policy, but in fact blacks were still predominantly messmen.

104. Nelson, pp. 19–21 ; L. D. Reddick, *Journal of Negro History* 32 (April 1947): 212–13.

105. *The Crisis* 52 (August 1945): 216 ; L. D. Reddick *Journal of Negro History* (April, 1947): 217 ; Walter White, Chicago *Defender,* August 11, 1945 ; Charley Cherokee, Chicago *Defender,* August 18, 1945.

106. Nelson, p. 164.

107. Selective Services, *Special Groups,* 1: 115–16.

5
The Black Press and the Armed Forces: In Defense of Black Servicemen

Conflict in the Camps

Once the War Department assured blacks that they would be utilized in all branches of the Army, the policy of the black press toward the Army was formulated out of a response to the treatment of black troops in the service. By the summer of 1941 this policy began to materialize, and eventually developed into a threefold program of protecting the troops from physical violence, of protecting them from discrimination in the military courts, and of upholding the honor of black combat troops. These functions were not unfamiliar ones, but they took on a special importance since it was the black press that had demanded that the Army organize black combat units, and had encouraged blacks to fight for the right to fight.

During the spring of 1941 black inductees began entering the Army in large numbers. Most of these men went to southern camps for training. The conditions confronting black soldiers in these camps assured that there would be violent outbreaks. Before these conflicts did erupt, black reporters visited the camps and predicted that existing conditions would insure eventual trouble.

P. L. Prattis, of the *Courier*, visited thirteen Army posts between May and November 1941. He called attention to the use of white MPs in black areas, and to the brutal treatment they often meted out to black troops. Black soldiers told him that they were often used to clean up one area of camp and then transferred to another area, usually the most inaccessible one.[1] Ollie Stewart, of *The Afro-American*, toured many camp sites and added to the concern of black leaders by his revelations. Blacks, he said, had too few camp recreational facilities, and, due to the limits of segregation in the Southern camp towns, they were afforded little opportunity for entertainment and relaxation. Stewart pointed out that prejudiced Southern white officers commanded black troops, and he called for more black officers to relieve this area of tension.[2]

These predictions of conflict proved, unfortunately, to be only too accurate. Within a few months the first major racial incident occurred at Fort Bragg, North Carolina. This clash originated in a conflict between white MPs and black soldiers. Black soldiers were on a bus going from town back to camp, when the white driver refused to move his vehicle until MPs arrived to quiet down some noisy passengers. The MPs arrived and began using their clubs freely, whereupon Private Ned Turman seized a pistol from one of the MPs and shouted, "Goddam it! I'm going to break up you MPs beating us colored soldiers."[3] The ensuing shooting resulted in the death of Turman and one MP.

A "Night of Terror" followed this shooting. MPs at Fort Bragg rounded up all black troops outside of their barracks and placed them in the stockade. Military trucks were sent into town to pick up the black soldiers on pass, and these men were also incarcerated in the stockade. Black soldiers claimed that the MPs

1. P. L. Prattis, Pittsburgh *Courier*, June 7, 1941 ; July 9, 1941 ; P. L. Prattis, "The Morale of the Negro in the Armed Services of the United States," *Journal of Negro Education* 12 (Summer 1943): 358–60.

2. *The Afro-American*, August 9, 1940.

3. Prattis, *Journal of Negro Education* 12: 355.

cursed, beat, and robbed them in the process.[4] The Army's reaction to the shooting, which smacked of hysteria, infuriated the black press. The Army, moreover, did not mollify the black press with its official report of the incident (the report was prepared by General Davis). The probe concluded that the MPs were just performing their duty and used their clubs only after meeting with resistance. The report also claimed that Turman was killed by a bullet fired from the same gun that he had seized and fired.[5]

This shooting gave rise to a serious debate within the black press about the advisability of having black troops stationed in the South. The *Afro* believed that the Army created problems when it sent Northern blacks to the Southern camps.[6] The *Afro* editor expressed satisfaction when he reported that the 366th Regiment (black) at Fort Devons, Massachusetts, would not go to North Carolina to participate in maneuvers. Although the government should protect troops everywhere, the editor wrote, it did not; until it did, the only safe policy was to keep Northern black soldiers out of the South.[7] The problem, however, was not simply that Northern black troops trained in the South. Turman, the soldier killed at the Fort Bragg incident, was a native of South Carolina. Later, racial violence erupted on Army bases in Oregon, Pennsylvania, and New Jersey.

This effort to remove Northern blacks from the South gained support when civilian police near Prescott, Arkansas, intimidated black soldiers of the 94th Engineer Battalion (mostly natives of Detroit and Chicago). On August 14, 1941, these men bivouacked on the edge of a highway near Prescott. State troopers were mistakenly informed that there was trouble in the area, and rushed to the bivouac site. One policeman yelled to an officer in charge of

4. *Ibid.;* Pittsburgh *Courier,* August 16, 1941 ; Lee, pp. 351–52 ; *Journal and Guide,* August 23, 1941 ; August 30, 1941 ; New York *Amsterdam News,* August 16, 1941 ; August 23, 1941 ; Savannah *Tribune,* August 28, 1941 ; California *Eagle,* July 17, 1941.
5. Chicago *Defender,* November 22, 1941 ; *Journal and Guide,* August 30, 1941.
6. *The Afro-American,* August 16, 1941.
7. *Ibid.,* October 18, 1941.

the troops to "keep those damn Niggers off the road," and another slapped a white Army officer who protested. White MPs in the area observed what took place but did not intervene.[8] There had been racial friction in this area previously, but this incident convinced many black soldiers that their lives were in jeopardy and their only hope for survival was to flee. Over forty men went AWOL, most of whom made their way back to Fort Custer, Michigan, where they had originally been stationed.[9]

The flight of these men impelled *The Afro-American* to call for a new policy on the part of blacks. The *Afro* believed that if the War Department ignored conflicts involving individuals, it could not ignore a situation where large numbers of soldiers deserted to avoid Southern discrimination. "Passive resistance is an effective weapon," declared the editor, and "a good deal of racial discrimination . . . will end when large numbers of our men refuse to be Jim Crowed." [10] This was perhaps the strongest statement of this sort made by any editor. It was the nearest thing to a call for black resistance to Army mistreatment.

Other papers refused to join the call to withdraw black troops from the South. The *Defender* believed that withdrawal would virtually condone the actions of Southern whites. This paper wrote, "If our democracy is worth saving, it is worth enforcing even if it means a repetition of [the] sacrificial bloodshed which gave it birth." [11] During the following weeks the *Defender* continued to write front-page articles demanding that the Army take steps to relieve the terror.

The *Courier* entered the debate and said that not only Northern blacks, but *all* black troops should be sent North.[12] George Schuyler commented on the *Defender*'s position and agreed that it had merit and much support within the black press. He said that the South would never welcome black soldiers, and that Roosevelt

8. Chicago *Defender,* August 23, 1941 ; Pittsburgh *Courier,* August 30, 1941 ; Savannah *Tribune,* August 21, 1941.
9. Chicago *Defender,* August 30, 1941 ; Lee, pp. 353–54.
10. *The Afro-American,* August 23, 1941 ; November 15, 1941.
11. Chicago *Defender,* September 6, 1941.
12. Pittsburgh *Courier,* August 30, 1941 ; September 13, 1941.

would not alienate the South. Schuyler believed that an honest view would see that it was a matter of discrimination in general, and perhaps blacks should advise their followers not to enter the military until it was fully democratic.[13] Schuyler was one of the few to hold this viewpoint even after the declaration of war.

Papers divided on this issue with no relation to their geographical location. The Norfolk *Journal and Guide* believed that the problems arose only because Northern blacks could not be expected to submit to Jim Crow regulations.[14] In New York, the *Amsterdam News* cried out on page one, "Terror Reign Sweeps Nation's Army Camps, Negroes Go A.W.O.L." This paper demanded redress, but believed that the call to take black troops out of the South was "nothing less than a plea for segregation."[15] When the Chicago *Tribune* joined those black papers seeking removal, the editor of the Oklahoma *Black Dispatch* denounced the *Tribune,* and declared that this was a paternalistic outlook. The *Dispatch* demanded that the federal government insure the safety of all troops, and said that a removal policy would be an admission that the government could not protect its citizens.[16] *The Crisis* commented, "Our boys must be protected or brought out."[17]

Despite the absence of a unified approach, the press continued to print vivid accounts of the friction and clashes on Army posts that persisted throughout the summer of 1941. This led to "avalanches" of letters and petitions pouring into the War Department and White House calling for the protection of black soldiers.[18] The Army, seeking an easy explanation, blamed the black press for magnifying incidents and printing rumors and false accounts of

13. George Schuyler, Pittsburgh *Courier,* September 6, 1941; September 13, 1941.
14. *Journal and Guide,* November 22, 1941.
15. New York *Amsterdam News,* August 23, 1941; September 6, 1941.
16. Oklahoma *Black Dispatch,* quoted in Savannah *Tribune,* October 9, 1941.
17. *The Crisis* 48 (July 1941): 215.
18. Lee, p. 355; Letters to F.D.R. in OF 93, Franklin D. Roosevelt Library.

the racial clashes. In June 1942 Army G-2 seriously considered censoring the black press.[19]

During the spring and summer of 1942 racial clashes broke out again, but they were not so serious as they had been the previous year. By the spring of 1943, however, serious racial outbreaks were again erupting. These clashes involved larger numbers of troops, with black soldiers often seizing the initiative.[20] Black papers continued to print articles about the violence, but a new tone was apparent. For one thing, major race riots broke out in the cities during the summer of 1943, and this occupied much of the press's attention. Also, by 1943 the black press was reeling from the heavy attacks upon it from all quarters and felt threatened with official censorship.

After the outbreaks of 1941, the Army had begun to develop better lines of communication with the black press. Army officials discovered that black reporters were hungry for news and were eager to print any information they could obtain.[21] Once news began to flow out of official Army sources, it was obviously less inflammatory. It was common knowledge among many blacks that by 1943 their newspapers were deliberately playing down incidents and avoiding many stories of open violence, and some editors did not hide this fact.[22] At this time the black press began to focus attention on the black troops in North Africa, and on the off-again-and-on-again FEPC hearings.[23]

Military Justice and the Black Serviceman

By the end of 1943 black papers were directing their attention toward another major problem confronting black soldiers: the dual

19. Lee, pp. 355, 361–62, 364, 383; Savannah *Tribune,* September 4, 1941, quotes letter of General Ulio to the NAACP.
20. Lee, p. 366.
21. *Ibid.,* pp. 383–84.
22. *Monthly Summary* 1 (November 1943): 22; (January, 1944): 22; Lee, p. 385.
23. Harry McAlpin, Chicago *Defender,* May 22, 1943.

system of military justice. There were no mass executions of blacks similar to those at Houston in 1917, but military justice proved to be extremely harsh in what often appeared to be a reaction against the growing militancy of black troops and their refusal to suffer quietly the indignities imposed upon them. During the war, black leaders became alarmed by the "excessive tendency to court martial and impose heavy sentences on Negroes. . . ."[24] Many of these incidents were spontaneous and involved hundreds of black servicemen—in one case at least 1,000 men—but the miltary authorities simply looked upon them as disobedience and often preferred charges of mutiny.

From the first awareness of the problem there was evidence that military justice was not the same for black and white. In December 1943 the *Courier* called attention to this dual pattern of military justice with the following examples. In Paris, Tennessee, sixty-four black soldiers used some military trucks to take a joy ride. This was, of course, a military offense, but not an uncommon one. The Army court martialed these men and sentenced them to from ten to fifteen years each. For whites justice did not appear equally harsh, especially when it involved whites and blacks. In Camp Swift, Texas, a white lieutenant was convicted of stabbing a black private and his punishment was an official reprimand.[25]

Not unexpectedly, the first military trials that the black press reported in detail were "rape" cases. Black soldiers were charged with rape in many areas of the world. The black press gave sustained coverage to two cases, because they appeared to be blatant

24. Walter White to F.D.R., December 26, 1944, Walter White Correspondence, James Weldon Johnson Collection, Yale University Library. A survey of the European Theater shows that their fears were not unwarranted. With slightly over 8 percent of the total number of troops in Europe at the end of the war, blacks comprised 21.4 percent of the 20,067 American servicemen convicted by courts martial during the war. There were 1,176 convictions for sex crimes, of which blacks made up 42.3 percent. Of the 5,008 convictions for violent crimes, 35 percent were black soldiers; and 74.1 percent of those receiving death sentences were blacks. See Jean Byers, *A Study of the Negro in Military Service* (Washington, D.C.: Department of Defense, 1950), p. 61.

25. Pittsburgh *Courier,* December 11, 1943.

miscarriages of justice. The Army eventually reversed the courts' original decisions in these cases due to the harshness of the penalties and the doubtfulness of the charges.[26] The events leading to conviction in one of these trials resembled those which occurred in the famous Scottsboro rape case in the early 1930s, and the press publicized this case as the "Army Scottsboro Case."

On June 15, 1943, a court martial at Noumea, New Caledonia, convicted Private Frank Fisher, Jr., 21, and Private Edward R. Loury, 22, of raping Louise Mounien, a resident of the island. Both received life sentences. The convictions were sustained a month later by the theater commander at Melbourne, Australia, and the two soldiers were shipped to the federal penitentiary on McNeil Island, Washington. Loury then contacted the NAACP and International Labor Defense (ILD) and told of their trial and conviction for allegedly raping a woman whom he said was a well-known prostitute. William Hastie, acting for the NAACP, and Congressman Vito Marcantonio, President of the ILD, took up the case, because they were convinced the two soldiers were innocent.

According to an affidavit signed by Loury, the following sequence of events occurred. On the night of May 2, 1943, Loury, Fisher, and an unidentified soldier were returning to camp from a carnival near Noumea and stopped in an area known as "Prostitute Hill." Here they spotted a man and woman emerging from the bushes near a parked jeep. The three approached the man, Lieutenant Robert L. Engels (white), and asked if they could "engage" the woman. Engels responded that she could make her own decision. She, in turn, agreed to go with the three soldiers into the bushes. While Loury was with the woman, a couple walked into the area where they were lying, and apparently, on seeing them, turned and walked away. Once finished with their transaction, the men paid the woman and departed.

On May 6, 1943, Fisher and Loury were placed under arrest and five nights of questioning and alleged threats and mistreat-

26. Chicago *Defender*, April 8, 1944. *The Crisis* 51 (July 1944): 217 has a brief summary of the various rape cases.

ment began. Each was questioned separately, with the interrogaters trying to force them to sign a statement in accord with Engels's deposition. Engels claimed that the men had brandished a .45 caliber pistol at him, beat him and the woman, tied him, and then raped the woman. During the interrogation Loury stated that the three officers questioning him threatened to use a blackjack on his head, and at one point said they would shoot him and report that he was killed in action unless he would sign the statement. His requests for legal aid were turned down. After the fifth night Loury, worn down and suffering with fever, signed a statement.

On February 3, 1944, Hastie and Marcantonio filed a brief with the War Department on behalf of Fisher and Loury. Since the original convictions were upheld by the theater commander, the only recourse available was to seek clemency from the Secretary of War. Hastie and Marcantonio found several contradictions in the testimony of Engels and the woman. They also discovered that important evidence bearing on the case was ignored. They contended that the woman was a prostitute who willingly sold her favors to the three soldiers and accepted money for her services. Apparently Engels, while waiting for the woman in his jeep, feared that he had been observed by the two passersby while the men and woman were in the bushes. Because of this, he insisted that the woman go with him to the military police to prefer charges of rape against the three soldiers. The first judicial official to hear the case was a French magistrate. The woman told him that she had had intercourse with Engels before the three men. She also said that she did not want to press charges but that Engels had insisted.

Investigating the details of the case for the Army was Captain John F. Saxton. He interrogated all those involved in the incident shortly after it occurred, and concluded that the evidence did not warrant the charges of rape. This report was ignored during the trial. Also not introduced at the trial were three medical reports that had been made following the alleged rape. These showed no signs of violence and nothing to indicate rape. One report revealed that the woman was infected with gonorrhea prior to her relations with Fisher and Loury.

The two men assigned to defend Fisher and Loury met with them for the first time less than a day before the trial. This gave them no time to study Saxton's report or to conduct their own inquiry. Defense counsel did not evidence a strong desire to bring to the court's attention all the evidence pertaining to the manner in which Fisher and Loury were interrogated. The three officers who conducted the interrogation were not put on the witness chair. Also, when Loury expressed his desire to give his own testimony, his counsel tried to dissuade him. Loury, however, insisted; but his lawyer offered no aid in preparing his testimony, nor did Loury recall his counsel's asking him any questions while he was in the witness chair.

In March 1944 the War Department reduced the sentences of Fisher and Loury to ten years and eight years respectively. In taking this action, however, Under Secretary of War Patterson emphasized that the reductions were due to the age of the two youths, not their innocence. Hastie and Marcantonio then filed an appeal with the White House for full clemency, but at the war's end the two were still in prison.[27]

A rape trial in England confirmed black fears that military justice was unfair and especially harsh when black personnel were involved. The Army accused Corporal Leroy Henry of raping an English housewife near her home. Henry claimed that he had previosly had relations with the woman, and on the evening of the alleged rape he had made arrangements to see her later during the night after her husband was asleep. Later, Henry said, she demanded more money than the agreed-upon sum; when he refused, she brought charges of rape against him. The women testified that Henry, a stranger, had knocked on her door late one night and asked for directions. She said that she walked down the road with

27. The black press furnished ample coverage of the case. A good summary of the events, along with reprints of Loury's affidavit and letter to the NAACP, can be found in *PM,* March 20, 1944 ; March 21, 1944. See also Marjorie De Armand, "Pacific Scottsboro," *New Masses* (October 17, 1944), pp. 9–10 ; International Labor Defense *News,* February 19, 1944 ; July 8, 1944 ; August 25, 1944 ; September 28, 1944 ; May 5, 1945.

Henry (in her nightgown), and when they were out of sight of the house he assaulted her.

A court martial found Henry guilty and sentenced him to death. This harsh verdict, based upon what appeared to be flimsy evidence, shocked many Britishers. They circulated petitions, gathering 50,000 signatures, calling for a reversal of the court's decision. General Dwight D. Eisenhower eventually reviewed the case and had the original decision reversed. The Army then returned Henry to duty. This action by Eisenhower made him an instant hero to the black press. Papers considered his action "Lincolnesque," because during the greatest invasion in history he had taken time to consider the case of one black soldier.[28]

As the rape trials were being contested by the black press, an incident occurred that initiated a series of events leading to the first major mutiny trial of the war and the largest in naval history. On the night of July 17, 1944, an accidental explosion shattered the harbor at Port Chicago, a small town on San Francisco Bay, killing over 320 people. Port Chicago was a naval ammunition supply depot from which goods were shipped to the Pacific theater. All of the men who loaded ships at Port Chicago were black, and all of the commissioned and petty officers were white. Almost all of those who were killed by the blast were black seamen loading the two ships in the harbor.[29]

After the explosion, the Navy split up the men in the units at Port Chicago, sending some to a nearby camp and keeping the rest behind to clean up the debris in the harbor. Within two weeks officers ordered the survivors to begin loading ammunition ships again. They refused to obey the orders and were placed in the brig. A few days later the Navy shipped over a hundred of these men to the South Pacific.[30]

Black seamen of the 2nd, 4th, and 8th Divisions, all involved

28. For details of the case see Chicago *Defender,* June 24, 1944; Pittsburgh *Courier,* July 1, 1944; *Journal and Guide,* July 1, 1944.

29. NAACP, *Mutiny? The Real Story Behind How the Navy Branded 50 Fear-Shocked Sailors As Mutineers* (New York, 1945), p. 5. Cited hereafter as *Mutiny;* Nelson, pp. 77–78.

30. *Mutiny,* p. 9.

in the July 17th disaster and afterwards transferred to other camps, were reassembled at Vallejo, California, and on August 9 were ordered to load ammunition ships. Out of 400 men assembled, over 250 refused to return to work.[31] The officers in charge tried persuading the men to return to work, but to no avail. Other officers and a chaplain tried their hand and were partially successful. All but 50 men finally returned to duty.[32] The Navy pressed mutiny charges against the 50. The trial lasted from September 14 to October 24, resulting in the conviction of all 50 men. The court handed down stiff sentences ranging from eight to fifteen years in jail.[33]

The NAACP sent Thurgood Marshall to investigate the case and file a brief before the court of review of the 12th Naval District in California. Marshall emphasized that prejudice was a factor in the conviction of these men, and that the men did not deliberately plot a mutiny. He said that the explosion was largely due to the negligence of the Navy, because it did not properly train the men for their hazardous duty. These men originally received seamen's training, and then were brought to Port Chicago as ammunition loaders. The only instructions they received in how to load munitions was the admonition "be careful." [34] Marshall also disclosed that the waterfront unions had warned naval authorities of a possible disaster if they employed untrained men. The unions offered to train these men but the Navy turned them down.[35]

Black newspapers followed the story closely and were furious with the outcome of the trial. "Fifty New Martyrs," headlined the *Defender* when the court returned its verdict.[36] This paper believed that the trial was also an effort to quiet the more militant black servicemen. The *Defender* wrote that the fifty men did not simply refuse to load ammunition, but protested against the policy of having only black men perform this type of duty.[37]

31. *Ibid.*, p. 10; *People's Voice*, September 16, 1944.
32. *Mutiny*, p. 10; Nelson, p. 78.
33. Nelson, p. 78.
34. *Mutiny*, pp. 2, 5, 10; Chicago *Defender*, October 7, 1944.
35. *Mutiny*, p. 7.
36. Chicago *Defender*, December 2, 1944.
37. *Ibid.*, September 23, 1944.

Some papers emphasized the traumatic effect of the explosion on the survivors, and the horror they experienced when they had to clean up the debris, which included the truncated bodies of their comrades.[38] A psychologist who testified for the defendants said that the men had been in a state of shock and did not have enough time to recover before the Navy ordered them to return to duty.[39] Some writers considered this duty itself as a form of murder.[40]

A naval review board declared that the trial had been conducted fairly and that the sentences would stand, despite the fact that the court delivered its decision after only 85 minutes of deliberation—which included the lunch hour of the members of the court—to consider 1,435 pages of testimony.[41] Marshall also discovered, after the first verdict was decided, that the prosecutor was the brother-in-law of one of the two white officers involved in the case.

Without the extensive coverage of the black press, it is doubtful that the black public could have obtained much information about the trial. *Time* magazine carried a small article about the trial with the observation that the trial had been "scrupulously conducted." *Time* pointed out that those who refused to return to work were "all Negroes," without emphasizing that only Negroes were assigned to this particular duty.[42] Encouraged by the black press, petitions and appeals continued to deluge the Navy Department until in January 1946 the Navy set aside the convictions and the men returned to active duty.[43]

The black press performed a great service for these men by publicizing their case, but many papers did exhibit an unequivocal stand that manifested a continuing opposition to direct action on the part of the masses. Even though all of the papers condemned the trial proceedings and expressed sympathy and understanding for the fifty men, some maintained that under any circumstances black servicemen should obey military orders.[44] The *Journal and*

38. Pittsburgh *Courier,* November 4, 1944.
39. *Mutiny,* p. 8.
40. Charley Cherokee, Chicago *Defender,* September 2, 1944.
41. Nelson, p. 80; *The Crisis* 52 (February 1945): 110.
42. "Trial's End," *Time* 44 (November 6, 1944): 68.
43. Nelson, p. 80.
44. Chicago *Defender,* December 2, 1944.

Guide was disturbed about the racial implications of the trial, but concluded, "No right thinking person can excuse desertion, disobedience of orders, [and] mutiny. . . ." [45] As black newspapers commented on the subsequent mass trials, this opinion cropped up in the editorials and columnists' discussions of these cases.

As the Port Chicago incident was reaching a climax, another event occurred that resulted in another mass trial. On August 14, 1944, a group of black soldiers in a labor battalion at Fort Lawton, Washington, raided the barracks where the Army billeted Italian war prisoners. One of the Italians was later bound and hanged and thirty men were injured in the melee. This raid took place after the black troops had become angry at the discrepancy between the treatment accorded black soldiers and that accorded white prisoners. The blacks were convinced that the Army was treating the Italian prisoners better than black Americans. The Army tried 43 of the men who took part in the raid, and after five weeks 28 were found guilty and received stiff sentences.[46]

The black press considered the raid as the inevitable result of the Jim Crow treatment accorded black soldiers. The Army transported prisoners in first-class coaches and hired them out to jobs that black civilians were unable to obtain. "There is a limit to all patience. That limit was reached in Seattle when post exchanges barred colored and admitted Italians." Blacks, said *The Afro-American*'s editor, would not forever submit to insults by prisoners of war and would not "quietly . . . see our enemies treated with greater dignity." [47]

Mass trials continued and began involving larger numbers of black military personnel. The services tried to conceal some of the trials and often news did not appear until months after the conclusion of the trials. Walter White, on tour of the Pacific area in July 1944, received an anonymous note in Hawaii telling him about a trial in process involving 73 black soldiers of the 1320th Engineers General

45. *Journal and Guide,* October 21, 1944.

46. "Lynching Bee," *Time* 44 (November 20, 1944): 67; Pittsburgh *Courier,* November 18, 1944; December 30, 1944; *The Crisis* 52 (January 1945): 8; New York *Amsterdam News,* December 23, 1944.

47. *The Afro-American,* September 2, 1944.

Service Regiment. These enlisted men got into trouble because they contested the Regiment's failure to promote black officers. The black officers had confronted the commanding officer about the lack of promotions and were subsequently replaced by white officers. When the enlisted men discovered this, they refused to report for duty.[48]

The commanding officer brought back one of the transferred black officers to call the men out for duty. They fell out and the 66th article of war was read to them. Still refusing to work, they returned to their barracks. Eventually a white colonel, who was more friendly with the troops, convinced them that they should return to work and they agreed to make up for the lost time. Despite this agreement, the Army a few days later brought charges against 73 of the men involved. All of the men were tried and convicted and the court sentenced all but one to 15 years. That one, considered the ringleader, received a 17-year sentence.[49] The black press did not find out about this trial until Walter White revealed the news in February 1945. After a rehearing of the case, the Army released all of the men from prison.[50]

While on his Pacific tour, White became involved in another mass trial of black troops, this time involving men stationed on the island of Guam. After a long period of friction between black and white troops, violence erupted on Christmas eve 1944 and a riot was barely averted. Black soldiers on pass went to the town of Agana, where white soldiers fired on them and forced them to flee for their lives. They returned to their camp and after informing their friends of the shooting, black troops commandeered some nearby trucks and set out to find one of their comrades whom they believed had been killed or wounded during the shooting in Agana. On the way to town they discovered that the missing soldier had safely returned to camp, so they turned their trucks around and dispersed peacefully. Shortly after this, however, white troops invaded the black camp, hurling debris and racial epithets. On Christmas day incidents continued to take place in town until

48. White, pp. 274–75; Chicago *Defender,* February 10, 1945.
49. White, p. 275; Pittsburgh *Courier,* February 17, 1945; *People's Voice,* February 10, 1945.
50. White, p. 276.

finally someone shot two black soldiers, killing one and wounding the other. That evening whites again raided the blacks' camp; this time both sides began firing. When the whites left the camp, the black troops boarded trucks and set out after them. The authorities headed them off on the road to town and placed 44 men under arrest.[51]

Walter White was in Guam when the trial of the men began. He consented to the court's request to represent the men despite his lack of legal qualifications and fear that the court was using him to protect itself against the possible charges of discrimination. The court convicted all 44 men after a three-week trial. White, who was taking this tour as a correspondent for the New York *Post,* filed his story on January 20, 1945, but the Navy marked it for release on July 11, 1945. White did not say anything about the case until July 7, 1945, when he made a nationwide broadcast, revealing the facts to the public for the first time and attacking Navy censorship.

The most surprising aspect of this episode was the failure of the black press to question White about his delay in breaking the story. (The press always maintained the position that one of its greatest functions was to expose failures in the leadership.) Black papers attacked the Navy for censoring White's story,[52] but never asked White why he waited for months before exposing the Navy's censorship. White, as everybody knew, had a weekly column in the *Defender,* access to *The Crisis,* and was at the time of the trial a correspondent for the New York *Post.* In 1946 the 44 men were cleared of charges and released from confinement.[53]

Black papers were not unaware of the possibility of using military justice to intimidate blacks who were outspoken in their demands for justice. The press expressed its fear that these trials, coming at the final stage of the war, would be used to discredit the contributions of the race to the war effort.[54] The press denounced the military trials and continued to express its sympathy for the

51. *Ibid.,* pp. 278–81 ; Pittsburgh *Courier,* July 21, 1945.
52. Chicago *Defender,* July 21, 1945.
53. Nelson, p. 83.
54. White, p. 223 ; Pittsburgh *Courier,* March 10, 1945.

men who acted under the pressures of service discrimination. But the press at the same time took a strong stand against *any* disobedience on the part of black troops. In 1941 the black press believed that the postwar status of blacks would largely depend upon an unblemished military record. These mass trials at the end of the war could discredit the entire race. This fear, along with the continuing reluctance of the press to confront authority with militant mass action, caused the press to reiterate its pleas to blacks to obey orders. "None of us," wrote the *Courier,* "condones disobedience of military orders, and this paper has repeatedly advised against it, no matter how unjust an order may appear to be." [55] The *Courier* objected that violators were not treated as individuals, but "*en masse* as Negroes."

The black press gave its total support to any action that did not result in a violation of military orders. At Port Hueneme, California, one thousand black Seabees of the 34th and 80th Construction Battalions went on a two-day hunger strike to protest the lack of promotions in their outfit. Their commander was a white officer from Meridian, Mississippi, who refused to promote blacks to higher rank. After the second day of the strike, officers told the men to eat or face mutiny charges. In order to avoid this offense the men complied.[56] This type of action was the kind the press was willing to accept without any reservations. P. L. Prattis applauded these Seabees because the men avoided refusing a direct order, which could have resulted in another mutiny trial.[57]

One of the most publicized trials of black service personnel involved four Wacs convicted after a sit-down strike at Lovell General Hospital, Fort Devons, Massachusetts. This case, more than any other, revealed the ambivalent attitude of the press in denouncing the discrimination that gave rise to such incidents, and then censuring the blacks involved for facing up to the issue.

On March 9, 1945, 54 Wacs refused to perform their assigned

55. Pittsburgh *Courier,* March 10, 1945.

56. *Equality* 2 (April, 1945): 1; Chicago *Defender,* March 10, 1945; California *Eagle,* March 8, 1945; *The Crisis* 52 (March 1945): 110.

57. P. L. Prattis, Pittsburgh *Courier,* March 31, 1945.

duties and staged a work stoppage. The strike began because black Wacs, trained as technicians, were given the job of cleaning the hospital, while white Wacs appeared to be receiving preferential treatment. The black Wacs were also protesting the open hostility of Colonel Walter H. Crandell, the hospital commandant, toward black personnel. They claimed that he refused to allow them to perform any duty except cleaning details. Eventually 50 of the women returned to work when they were informed of the consequences of their action, but four remained adamant and were brought to trial.[58]

The court convicted and sentenced these four women to one year in prison. The Boston branch of the NAACP criticized the Wacs and in an official statement said, "We deplore the action of the colored Wacs." In response to this statement, the Boston branch of the ACLU intervened and chastised the NAACP for its timid role in the trial and its public comments denouncing the Wacs, whom it might have been expected to defend. The ACLU was firmly convinced that it was a clear case of discrimination that prompted the sit-down strike. "There is nothing intrinsically sacred about patriotism or army discipline," commented the ACLU.[59] Black papers in general did not share this point of view, although some columnists were beginning to applaud this type of action and were pleased with the resistance displayed by the four Wacs.

Many black papers agreed with the Boston NAACP. The editor of *The Afro-American,* commenting on the conviction, said that if the discrimination charges were true, Crandell had to be dismissed; but, he added, "On the other hand refusal by Wacs to . . . [follow orders] cannot be completely ignored." [60] Ralph Matthews, Washington editor of the *Afro,* said, "refusal to obey military orders, [it] matters not what the motivation, is always wrong. Even my

58. *The Afro-American,* March 31, 1945; Pittsburgh *Courier,* March 24, 1945.

59. *The Afro-American,* April 21, 1945; "The Case of the Negro Wacs," *The Negro* 3 (February 1945): 8; New York *Amsterdam News,* March 24, 1945.

60. *The Afro-American,* March 31, 1945.

love of my kinsmen will permit me no compromise with this basic premise."[61]

The *Courier* offered its sympathy, but not its support for the Wacs. "While the Pittsburg *Courier* never condones disobedience of military orders, we cannot but feel that there was some justification, however slight, for the action of the four Wacs." The editor thought the four had rightfully protested discrimination, but "they should have obeyed the orders given them," despite the justice of their claims. The *Courier* believed that the Army should have been *equally* condemned for this affair.[62]

Some columnists for the *Courier* (always considered one of the most "inflammatory" black papers) joined their editor in denouncing the disobedience of military orders. P. L. Prattis said that the Wacs had the right to complain about dirty work, but when direct orders were issued, a new factor entered the case: "They do not have the right to refuse a direct order." Prattis was convinced that the military had tricked the "mutineers" at California, Hawaii, and Devons in order to bring discredit upon the race.[63] It is unlikely, though, that the authorities at Devons were trying to trick the Wacs. They had asked them to return to duty time and again before they preferred charges. These four women refused their orders because they wanted to confront the issue of discrimination directly and in the open. One of them said before the trial: "If it will help my people I will take a court martial"[64] Prattis was not alone in his view; others expressed the opinion that the Wacs had been tricked.[65]

Adam C. Powell, Jr., directed action from his congressional seat in Washington that eventually resulted in the release of the four Wacs. At the same time, the *People's Voice,* Powell's newspaper, assumed a less militant posture. This paper editorialized that the Wacs had "committed a serious offense," and "no matter

61. Ralph Matthews, *The Afro-American,* March 31, 1945.
62. Pittsburgh *Courier,* March 31, 1945.
63. P. L. Prattis, Pittsburgh *Courier,* March 31, 1945.
64. Schomburg Vertical Files: U.S. Army, Women's Army Corps.
65. Charley Cherokee, Chicago *Defender,* March 31, 1945.

how serious the provocation, they should not have defied military discipline. . . ." [66]

A few columnists and editors did applaud the action of the four Wacs and the other "mutineers" as the beginning of a new militancy that should be encouraged. Harry Keelan, an *Afro-American* columnist, said, "For the first time in America colored Americans have . . . chosen prison rather than compromise with their ideals." He compared the Wacs to Gandhi and Nehru, and attacked the NAACP for claiming that they had received a fair trial.[67] Schuyler, of course, praised the Wacs and all others who refused to submit to discrimination, and said only a "slavish craven" would ever accept such conditions.[68] The California *Eagle* called the action of the Wacs a new approach in the fight for desegregation.[69] These were the exceptions; most writers were not yet ready to support direct action and discouraged any disobedience to the military.

Combat Efficiency of the Black Soldier

Black papers feared that these trials could eventually discredit all black soldiers. As these trials were in progress, the Army was taking steps that would in effect help defeat the wartime program of the black press and further discredit the wartime services of blacks. In the spring of 1944 the press suddenly became aware of the fact that as more and more blacks were drafted, the Army was decreasing the number of black infantry soldiers. The *Defender* reported that between August 1943 and February 1944 the number of black infantry soldiers declined from 57,323 to 44,022, while the total number of blacks in the Army rose from 582,861 to 664,066.[70] Reports were also filtering out that the Army was con-

66. *People's Voice,* March 31, 1945.
67. Harry Keelan, *The Afro-American,* March 31, 1945.
68. George S. Schuyler, Pittsburgh *Courier,* April 21, 1945.
69. California *Eagle,* April 5, 1945.
70. Chicago *Defender,* May 27, 1944.

verting black combat units into service battalions.[71] Many papers began to express their uneasiness that, after two years of war, the Army had not yet committed black troops to combat.

Congressman Hamilton Fish, always ready to embarrass the Democrats during an election year, wrote to Secretary of War Henry L. Stimson and raised the question of the failure to utilize black combat troops. Fish released Stimson's reply to the black press and it caused an immediate outcry against the Secretary, raising demands for his dismissal. Stimson wrote that a large percentage of black inductees were in the lower educational classification, "and many of the Negro units accordingly have been unable to master efficiently the technique of modern weapons." [72]

"Too Dumb to Fight" was the reaction of the black press to Stimson's letter. These papers expressed astonishment and dismay at the Secretary's comment. The *Courier* likened it to a "bombshell to Negro morale. Negro people who have been supporting the war effort a hundred percent have been stunned by the charges." [73] It convinced Horace Cayton and others that the Army would never really change, and that the press could not lessen its vigilance or there would be no black combat soldiers.[74] The *Defender* considered Stimson's letter a "terrific blow to the morale of the Negro people," and said that if Chinese and Russian peasants could master modern weapons and hold back the more intelligent troops of the Japanese and German armies, Stimson's charges were unacceptable. The truth was, said the *Defender*, that the Army did not want to use black combat units and Stimson was using intelligence tests to prevent them from receiving combat training. The editor believed this "vicious and unwarranted attack" by Stimson to have caused a greater demoralization and bitterness than any other action of the Army.[75]

71. Chicago *Defender*, March 4, 1944; March 25, 1944. As early as October 1943, G-3 ordered that no further Negro combat units be organized. See Lee, pp. 426–27.
72. Pittsburgh *Courier*, March 4, 1944.
73. *Ibid.*, March 11, 1944.
74. Horace Cayton, Pittsburgh *Courier*, March 11, 1944.
75. Chicago *Defender*, March 11, 1944; March 18, 1944.

Black papers had placed their hopes for the future on an exemplary war record earned by black troops. By early 1944 the Army seemed to be repeating its World War I policy. Stimson's assumptions about the effectiveness of black combat units were based largely upon the post-World War I reports that blacks made poor fighters unless "competent and sympathetic white officers" led them.[76]

In the fall of 1944 the Army raised the hopes of the press somewhat when elements of the 92nd Division (black) began to engage the enemy in the Italian theater. Their mission was primarily defensive, but they initiated small offensive actions. The 92nd launched one large, but unsuccessful, attack in February 1945.[77] Black newspapers eagerly printed front-page articles telling of engagements and advances into enemy territory. The white press, on the other hand, had different stories to report about the 92nd. A *Defender* columnist described the situation: when the 92nd advances, the black press yells heroes; when it retreats the racists yell cowards.[78]

In February the 92nd received national publicity in *Newsweek* magazine. *Newsweek* condemned the outfit as a complete failure. This magazine reported that black troops had quickly acquired a poor reputation among white troops, who considered them "trigger happy." *Newsweek* also said that the 92nd "crumbled" during the Serchio River offensive in December. The black press was alarmed by this story and others, which it viewed as an attempt to slander black troops. When white troops were sent reeling back at the Bulge, retorted the *Defender,* the white press did not condemn these white soldiers as being inept or cowards.[79] Before *Newsweek* covered the 92nd, black papers were fearful about the possibility of bad publicity. "Will They Try to Discredit Our G.I.'s?" pondered the *Amsterdam News* editor. Recalling the experience of World War I and the discrediting of black troops then, the editor feared

76. H. L. Stimson and M. Bundy, *On Active Service in Peace and War* (New York: Harper & Bros., 1947), pp. 461–64.

77. Lee, pp. 536–75.

78. Charley Cherokee, Chicago *Defender,* February 24, 1945.

79. Chicago *Defender,* March 4, 1945.

that history might repeat itself at the end of World War II.[80]

A few months before the war in Europe ended, the reverses of the 92nd gave rise to a cause célèbre centering around Truman K. Gibson, the black Civilian Aide to the Secretary of War. When Hastie received the appointment as Civilian Aide, Gibson went to the War Department as his assistant. After Hastie resigned in early 1943, Gibson reported to the black press that he too was anxious to resign. He said he was going to remain temporarily until the War Department found a replacement for Hastie, and emphatically denied any ambitions to fill Hastie's position.[81] Gibson did not resign, and his ability to get along well with the Army eventually resulted in his appointment to Hastie's vacant post.[82]

Until 1945 the black press had little to say about Gibson, but the few times his name appeared it was not in a favorable light. In 1943 the New York *Age* wrote Gibson inquiring about the Army's plans to ease tension in the Southern camps. Gibson responded with a memorandum charging the black press with magnifying racial incidents, and asked the *Age* not to use his name in its story. The *Age* denounced Gibson for his memorandum and his request not to reveal his name. Columnist Frank Griffin felt that Gibson was a poor substitute for Hastie because he had never made any complaints against Army discrimination. Gibson was also conspicuous at the 1943 NNPA meeting for calling on the press to tone down its articles dealing with Army discrimination.[83]

Gibson, at the request of Assistant Secretary of War John McCloy, planned a personal visit to the Italian zone to investigate the 92nd firsthand. He arrived on February 26, 1945, and visited with General Mark Clark and other high Army officials. Afterwards he reportedly spoke to about 800 black officers and "hundreds" of enlisted men before filing a report on his findings on March 12.[84]

80. New York *Amsterdam News,* December 2, 1944.
81. Chicago *Defender,* January 23, 1943; January 30, 1943.
82. Lee, pp. 174–78; Stimson and Bundy, p. 464; *Negro Digest* 1 (August 1944): 17.
83. New York *Age,* July 3, 1943; March 11, 1944; *PEP* 1 (July 1943): 10.
84. Lee, p. 576.

Two days later he held a press conference in Rome. This conference was a disaster for Gibson and—the black press claimed—for the entire race.

There was no transcript of Gibson's remarks, but the press, white and black, reported his comments extensively. Gibson confirmed earlier reports that the 92nd had "a rather dismal record" and that elements of the Division had engaged in "more or less panicky retreats." He also said, in the most evocative of his comments, that units of the 92nd had "melted away" before enemy advances. Gibson did not fail to discuss the important fact of discrimination, but he emphasized the low intelligence levels as one of the most important elements in the failures of the 92nd. Most of the men were in class IV and V, which included illiterates and semi-literates. Milton Bracker, the New York *Times* reporter covering the Rome conference, said this appraisal had to be taken "most seriously," since Gibson was a War Department official and a Negro.[85]

The response of the black press was immediate and loud. A *Defender* editorial roared, "Somebody's Gotta Go!" The editor attacked Gibson as a "new enemy," an "uncle Tom," and characterized him as the typical Negro who was black but thought like a white man. Gibson's motives, he added, had been suspect ever since Hastie resigned, and it was now clear that he had used Hastie's exit to slip into a soft job. The *Defender* concluded that Gibson was an official apologist for the War Department.[86] Most black papers felt the same as the *Defender*.

George Schuyler wrote, "Such a Negro is a liability to everybody except the Army Command." [87] Cayton was more philosophical. He believed that the Army had duped Gibson and maneuvered him into saying what he did at Rome. Gibson's emphasis on the 92nd's "failures" and low intelligence levels were the excuses the Army had always used when the black press demanded equal treatment. Cayton felt that Gibson should have resigned when

85. New York *Times*, March 15, 1945; "Report on the Negro Soldier," *Time* 45 (March 26, 1945): 22.
86. Chicago *Defender*, March 24, 1945.
87. George Schuyler, Pittsburgh *Courier*, March 31, 1945.

Hastie left office. Instead, he said, Gibson "found himself taken step by step until the final and logical conclusion of his act—a public statement about the failure of Negro soldiers." Granting that Gibson might have achieved much by remaining in office, Cayton concluded, "nothing that has been accomplished will make up for this one-sided indictment of Negro soldiers by a Negro spokesman."[88]

Arthur P. Davis reprinted a letter from a soldier of the 92nd in his *Journal and Guide* column, which poured out the feelings of many in that ill-fated division. These men first found out about the Rome conference in the *Newsweek* article of February 26. As the story spread, "hot indignation swept everyone" in the outfit. The only relief they felt was in reading the continuing attacks against Gibson by the black press. "The harm has been done" already, wrote this soldier, and he suspected an undeclared conspiracy to ruin the reputation of black combat troops. The soldier believed that trouble could have been avoided by totally integrating the Army, or forming all-black units with all-black officers.[89]

Powell, writing in the *People's Voice,* declared that Gibson had let the Army use him. He revealed that he and Gibson had conferred a month prior to his Rome conference. Gibson told him at that time the same things he later said at the Rome conference, which was supposed to be the result of information sifted from interviews with "hundreds" of black soldiers and over 800 black officers. Therefore, Powell concluded that the Army sent Gibson to Rome to say something he was told to say in Washington.[90] There is little reason to believe that the Army told Gibson what to say, but there is evidence that Gibson left for Italy with certain conclusions about the 92nd already formulated.

In November 1944 Gibson asked Major Oscar J. Magee of Intelligence to gather information about the 92nd. After visiting the Italian theater, Magee reported, in December, that too often the infantry "melts away" under fire. He also said that white officers

88. Horace Cayton, Pittsburgh *Courier,* March 31, 1945.
89. Arthur P. Davis, *Journal and Guide,* May 5, 1945.
90. *People's Voice,* March 31, 1945.

were unhappy with their assignment to black units. General Edward M. Almond, Commanding General of the 92nd, reported to General Clark in November 1944 that the "melting away tendency" was apparent when black troops confronted the enemy.[91] Gibson was in Italy less than two weeks before the conference, and yet he claimed he gathered his information from interviewing over a thousand soldiers. Gibson had a long history of speaking for the Army, and he appears to have adopted the Army "line" in Rome, especially when he spoke of melting away and low intelligence levels.

Earl Brown, columnist for the *Amsterdam News,* commented acutely on the Gibson fiasco. Illiteracy, he wrote, was not the reason that the black soldier was not a good soldier. The real problem was the depressing morale of black troops and the trying conditions of fighting for an Army that seemed to despise the entire race. The Army, he said, had nothing but praise for Gibson, which in itself was *prima facie* evidence to most blacks that Gibson sold out. Brown, like Powell, revealed that for months Gibson had been saying the same thing in his Washington office that he later told reporters in Rome.[92]

Gibson's predecessor had some comments about his press conference. Carefully declaring that he was not yet ready to believe the statements attributed to Gibson, Hastie avoided making personal remarks about his successor. The importance of the conference, Hastie noted, was that the American people would believe that black combat troops did not perform well, which would be a serious error and a "gross libel" against the race.[93]

Elements of the 93rd Division, the other all-black infantry division, engaged in combat in the Pacific theater. Although this division did not receive the same degree of publicity in the press as the 92nd Division, accounts relating to its combat effectiveness were substantially the same as those which were circulated about the 92nd. When Walter White toured the Pacific in 1944–45, he

91. Lee, pp. 560–61.
92. Earl Brown, New York *Amsterdam News,* April 24, 1945.
93. New York *Amsterdam News,* March 31, 1945.

encountered so many "viciously false statements regarding the 93rd Division . . . and Negroes as combat troops generally," that he became convinced that "a deliberate if not an organized campaign" was being conducted to smear the reputation of black soldiers. Rumors were rife that blacks of the 93rd were "no good as combat troops," and that they broke and ran under fire. Eventually these stories reached the War Department. The Assistant Secretary of War told White that he had heard that the 93rd failed to take an easy beachhead at Bougainville.[94] General Marshall said after the war that the black troops on Bougainville "wouldn't fight." [95]

The basic premise of the "Double V" program was that for services rendered and battlefield bravery, liberal white Americans would discover the paradox within their own democracy and join the struggle for civil rights. The Army did little to allow blacks to perform fully under conditions similar to those enjoyed by whites. Black divisions were destined for failure not because of low intelligence levels, but due to the country's unwillingness to confront the homefront crisis as forcefully as it was willing to face the enemy abroad. Black soldiers received little praise from their white countrymen at the end of the war. In May 1945 the Army sent questionnaires to various commands to determine the effectiveness of black troops. The responses revealed that the World War I racial stereotypes were still firmly rooted in the military.[96] In Congress, Senator James Eastland, in attacking the proposal for a permanent FEPC, pointed to the poor record of the black soldier as proof of that race's "inferiority" and unworthiness. To support his contention he said that "a Negro from the War Department" had confirmed the failure of the 92nd Division.[97]

In 1945 the Army established a three-man committee (Gillem Board) to review its policy toward black soldiers. It made suggestions to alleviate some problems, but did not question the policy

94. Memorandum from Walter White to F.D.R., February 12, 1945, Hollandia, Dutch New Guinea, Walter White Correspondence, James Weldon Johnson Collection, Yale University Library.

95. Quoted in Lee, p. 512.

96. Dalfiume, p. 148.

97. Quoted in Pittsburgh *Courier,* July 7, 1945.

of segregation. In fact, it confirmed, in somewhat temperate language, the general feeling that blacks were least effective in combat situations.[98] The Board also called on the Army to maintain black troop strength at the 10 percent level. By 1945 this was no longer acceptable to the black press, which at this time was calling for an end to quotas and segregation.

Segregation ended in the Army not because liberal whites were grateful to blacks for their World War II performance. It ended for other reasons. The segregation policy was shaken a little when blacks threatened mass resistance to the 1948 peacetime Draft Act.[99] Threatened with massive civil disobedience in an election year and with the onset of the Cold War, President Truman, in June 1948, issued Executive Order 9981 calling for equality of treatment in the armed forces, and set up the Fahy Committee to make the necessary recommendations to implement the order. Even this effort did not bring an end to segregation in the Army. When the Cold War heated up in Korea, segregation in the Army finally began to crumble.[100]

98. *Report of Board of Officers on Utilization of Negro Manpower in the Post War Army. February 26, 1946*. Printed in Selective Service: *Special Groups,* 2: 159–69.

99. L. D. Reddick, "The Negro Policy of the American Army Since World War II," *Journal of Negro History* 38 (April 1953): 196–214.

100. Dalfiume, p. 201.

6
The Black Press and World War II

The European Belligerents

When the war in Europe broke out in 1939, the response of the black press revealed the contradictions of a minority race living under a fairly rigid caste system within a democratic society. The attitude of the press toward the Allies and the Germans exhibited the dual nature of the black man as an American, and as a non-white belonging to that majority which throughout the world was under the domination of white Europeans now fighting among themselves. These ambivalent feelings were heightened because of the nature of the belligerent societies. The Allied powers controlled a large portion of the world's colored population, while Germany, with no colonial possessions, was governed by a dictator with the most extreme racist ideology to be espoused openly by any major wartime leader.

The outlook of black papers toward the warring nations was ultimately affected more by the ideological basis of Nazi racism than by the historical actions of the Allies toward the world's colored majority. What Adolf Hitler stated about non-Aryans caused greater concern among black editors than all of the acts of oppression perpetrated by the English, French, Dutch, and Belgians upon their subject nonwhite people over the previous decades and centuries. The black press was democratic and assimilationist, and as such could relate better to the democratic Allies than to Germany, which at the time was not guilty of oppressing blacks. But this did not preclude the press's launching a sustained attack on the colonial powers during the early stages of the European war.

These contradictions became evident during 1939 and 1940 when the press, despite its greater fear of Germany, had more of a basis from which to attack the Allied powers than the Axis countries. When the pro-Allies white writers tried to gain the support of blacks by warning them of Hitler's plans for non-Aryans, black writers responded by pointing to the similarity between Germany and Georgia. The only difference between the two that the press would concede was that Germany was planning to do what the South had already put into effect.[1] The black press assailed the Allies' colonial policies relentlessly, but on the other hand few writers wanted to see the Allies go down to defeat. A few black writers did maintain a consistent position of favoring neither Germany nor the Allies, but most, despite the contradictions, believed the future hope of the world's blacks to lie with the colonial powers.

Since black papers were read as supplements to the daily papers, the views expressed offered a different perspective. Much of the discussion dealing with the war centered on its effects on the world's colored peoples. The relationship of the war to American security (a primary topic of debate between white isolationists and interventionists) was not, with a few exceptions, a major area of discussion. Also, despite their ultimate fear of Hitler, black writers generally hoped that Germany would be able to weaken (but not destroy) the Allies to such an extent that their grip on their colonies would be shattered permanently.

Thus, when the European war commenced, the black press presented an ambivalent picture, but one quite different from that

1. Pittsburgh *Courier,* March 15, 1941 ; Horace Cayton, Pittsburgh *Courier,* March 22, 1941.

of the white media. No position differed more from that of the white majority than the outspoken pleasure with which many black editors received the news of the war. Papers immediately wrote of expected economic benefits at home, and political benefits to blacks throughout the world.

The leading black interventionist paper, *The Afro-American*, welcomed the war in an editorial entitled "Why We Are For War." First, the editor wrote, it would stimulate black migration to the Northern industrial states; a benefit to the race. Secondly, it would mean eventual freedom for the African. The Allies would of necessity train African soldiers, and "After an African native has discovered in Europe what a modern rifle will do, does anybody imagine he'll be satisfied to go back home to a bow and arrow or spear?" War was "savage and barbarous," but tyranny and oppression "never yield except at the muzzle of a cannon." After a tirade against the Allies, the editor concluded: "We are against Hitler because of his race hatred of Jews." [2]

Other papers, less militant than the *Afro*, also expressed no displeasure when writing about the war in Europe. A war editorial in the New York *Age* emphasized that the Allies would be forced to use their colonials to fight Germany. This would allow the subject people to "bargain" for concessions for their services rendered. A parallel was drawn between black Americans and the blacks under the domination of the Allies. Should the United States be drawn into the war, the black American would be offered an "unprecedented opportunity to advance his status." [3] When papers spoke of opportunities for Africans to gain freedom, they meant freedom after the war. The idea that black Africans should revolt and strike for freedom while the colonial powers were under siege was not expressed by any editor.

At once writers began to attack Allied colonial practices. England, they said, had placed the black man on a par with animals. It had kept India divided and subdued, and East Africa enslaved.

2. *The Afro-American*, September 16, 1939.

3. New York *Age*, September 9, 1939; see also Rayford Logan, New York *Amsterdam News*, September 9, 1939.

France, more liberal than England, still committed "certain errors" in its colonial policies. "Our wholehearted sympathies were with France," wrote Lucius Harper. Hitler was another matter; he had to be destroyed. But—and here Harper expressed the feeling of many black observers—in the process of destroying Hitler, he wanted to see England turned "inside out." Harper was convinced that the war would be beneficial to black people.[4]

The hope that the war in Europe would weaken the Allies and enhance the future prospects of colonial freedom, was expressed side by side with the ultimate fear that Hitler would emerge triumphant. This phenomenon reoccurred when the United States entered the war. Many black writers then expressed their full support of the American cause, along with the desire that the war would continue for many years.

A few black papers were less oblique in their support of the Allied cause, and initially offered no critique of their colonial policies. These papers simply called for all-out aid to the British and French. Eventually even these black papers voiced criticism of the colonial policies practiced by the Allies, but strong support for the democracies was never absent from their comments.

From the *Defender's* initial comments came unequivocal support for England and France. Criticizing those black Americans who were indifferent to the fate of the Allies, the editor warned that nobody was exempt in the struggle between fascism and democracy. Blacks had no other choice than to align themselves with the democratic cause. The editor demanded an end to the "bogus neutrality" laws hampering the "other two democracies" so that the United States would not have to bear the responsibility for the demise of the cause of freedom. The *Defender* did not ignore the brighter aspects of a European war such as the enhancement of the economic condition of the black man in America.[5]

No black paper expressed a more consistent and categorical

4. Lucius Harper, Chicago *Defender,* September 23, 1939; Pittsburgh *Courier* correspondent Walter Merguson wrote many articles from the front lines telling of black colonials fighting with the French forces. See December 2, 1939; March 2, 1940.

5. Chicago *Defender,* September 23, 1939; September 30, 1939.

sympathy with the Allies than the *Journal and Guide.* The Allies were democracies and as such had the backing of the editor. Moreover, if war should come to the United States, he expressed no concern about the response of the black community. At such times, the black man "invariably forgets the bitter social, economic and political repressions . . . and dives, head first, for the nearest rifle. . . ." [6] Thus, from the very first consideration of the possibility of United States involvement in the war, the *Journal and Guide* expressed a close-ranks position.

Four months prior to the outbreak of war, William Pickens, an ANP columnist appearing regularly in the *Journal and Guide,* predicted that the United States would be unable to "stay out of a war with Democracy fighting a Life and Death Fight on one side of it. . . ." Week after week Pickens hammered away at his readers that "The Allies' War is Our War. . . ." Yes, it was true that Great Britain was "a great sinner," but "Germany was the worst" sinner.[7] Pickens was one of the first black writers to identify the Allied cause with American security. Most black writers did not make this connection until after the fall of the Low Countries and France. Pickens immediately espoused this line of thought and insisted that should the Allies fall, the first line of America's defense would be breached. He was careful to state that he did not approve "absolutely" of the Allies, but he believed that the interest of the entire world and human liberty were at stake, and hung upon an Allied victory.[8]

Joining Pickens on the feature page of the *Journal and Guide* were Gordon B. Hancock and Kelly Miller. Hancock was as apprehensive about a German victory as Pickens. Desiring American involvement as quickly as possible, he was anxious to send United States troops to Europe before the war spread to the Western hemisphere.[9] By the fall of 1940 he was growing increasingly alarmed about the future of the Allies and the United States.

6. *Journal and Guide,* September 16, 1939.
7. William Pickens, *Journal and Guide,* April 29, 1939; September 23, 1939; October 28, 1939.
8. *Ibid.,* December 30, 1939.
9. Gordon B. Hancock, *Journal and Guide,* December 30, 1939.

To avoid the defeat of the Allies, and eventually the United States, Hancock proposed giving the President dictatorial powers: "There is no need to have a power reposed in a people who do not understand how and why it is to be used." [10] This columnist was one of the few who, during this period and later when the United States entered the war, maintained that blacks should forget their grievances until the emergency ended.

Miller was more restrained in his pro-Allies stance. He was sure that the sympathy of black Americans was with the Allies, albeit a passive sympathy.[11] Miller believed that United States involvement was inevitable and tried to define an approach blacks could pursue that would avoid the "close ranks" policy of World War I. Miller stressed the difference between forgetting grievances and holding them in abeyance until the strife ended. When DuBois, in 1918, told his audience to forget their grievances, he obviously meant only for the duration of the war. This, in effect, was a call to put grievances in "abeyance." Miller asked his readers to contribute patriotically in any national emergency and importuned his country not to belie its lofty ideals.[12] Miller was edging toward a "Double V" approach, but as yet was unwilling to call on blacks to press for an end to discrimination during an emergency. It was not until shortly after America became a belligerent that the press realized that the "Double V" was the most effective way to encourage blacks to "close ranks" for the war effort.

Most black papers did not view the war in Europe primarily as a struggle between democracy and dictatorship, but rather a continuation of the imperialistic quarrels of World War I. This meant that the battle to control colonial markets would eventually center on Africa. The *Amsterdam News* condemned both England and Italy for their control of African states. The Germans, of course, had no colonial possessions in Africa, but they had "robbed and are trying to rob again the Africans the same as the English and Belgians have always done." [13] France, a major colonizer of Africa

10. *Ibid.*, October 20, 1940.
11. Kelly Miller, *Journal and Guide,* October 14, 1939.
12. *Ibid.*, October 28, 1939.
13. New York *Amsterdam News,* September 9, 1939.

and Asia, was almost immune from criticism from the black press, since most editors did not consider France a "racist" country. Despite the *Amsterdam News'* dislike of both England and Germany, its sympathies were with the Allies, and it attacked the "fallacious reasoning" that said that both sides were equally bad.[14] In choosing sides, black papers were faced with a choice of the lesser evil, and France did much to tip the balance to the Allies.

The most devastating attacks on the democratic powers came from the *Courier* and its columnists, with George S. Schuyler, the "Dean" of black columnists, leading the way. Even before 1939 he expressed amusement with all the concern about Hitler's use of force in seizing foreign territories. Schuyler reminded his readers that England, France, Portugal, and Spain had all used force to acquire their empires. The United States, too, had applied force to maintain its Philippine protectorate. For Schuyler, there was no difference between Hitler's treatment of minorities and "the treatment of minorities in the democ(k)racies." [15]

According to the editor of the *Courier,* the British Empire was the "keystone of race prejudice and discrimination in the modern world." [16] Robert Vann, publisher of the *Courier,* expressed no fondness for the Allies, but disliked Germany more than England and France. He favored letting Hitler know at once that he was disliked, and would receive no help from the United States. Vann, as late as August 1940, believed that England would destroy Germany.[17] This could explain why, despite the publisher's greater fear of fascism, the paper did not express much anxiety about Germany's racist ideology, and emphasized instead English imperialism during the early stages of the war. The *Courier,* one of the most militant black papers in exposing America's democratic pretensions, attacked relentlessly the Allied colonial practices. Editorials denounced English colonial policy as the worst form of dictatorship. The war was one of rival imperialisms, not a war

14. *Ibid.,* September 23, 1939.
15. George Schuyler, Pittsburgh *Courier,* March 25, 1939.
16. Pittsburgh *Courier,* June 24, 1939.
17. Robert Vann, Pittsburgh *Courier,* October 7, 1939; August 24, 1940.

between democracy and totalitarianism. How many Africans, pondered the editor, would mourn the downfall of white civilization? [18]

Schuyler became the leading proponent of the view that the war would weaken white civilization and therefore be a factor in liberating blacks. "If the white world begins mass suicide, the dark world has but to bide its time, scheme, and at the opportune time, revolt." [19] He hoped for a long war, and continued to hold this desire after the United States entered the war. Until the United States became a belligerent, he expressed his hope for a British defeat. After the German conquest of the Continent, most black writers came out openly in support of England, but Schuyler remained adamant and attacked black leaders who were willing to go to war to defend the British Empire.[20]

At first, many *Courier* columnists joined Schuyler in desiring a weakened white civilization, including America. Joel A. Rogers differed only in emphasizing the opportunity for blacks to "bargain" rather than revolt while whites were backed against the wall. The conservative executive editor of the *Courier*, P. L. Prattis, was alarmed at the avid pro-Allies sentiment among America's whites. He believed it was rooted in the Anglo-Saxon desire to act as the world's policeman in the postwar period. This, Prattis wrote, was just an "imitation of Hitler and his policy." [21]

With the spread of the Nazi legions across continental Europe, both East and West, came a shift in the writing of most black newspapermen. Rogers began expressing more alarm about Germany, and finally concluded that Hitler was "the worst threat to the American Negro." [22] Prattis declared that "the majority among us agrees that Great Britain is the friend we wish to help." [23] These writers did not delude themselves into thinking that many blacks

18. Pittsburgh *Courier*, May 13, 1940.
19. George Schuyler, Pittsburgh *Courier*, September 2, 1939.
20. *Ibid.*, September 16, 1939; August 24, 1940; January 25, 1941; October 4, 1941.
21. J. A. Rogers, Pittsburgh *Courier*, October 19, 1940; P. L. Prattis, Pittsburgh *Courier*, January 25, 1941.
22. J. A. Rogers, Pittsburgh *Courier*, September 27, 1941.
23. P. L. Prattis, Pittsburgh *Courier*, October 4, 1941.

shared their view, and began to express their concern about the apathy of the black masses toward the threat of Hitler. Writers began to emphasize the need to convince the masses that the Nazis would destroy any chance for democracy.[24]

In 1939 most editors and columnists made clear their ultimate fear of a victorious Hitler, but concentrated their attention on Britain's imperialistic policy. After the Nazi conquest of the Continent, a noticeable shift occurred, and Hitler began to receive more attention. During the first year of conflict the black press stressed the imperialistic nature of the war, but this too changed by the end of 1940. By this time writers were saying that despite England's disgraceful colonialism, it was the last hope for democracy.[25] This shifting emphasis did not imply an open embrace of England. It was a surfacing of latent or implied feelings present since 1939, brought on by the swift victories of Germany. Perhaps DuBois expressed what many writers believed when he wrote, "If Hitler triumphs the world is lost; if England triumphs the world is not saved."[26]

The shift of opinion about the nature of the war, along with the growing concern about black indifference to a Nazi victory, is best illustrated by Randolph's conversion to an open pro-Allies position. In early 1940 Randolph, in an address to the third National Negro Congress convention, denounced all of the belligerents in strong terms. He said that the "fingers of England and France [are] dripping with the blood of black, yellow and brown colonials." Japan and Russia were also empires that subjugated millions of dark people. "Negroes," Randolph concluded, "should oppose America's entrance into war. . . ."[27] By late 1940 Randolph, now a member of the Committee to Defend America by

24. Marjorie McKenzie, Pittsburgh *Courier,* October 4, 1941 ; see also Lester Granger, New York *Amsterdam News,* June 21, 1941.

25. Lester Granger, *Journal and Guide,* June 21, 1941 ; A. P. Randolph, Pittsburgh *Courier,* February 8, 1941.

26. W. E. B. DuBois, New York *Amsterdam News,* April 19, 1941.

27. A. Philip Randolph, *The World Crisis and the Negro People Today.* This address was delivered to the National Negro Congress in April, 1940.

Aiding the Allies, began publishing articles in the press with the apparent aim of convincing blacks that they had a vital concern in the outcome of the European war. He conceded that English colonial policy had been disastrous for nonwhites, but he said that Hitler would be infinitely worse. "If Britain loses, democracy and liberty lose." Britain had betrayed black people, but at least the British considered blacks as humans, whereas Hitler looked on them as half apes. By early 1941 Randolph had concluded that "England's Fighting Our Cause." [28]

The *Amsterdam News* attacked those blacks who were happy to see whites killing each other. This paper encouraged blacks to join with their white countrymen in times of crisis. The danger to all was fascism. When German troops invaded Scandinavia, the paper became alarmed, but it was apparent to the *Amsterdam News* that its readers did not display the same concern about the defeat of white nations by Germany. The editor condemned both English and German imperialism, but said there was at least a difference "of degree" in the treatment meted out by the two countries to their subject peoples.[29] England's most hostile critic, the *Courier*, joined the growing chorus of pleas in the black press warning blacks to awaken to the impending disaster of an Axis victory. In March 1941 an article appeared entitled "If Hitler Wins." The article informed blacks that intermarriage would be prohibited, all political rights would cease, and Jim Crow would be made complete and rigid.[30]

By December 7, 1941, the black press had identified Germany as the major threat to nonwhites. England, while no friend to blacks, was at least similar to the United States in that it was an imperfect democracy with possibilities of improvement. France, a colonial power, was generally considered friendly and humane in its relations with nonwhites. Lack of any expressed hostility, and

28. A. Philip Randolph, *Journal and Guide,* August 31, 1940; Pittsburgh *Courier,* February 8, 1941; *The Black Worker,* September, 1940; May, 1942.
29. New York *Amsterdam News,* April 20, 1940.
30. Pittsburgh *Courier,* March 8, 1941.

often open praise, were reserved for Russia. Most black papers throughout the entire war considered Russia to be the one country that had "solved" its minorities problem.

Most black papers expressed no fear of communism or Russia, which was evident in various white newspapers. Quite often, black writers came to the defense of Russia against the attacks of the white press. The conservative Washington editor of *The Afro-American*, Ralph Matthews, wrote: "Russia has done nothing particularly harmful to either nation [the United States and Great Britain] except perfect a way of life for her own people. . . . That of course makes Russia a very dangerous force."[31] Race relations within the Soviet Union were pointed to as a model that the United States should emulate: "In this equality and impartiality in military as well as civil life is doubtless one of the greatest sources of strength and soundness of the Soviet Russian state."[32] The California *Eagle* declared that Russia was the only nation in the world where there was no racial discrimination.[33] Black papers usually expressed their satisfaction that Russia would be included in the peace negotiations at the end of the war. Russia, they believed, would exert a beneficial influence in opposing the old imperialistic ideas and in favor of worldwide racial equality.[34]

Japan

Before the bombing of Pearl Harbor there was little discussion in the black press about Japan or Japanese-American relations. When black papers did turn their attention to Japan, there was no expression of fear and little hostility. Quite often, in fact, papers openly praised the Japanese. If the black press did expect trouble

31. Ralph Matthews, *The Afro-American,* October 11, 1941 ; see also California *Eagle,* February 22, 1945.
32. Chicago *Defender,* March 18, 1944.
33. California *Eagle,* July 17, 1945.
34. Horace Cayton, Pittsburgh *Courier,* November 6, 1943 ; *People's Voice,* January 9, 1945 ; J. R. Badger, Chicago *Defender,* September 4, 1943.

between the United States and Japan, it rarely discussed it in its columns. This was true even after tensions heightened after the creation of the Axis alliance in the fall of 1940.

Japan's expansionist designs in the Far East were aimed at replacing white European hegemony in the area. Few black writers were disturbed by these intentions, and many were quite pleased by the prospect of seeing the white overlords chased out of Asia. This did not mean that black writers believed that the Japanese were trying to free Asia from all exploitation. Many viewed it as merely a change of exploiters, with a nonwhite nation doing some exploiting for a change. There appeared to be a complete acceptance of Japan as the dominant nation of the Eastern area of the world, just as the United States was accepted as the dominant nation of the Western hemisphere.

Black writers did observe their countrymen's fears vis-à-vis the Japanese, and the racial issue dominated the discussion. *The Afro-American* had "A Good Word for the Japs," and wrote that if Japan pushed the Dutch out of Asia, black people would shed no tears. If Americans held to the proposition of America for the Americans, why should this country become upset at the idea of Asia for the Asiatics? The United States had no more right to resist Japan in China than the Japanese had to violate the Monroe Doctrine. Asia was considered Japan's natural sphere of influence, and as long as the Japanese did not expand beyond Asiatic limits, the United States should not interfere.[35]

DuBois added depth to the discussion of Asia when he analyzed America's motives in that area. Was this country really interested in trying to help the people of China and the Dutch East Indies? DuBois did not think so. He was convinced that the primary concern of the United States was to keep the other powers from dominating the Far East. If Japan became the dominant power in the area, that country could threaten United States' economic penetration of Asia. The economic encirclement of Japan by the United States and Great Britain and the psychology of race were

35. *The Afro-American,* December 13, 1940.

major threats to Japan. Both of these factors played a major role in goading Japan into its expansionist policy.[36]

Just as the black press viewed the European war as one of rival imperialisms, it considered friction in the Far East basically similar, with the exception of the race issue. Many papers believed that Asia was Japan's natural sphere of interest, expressed no displeasure in seeing a colored nation replacing white colonial powers, and emphatically stated that the United States should not become involved. The *Courier* put it rather bluntly: "Japan has white imperialism on the run—the white imperialists don't like it but they'll have to lump it." [37] When Secretary of State Cordell Hull notified Japan that the United States was terminating the Mutual Trade Pact, black writers were disturbed and considered it a provocative action. Again, race and imperialism were felt to be the primary motives behind the moves to counter the Japanese program. The United States boycott was implemented in order to aid white European powers against the Japanese. Why didn't the United States take similar drastic action when white Italy invaded colored Ethiopia? Only when a nonwhite nation became self assertive, it appeared, did the United States stir itself to action.[38]

A few black papers remained outside of this general trend of thought about Japan. The *Journal and Guide* wrote that the Japanese claim to lead the world's colored people was nonsense. "Tokio is as heartless as London, Paris, Rome and Berlin. . . ." [39] It had subjugated Korea, Manchuria, and other Chinese provinces, and offered the world's colored population the choice of jumping from the frying pan into the fire. For the *Defender*, a fascist Japan only added to the threat of a fascist Germany.[40] Schuyler voiced his disapproval of fascism, white or colored. He expressed no pride in Japanese conquests, but rather had equal contempt for that

36. W. E. B. DuBois, New York *Amsterdam News*, January 25, 1941; W. E. B. DuBois, "A Chronicle of Race Relations," *Phylon* 2 (Second Quarter 1941): 179–80.
37. Pittsburgh *Courier*, April 8, 1939.
38. *Ibid.*, August 5, 1939.
39. *Journal and Guide*, July 22, 1939.
40. Chicago *Defender*, July 27, 1940.

country and all Caucasian exploiters. Japan, he wrote, was long the "hired gunman of Anglo-Saxondom," helping to keep Russia checked in the Far East and undermining China. But when the "Nipponese bandit went into business for himself," he became a problem to the white overlords.[41]

Despite an awareness that Japan was a fascist state and an expansionist power, the emphasis of black papers remained on the racial aspects of international politics. The day before the Japanese attacked Pearl Harbor, *The Afro-American* discussed the growing United States-Japanese tensions from this racial perspective. The editor continued to insist that Japan was simply carrying out its own Monroe Doctrine in Asia and that the United States had no right to deny this colored nation political hegemony in the area.[42] Ralph Matthews was convinced that the United States' opposition to Japan was racism pure and simple:

> Of course the most important element in the whole Far Eastern crisis is not so much one of material spirits as it is the first great challenge by any darker race to the white man's right to rule the world. . . . Japan therefore must be crushed—not to save democracy, not to halt aggression. . . , but to keep intact the idea of Nordic invincibility and to roll back for another century the rising tide of color.[43]

P. L. Prattis, in a column published on December 6, 1941, elaborated a theory that would later be called the United States' "Back Door" approach to war. Prattis was for "all-out defense" against the Germans, but was concerned about the way F.D.R. seemed to be edging the country toward belligerancy. "In the current emergency it will be much easier to unite the American people in a warlike attitude toward Japan than it will be to get them to go to war against Germany. The element of prejudice is involved." Prattis, in fact, seemed to imply that United States-Japanese friction

41. George Schuyler, "The Caucasian Problem," *What The Negro Wants,* ed. Rayford Logan, p. 283.

42. *The Afro-American,* December 6, 1941.

43. Ralph Matthews, *The Afro-American,* December 6, 1941.

was in large part the fault of the Chinese for preferring "whites to boss them rather than Japanese." He believed that China should have joined with Japan, but instead they behaved like "Uncle Toms" and "would rather flunkey for the white than allow the Japanese to set up a 'Monroe Doctrine' for Asia." Prattis, along with most black commentators at this time, did not have any illusions about America's desire to preserve Chinese independence. He too spoke of the government's fear of being closed off from the Chinese market as the motivating force behind the administration's Far Eastern policy.[44]

Pearl Harbor and After

Once the United States entered the war, the outlook of the black press underwent a major change in viewpoint. The emphasis shifted toward the proposition that it was *not* a "white man's war," and that it was a war for freedom rather than one of rival imperialisms. Throughout the war, the attention of the black press remained focused on the European theater, where the bulk of black troops going overseas were sent. Comments on Asia usually dealt with China's efforts to free itself from Japanese control.[45]

The immediate response of the black press to the bombing of Pearl Harbor was one of outpourings of support, with connotations of, and often outright calls for, closing ranks. Only when the press discovered after a few weeks that its readers were apparently less responsive to appeals for unity did it back away from this position and adopt the "DoubleV" program.

"Mr. President, Count on Us," proclaimed *The Afro-American*. Blacks were Americans and would join in the defense of their country. The editor pleaded for guns instead of mops and aprons,

44. P. L. Prattis, Pittsburgh *Courier*, December 6, 1941.

45. Lin Liang-mo appeared on the feature page of the *Courier* during the war. His columns almost exclusively dealt with the problem. At the end of the war his column was discontinued when the *Courier* received reports about China's "disdain" for blacks; see *PEP* 2 (May 1945): 18.

saying that blacks would forget the past and "without bitterness for what has happened in the past, offer themselves to the [President] . . . and say Mr. President, you can count on us." [46] *The Afro-American* was not the only paper willing to forget the past; others joined in it declaring their total support for the country in its time of peril.

"The Black Tenth is Ready" to help crush the Axis powers, reported the Savannah *Tribune*. Blacks, according to this editor, were not just ready to fight, they were anxious. The *Tribune*'s only fear was whether the country would permit blacks to fight.[47] Black Americans, reported the Chicago *Bee*, had no ties to the Axis; America was the only country they supported.[48] The California *Eagle* declared that the war would change its preoccupation with the "Negro problem" in its columns, since it would no longer dominate the thoughts of the black community. The paper's emphasis would shift from its campaign for full citizenship rights to the exercise of full citizenship duties. The *Eagle* said it would not forget segregation and discrimination; but it stressed that blacks in the United States, despite these things, had more freedom than other blacks. If America was not a full-fledged democracy, at least it was a "quasi democracy," and superior to fascism. The fight for Negro rights would be resumed after the war.[49]

A few papers openly called on their readers to "close ranks" for the war effort. The *Journal and Guide* did not hesitate to write that blacks would defend the country "without regard to any notions formerly held concerning the correctness of . . . [the country's] domestic policies." Black citizens, this paper believed, should trust the authorities and adjourn debate for the duration of the war. The time had come to "close ranks and join with fervent patriotism in this battle for America." [50]

Reservations were expressed by the *Defender*, but it too joined in the call for unity. "The heart of the American Negro people

46. *The Afro-American*, December 13, 1941.
47. Savannah *Tribune*, December 11, 1941.
48. Quoted in *ibid.*, December 18, 1941.
49. California *Eagle*, December 11, 1941.
50. *Journal and Guide*, December 13, 1941; December 20, 1941.

beats as one with the heart of other citizens of the land. It is no less our burden than it is the white man's." Blacks did not intend to hinder the war effort, but on the contrary desired to serve as full-fledged American citizens. This editor, along with many others, emphasized the loyalty of the black press, but added to this a reminder of its duty to continue to protest without subversive intent, which would impair the national will. "The hour calls for a closing of ranks, for joining of hands, not for a widening of racial gap. . . . "[51]

Both the *Courier* and *Crisis* hesitated to jump on the unity bandwagon as completely as the other papers. They both pledged their full support but stressed the need to continue the struggle against racism at home. The *Courier* called on the President to use his emergency powers to end segregation in the armed forces. Knowing that the President would not heed its plea, the paper asked for black officers to lead black troops if segregation was to remain the policy. Nevertheless, the *Courier* evidenced a conciliatory tone and argued that blacks had to improve their status through service to the country during the wartime crisis.[52]

The Crisis was the one journal to express a great degree of caution in offering its support to the nation. It was this magazine that in 1918 had called on blacks to "close ranks," and that ever since had been under attack for this "sell-out." Also, being a monthly journal, it had more time to reflect on its wartime editorial position. Within a few weeks of the disaster at Pearl Harbor, many papers had already begun to voice reservations about the call to forget grievances while uniting with whites for the duration. Thus, it was *The Crisis* that took the most uncompromising position in its first war editorial, entitled "Now Is Not the Time to Be Silent." The fight against Hitlerism had to begin at home, since blacks in America were almost in the same situation as Jews in Germany. The major struggle was not against the Axis, but for a true peace. The fight, therefore, had to begin at once and in this

51. Chicago *Defender,* December 13, 1941 ; December 20, 1941.
52. Pittsburgh *Courier,* December 13, 1941 ; December 20, 1941 ; December 27, 1941.

country.[53] Walter White urged blacks not to go overboard, and to remember the broken promises of World War I. But he did not neglect to remind his readers that, as bad as things were in the United States, they would be worse if Hitler won the war.[54]

Columnists joined their editors in pledging full support on behalf of the black community. Emmet J. Scott told his readers that "all grievous wrongs are subordinate to the National Will and Purpose" during the war. When the war ends, Scott wrote, then blacks will be able to seek a solution to their problems.[55] J. D. Bibb was sure that black people were willing to forget for the duration of the war the failure of America to deal fairly with its black minority, and J. A. Rogers stressed the many opportunities for black people to serve their country.[56] Randolph wrote that if America lost the war, the black man would be through in the Western world. Limited though this country's democracy was, Randolph reminded his readers, the black man had "the right to fight for his rights." [57]

A few voices in the press spoke out against the enthusiastic display of patriotism emanating from the columns of black papers, but in general the press responded to World War II in its initial comments as it had to World War I. George Schuyler expressed his concern with this and denounced black editors for their enthusiasm to serve. His view on the war, he affirmed, would not change. For Schuyler, the principal struggle would remain the one at home.[58]

Shortly after the United States declared war on Japan, the editor of the *Interracial Review* observed that the black press had exhibited an unusual shift of opinion after December 7.[59] A few months later, Ernest Johnson, a black reporter, conducted a survey for this journal of twenty-four war editorials in the black press. These papers, he concluded, generally did not display a militant posture. Of the twenty-four papers studied, sixteen were considered

53. *The Crisis* 49 (January 1942): 7.
54. Walter White, *The Afro-American,* December 20, 1941.
55. E. J. Scott, Pittsburgh *Courier,* January 10, 1942.
56. J. D. Bibb, Pittsburgh *Courier,* January 10, 1942.
57. A. Philip Randolph, Pittsburgh *Courier,* January 10, 1942.
58. George Schuyler, Pittsburgh *Courier,* January 3, 1942.
59. *Interracial Review* 15 (January 1942): 2.

definitely "weak." These papers concentrated on discussions of political ideology rather than "Negro matters." Their discussions centered on national unity and the great loyalty of the black masses. Complaints involving injustices on the national scene were omitted. Eight of the papers had called on their readers to forget their grievances. Only three were placed in the "complaint first" category. Johnson wrote his article after the press had shifted to the "Double V" approach and he had the aid of hindsight to guide him. But his study did reveal that the initial war editorials of the black press did not convey an accurate reflection of the mind of the black masses. Johnson concluded that the editors had failed to observe the true feelings of the black community and reflected more of an "anxious concern of editors to conform to the national pattern."[60]

The press had temporarily moved away from the masses. It had displayed a "close ranks" attitude as its first reaction to the Pearl Harbor debacle. The black community, apparently, was not yet ready to "close ranks," nor were blacks as fearful of Hitler as the press.[61] In an article written a week prior to December 7, 1941, Chandler Owen analyzed the attitude of black people toward Hitler. He wrote that the "average or mass group Negro is almost pro-Nazi." Owen compared the masses to the more "balanced" thinking of the "intelligent Negro," who weighed "the situation with poise and even temper" and said, "conditions are bad but they could be worse." He denounced those blacks who claimed that "things couldn't be any worse under Hitler."[62]

The "Double V" was the program that brought together once again the black press and the black masses. The "complaisance and disinterest and cynicism" of black people were the backbone of the double crusade preached in the press. The masses would not become enthusiastic if they were told to forget their grievances, and only if the war abroad was part of an overall struggle for

60. Ernest Johnson, "The Negro Press Reacts to the War," *Interracial Review,* 15 (March 1942): 39–41.
61. See chapter 3.
62. Chandler Owen, *Journal and Guide,* December 13, 1941.

freedom on all fronts would they join in and "close ranks" with the rest of the country.

The California *Eagle* epitomized the general shift of the black press. Its December 11 war editorial announced that the paper's preoccupation with the "Negro problem" was going to cease for the duration. Until the war reached a successful conclusion, the *Eagle* was going to drop its emphasis on "full citizenship rights" and remind its readers of their responsibility to their country. The paper attacked the complacent feelings of blacks and told them not to let personal problems hamstring the country's war effort. Within two months the *Eagle* adopted the "Double V" program and citizenship rights were once again placed on a parity with citizenship duties.[63]

The leaders were catching up with their followers.

During the European stage of World War II, a large segment of the black press expressed the belief that the war was one of rival imperialisms. Papers wrote or implied that it was a "white man's war" and of no interest to black Americans who had enough problems of their own. When, in 1941, Roosevelt and Churchill signed the eight-point Atlantic Charter, black newspapers were unimpressed. DuBois did not believe it was a proclamation for world freedom, but evidence of the "hypocrisy" of the white powers. For DuBois, the Charter was the reiteration of America's Open Door policy, which gave this country the "right to exploit" the world's backward countries.[64] DuBois did not neglect to point out to his readers that the two countries had conveniently omitted including any of the black colonies in the Charter's statement of freedom.

After Pearl Harbor, DuBois wrote of the shifting Allied war aims, with race relations moving to the forefront. Roosevelt, in the interim, had contradicted Churchill and declared that the Atlantic Charter applied to all nations of the world. Roosevelt's new position

63. California *Eagle,* December 11, 1941 ; February 19, 1942.

64. W. E. B. DuBois, New York *Amsterdam News,* August 30, 1941 ; W. E. B. DuBois, "A Chronicle of Race Relations," *Phylon* 2 (Fourth Quarter 1941): 389–90.

was "the admission of a world revolution which involved the relation of the white and colored peoples."[65] Adam C. Powell, Jr., commented on the changing nature of the war. The war started out as a white man's war in the United States, but blacks decided to make it a people's war with their "Double V" program.[66] Powell's *People's Voice* always spoke of the war as a "People's War." *Congress Vue,* the black journal of the Communist party, also used the slogan "People's War" and stressed the connection between the subjugated colored people throughout the world.[67] A "People's War" was one way of saying it was no longer a "white man's war." Essential to the "Double V" approach was the understanding that fighting the war was not the exclusive responsibility of whites. This was a difficult task facing a black press which during 1940 and much of 1941 had insisted that the war was a white man's affair.[68]

Walter White admitted the enormity of the problem and called on the leaders of the race to correct the erroneous view of the masses that it was a "white man's war." White related the reaction of a black audience to a speech of his when he quoted a black college student who said:

> I hope Hitler wins. The Army Jim Crows us. The Navy lets us serve only as messmen. The Red Cross refuses our blood. Employers and labor unions shut us out. Lynchings continue. We are disenfranchised, Jim Crowed, spat upon. What else could Hitler do?[69]

White was about to tell the audience that this was a shortsighted and dangerous view; but before he was able to do this, the people burst into a sustained applause. It took over a minute to quiet

65. W. E. B. DuBois, "A Chronicle of Race Relations," *Phylon* 3 (Second Quarter 1942): 206, 207; (Third Quarter 1942): 320.
66. Powell, *Marching Blacks,* pp. 127–29.
67. *The Congress Vue* 1 (April 1943): 1–2.
68. New York *Amsterdam News,* April 26, 1942.
69. Walter White, "What the Negro Thinks of the Army," *The Annals of the American Academy of Political and Social Science* 223 (September 1942): 67.

down the audience so that he could explain his purpose in relating the disgruntled statement of the black youth.

When the war was a European affair, black papers said it was not a black man's problem. After the United States became a belligerent, part of the "Double V" idea was to encourage blacks not to permit it to remain a white man's war. A white man's war would only result in a white man's peace. A basic factor of the double struggle was the participation of blacks in every aspect of the war, and a refusal on their part to let the war continue to be for whites only.

Horace Cayton commented that after Pearl Harbor many blacks were at first "sullen and wished to see their country brought to its knees." He wrote of a large segment of the black community that was not willing to participate until discrimination ended first on the homefront. In Philadelphia a black man was arrested and held for treason for saying "this is a white man's war." Cayton said this view was prevalent at first, but black people had forced the country to alter its war aims by demanding that the minority race participate fully in the war program.[70]

The "Double V" attempted to prevent pitting black against white in the United States. It concentrated on getting blacks to serve fully and faithfully so they would be able to seek concessions later from the country. No paper or columnist spoke of revolution in the violent sense of the term and most stressed the view that violence was futile because blacks were a small minority in the United States. The black press hoped to gather support from enough liberal whites to begin to attack the caste system within the country. Blacks would not struggle against whites, but with liberal whites for a "People's Victory." The dilemma of black involvement in a "white man's war" was solved by converting it to a "People's War," a war for freedom rather than one of imperialism. Black writers conceded that it had begun as a white man's war for imperialistic spoils, but by 1942 this had changed

70. Horace Cayton, "The Negro's Challenge," *The Nation* 157 (July 2, 1943): 10–11; Horace Cayton, Pittsburgh *Courier,* February 28, 1942.

because black Americans refused to go along on this premise. Also, by then, many liberal whites were awakening to the contradiction of fighting Hitler abroad while continuing racist policies at home.[71]

When black papers converged around the "Double V" program in early 1942, much of the discussion about the nature of the war disappeared until late 1944 and early 1945. Continued discrimination in the services and defense industries, the FEPC, the attack on the black press, and race riots filled most of the columns during these years.

In late 1943 a debate arose in the black press which, while it did not deal directly with the nature of the war, took into account the war and its effect on black people in the United States. For a few months black writers contended with each other over the benefits to be gained by blacks from a longer or shorter war. By 1943 there was no denying the benefits accruing to blacks as a result of the war. The Army and Navy had finally opened to blacks. White liberals, especially after the bloody homefront riots of 1943, were beginning to speak out on behalf of better race relations in a new postwar world. The wartime economic benefits were the most obvious gains and new jobs were what the press was most concerned about losing with the conclusion of the war. The specter of postwar unemployment haunted the pages of the black press. As the war was nearing its end, there seemed to be a panic feeling in the press, and "Hold Your Job" campaigns were started.

But along with these benefits—some of which would apply to whites—there was an undercurrent of hostility and anger that surfaced after the riots of 1943. The FEPC, once considered the "second emancipation," was languishing. Economic conditions were improving, but segregated industrial patterns were often imposed even in the North. When black workers moved into an

71. Alain Locke, "Color: The Unfinished Business of Democracy," *Survey Graphic* 31 (November 1942): 456; Adam C. Powell, Jr. "Is This a White Man's War?" *Common Sense* 2 (April 1942): 111; Ralph Matthews, *The Afro-American,* December 20, 1941; P. L. Prattis, Pittsburgh *Courier,* February 28, 1942.

industry for the first time, such as at Sun Shipyards in Chester, Pennsylvania, they were often located in all-black sections. Few blacks would agree that the Army was a paragon of successful race relations. Mordecai Johnson, President of Howard University, openly expressed the angry feelings of many black people when he said it might be better if the war would last five to ten years in order to give whites time to wake up to the homefront crisis.[72]

This attitude, of course, was a fundamental contradiction of the principle that it was not a "white man's war." The proposition that a long war would humble the white oppressor actually confirmed that it was a "white man's war," with the world's nonwhites waiting for white people to exhaust themselves. Marjorie McKenzie said that "the oppressed have been watching . . . [the] oppressors suffer—just retribution." [73] Blacks could not help this feeling, she added; it was an involuntary reaction on their part.

From every sector of the political spectrum advocates elaborated on the advantages of a long war. Arthur P. Davis was convinced that many blacks were willing to see the war last indefinitely, and he agreed with them. Davis, though, was not thinking about retribution; he was appalled by the millions of war casualties. But it was only through wars, riots, and mob violence that blacks would advance. He was not calling on blacks to engage in violent action, since he was obviously referring to the 1943 race riots where blacks were in most cases the victims of white violence. Davis believed this violence would "focus the national attention and arouse the latent [white] American conscience." [74] Others were convinced that a longer war would awaken white America to the dangers of racial strife at home, while at the same time make blacks more race conscious and develop more able leadership.[75]

By the end of 1943 the long-war-short-war debate was widespread enough for the *Negro Digest* to conduct a survey on the issue. The *Negro Digest* indicated that blacks favored a long war

72. Pittsburgh *Courier,* March 4, 1944.
73. Marjorie McKenzie, Pittsburgh *Courier,* September 16, 1944.
74. Arthur P. Davis, *Journal and Guide,* September 11, 1943.
75. J. A. Rogers, Pittsburgh *Courier,* November 27, 1943.

by fifty-four percent of those queried.[76] *The Crisis* held its own forum on the question and invited George Schuyler and Benjamin Quarles to participate. Schuyler favored a long war and was convinced that most blacks felt likewise. He believed that millions of whites were ready to end the caste system, and only during a major upheaval would they seize the opportunity to act. World War I did not last long enough for this to happen. Schuyler, for once, was optimistic. He believed a long war would end Jim Crow in the Army and discrimination in industry. The postwar American Empire, he added, would require every American to defend it, and a color line would be "suicidal." [77]

The *Defender* argued against this reasoning, calling it "racial suicide." This paper pointed to the obvious contradiction of favoring a long war and espousing the "Double V." This view, the editor warned, said blacks were blacks first and Americans second. Blacks who adhered to this were "isolationists" (that is, black chauvinists), and those favoring integration had to oppose the long-war proponents since it was against the best interests of all the people. It would also brand blacks as subversive and "un-American." [78] Benjamin Quarles feared a long war for other reasons. It would exhaust the country and prevent it from facing the homefront crisis.[79] Black members of the Communist party also opposed the long-war view.[80]

Despite the debate among editors and columnists about the benefits of a longer or shorter war, it was apparent that those discussing the issue were under the impression that a majority of blacks favored the longer war argument. The editor of the conservative *Brown American* was apologetic when he wrote of the lack of joy among many blacks when the war in Europe ended. He

76. *Negro Digest* 2 (November 1943): 8. The question was as follows: "Will a long war aid the Negro?" The response was 54 percent yes, 33 percent no, 13 percent undecided.

77. George Schuyler, "A Long War Will Aid the Negro," *The Crisis* 50 (November 1943): 328–44.

78. Chicago *Defender,* October 9, 1943.

79. Benjamin Quarles, "Will a Long War Aid the Negro?" *The Crisis* 50 (November 1943): 288.

80. Doxey Wilkerson, "Freedom Through Victory," *What the Negro Wants,* ed. Rayford Logan, pp. 198–200.

explained this as a condition arising from the small margin of economic security gained by blacks during the war years and their mistrust of "the blessings of peace." [81]

Once the successful Allied landings in Normandy indicated the inevitability of an Allied victory, the black press again turned its attention to the nature of the war, the problems of peace, and the black man's role in the postwar world. The initial comments in the resumed discussion again focused on the British and their empire. After December 7, 1941, the hostility widely evidenced in the black press toward Britain became less visible. Papers began to make distinctions between the British people and their leaders. Black soldiers stationed in England were often treated with greater dignity than they were in many sections of the United States, and the black press did not fail to report favorably of the British subjects who ignored the United States Army's racial preoccupations.

Winston Churchill remained the foe of all colored peoples. His comments early in the war that the Four Freedoms applied only to Nazi-occupied Europe and his stated refusal to preside over the dismemberment of the British Empire were widely reported and attacked in the black press. P. L. Prattis, in a column acutely gauging the British political situation, wrote that Churchill was not the leader for a postwar world sought by the common people. Once victory over the Axis was achieved, "Mr. Churchill will be laid aside and honored," but will not be chosen to lead the nation in peace.[82]

By late 1944 the idea of a "People's War" and a "People's Peace" appeared more and more illusory both at home and abroad. While the United States Army was dashing the hopes of the black press for a chance to prove the capability of black soldiers, Allied victories in Europe did not give the appearance of enhancing the opportunities for a "People's Victory" abroad. The British government's actions in occupied Europe were alarming. *The Afro-American* denounced Churchill as a "Pious Fraud" for claiming that the Allies had "trusted the mass of the people in almost every

81. *The Brown American* (Spring 1945): inside cover.
82. P. L. Prattis, Pittsburgh *Courier,* April 3, 1943.

[liberated] country." Instead of concentrating his armies against Germany, the *Afro* wrote, Churchill was using English soldiers to prevent democratic rule in Belgium, Italy, India, and West Africa.[83]

English actions in these areas were viewed as a recrudescence of the old colonial world structure, imposed upon the peoples of these countries against their wishes.[84] The press drew parallels between the Greeks oppressed by Britain and blacks oppressed at home. A postwar reaction, it seemed, was about to set in throughout the world even before the war ended. Papers began emphasizing the similarities of the caste system in the United States and the colonial structure in the world.[85] "The Negro is the colonial of America, exploited and robbed. . . ," and all people had to be free before any group could enjoy a "People's Peace." [86]

Many black writers immediately connected the United States to Britain's suppression of leftist movements in the liberated countries of Europe. English actions abroad went hand in hand with the rising anti-Communist crusade and racial policies of the United States. Black papers believed that these developments were part of a worldwide movement of reactionaries trying to reimpose the *status quo ante bellum*. The United States, with its segregation and lynchings, had its own brand of domestic imperialism and Nazism; and reactionaries in the United States who opposed change applauded Britain's actions abroad.[87] The suppression of elements within the liberated European countries, the black press feared, was a portent of future policy to be applied to African and Asian colonies struggling for their independence.[88]

83. *The Afro-American,* December 16, 1944. For a complete account of Allied actions in suppressing popular movements in occupied areas of western Europe see Gabriel Kolko, *The Politics of War: The World War and United States Foreign Policy, 1943–1945* (New York: Random House, 1968), pp. 43–63, 96–98.

84. Adam C. Powell, Jr. *People's Voice,* December 6, 1944.

85. *Monthly Summary* 2 (December 1944): 119; George Schuyler, "More Race Riots Coming," *The Negro* 3 (February 1945): 22.

86. Chicago *Defender,* March 10, 1945.

87. Earl Brown, New York *Amsterdam News,* December 16, 1944; J. A. Rogers, Pittsburgh *Courier,* December 30, 1944.

88. Horace Cayton, Pittsburgh *Courier,* December 30, 1944.

When Prime Minister Churchill lost his bid for reelection in the summer of 1945, there was jubilation in the black press.[89] It took but a short time however, to discover that Britain under a Labor government was no less desirous of holding on to its colonies. Soon after taking office, the Labor party announced that Malay and Singapore would reenter the Empire, and India's status would not be independent. Not only England, but Holland, Portugal, and France were planning to continue their colonial empires.[90]

The European imperialists were highly visible targets and the black press attacked them vigorously. At the same time, some black writers began expressing their concern about America's relationship with the Third World countries. George Padmore offered a cogent insight to the future of America's world position. This country would "emerge from the war as the dominant imperialist power, whose needs for new markets, sources of raw materials, air and sea bases . . . will have to be satisfied." Padmore showed that the productive capacities of the United States had enormously increased during the war, which in turn required overseas markets to keep it operating. The new American Empire, though, would support the political aspirations of the world's colonized people for independence. "Dollar diplomacy can secure the United States all the advantages it seeks without the responsibility of policing overseas territories with Marines." [91]

DuBois expressed his doubts about President Truman's claim that the United States did not desire "one piece of territory out of this war," and observed the many new outposts ranging over thousands of miles of the Pacific that could be "turned into fortresses to dominate the Pacific." He did not fail to point out that the recently ratified United Nations Charter made provisions for the United States to retain these islands without any international controls.[92] Walter White also expressed anxiety about his country's

89. California *Eagle,* August 2, 1945; Harry Keelan, *The Afro-American,* August 11, 1945; Marjorie McKenzie, Pittsburgh *Courier,* August 4, 1945; Pittsburgh *Courier,* August 4, 1945.

90. New York *Amsterdam News,* September 15, 1945.

91. George Padmore, "Anglo-American Plan for Control of Colonies," *The Crisis* 51 (November 1944): 355–56.

92. W. E. B. DuBois, Chicago *Defender,* August 11, 1945.

postwar empire in the Pacific. He wrote of the billions of dollars spent and thousands of American lives lost in the Pacific theater only to return the old colonial powers to their former position of domination. What bothered White was the apparent refusal of the Americans and Europeans to consider any alternative to the old world structure. Added to this, America's involvement in colonial politics seemed to be expanding as a result of the war.[93]

Black press representatives attended the United Nations conference at San Francisco in the spring of 1945 and began to draw the lines of future conflicts as they observed the deliberations. As they saw it, on one side stood Russia with the moral leadership of the world, and on the other the colonial powers, with United States support, seeking compromises.[94] The *Defender's* editor accused the United States delegation of knifing colonial freedom when it joined Britain and France at the conference in maintaining the status quo.[95] Walter White, writing from San Francisco, said that the United States' actions at the Conference were appalling. He denounced this country for refusing the Russian and Chinese request to amend the Dumbarton Oaks draft to pledge independence as well as self rule for the colonies. It was the United States' vote that broke the tie in favor of the colonial powers.[96] Even the *People's Voice,* a strong supporter of the administration, was discouraged with the United States' policy toward the colonial people, and its support of reactionaries in Europe.[97]

In the view of many black writers, white imperialism had emerged from the war strengthened and in the complete control of the Anglo-Saxon powers. America had become the world's first superpower, and with its bases all around the globe, its huge Navy, and its atomic bomb, the country was becoming "heady" with power. "A world completely dominated by the whites, with complete control over Japan," was "a dread prospect." [98]

Throughout their discussion of the war, most black papers had

93. Walter White, Chicago *Defender,* May 26, 1945.
94. *Monthly Summary* 2 (June 1945): 341.
95. Chicago *Defender,* May 26, 1945.
96. Walter White, Chicago *Defender,* May 26, 1945.
97. *People's Voice,* June 2, 1945.
98. Layle Lane, New York *Age,* March 17, 1945.

made an effort to make their readers conscious of the relationship of blacks at home and black colonial people abroad. Both groups were oppressed people held in check by reactionary forces. A defeat abroad was considered a prelude to defeat on the homefront—thus the "Double V." When the Allies crushed the Axis militarily, it looked as if the reactionary forces were successfully implementing a return of the old order. On the homefront the picture was no brighter. Reactionary forces here were operating to insure the defeat of progressive forces seeking a "People's Peace." Black troops were under attack in the press, in military courts, and in the congressional halls, and the permanent FEPC Bill was defeated in Congress.

"Victory," commented the editor of the *Amsterdam News* after the defeat of Japan, but "Not Without Sadness." "A somber and haunting spectre crowds hard upon the heels of victory. The battle against second rate citizenship looms ever more threatening."[99] As blacks return from the war they will ask "Is it really the land of the free and the home of the brave?"[100] When the Allies terminated all race laws in Germany, the *Journal and Guide* headline read, "Race Discrimination Ends—In Germany—*Not* America."[101] The *Courier* displayed little exhilaration when commenting on the war's conclusion: "War Ends—We Face Job Crisis."[102]

The view of the nature of the war held by the black press had come full cycle back to where it had been in 1939. First analyzed as a war of "rival imperialisms" and a "white man's war," the press by 1942 began to envision a "People's War." The expectations of a "People's Peace" did not materialize. By 1945 the European colonial powers proved intent upon clinging to their colonial territories, and, worse yet, the United States was acquiring its own empire and apparently aiding the forces of reaction in restoring "order" to the devastated world.

99. New York *Amsterdam News,* August 25, 1945.
100. *Ibid.*
101. *Journal and Guide,* August 11, 1945.
102. Pittsburgh *Courier,* August 18, 1945.

Conclusion

During the war years the black press performed several essential services for the black community. Most black adults read black newspapers throughout this period because the white media usually disregarded the activities of the black minority. Black papers provided information about black servicemen and interpreted the war, emphasizing the nature of the conflict as it affected the nonwhite majority of the world. Also, the black press refused to relent in its call for complete equality, and continued to remonstrate against discrimination despite the efforts of friend and foe alike to restrain its protest writing. At its best, the press maintained a constant vigilance against the blatant discrimination in military camps and military courts, and was ever alert to the attempts of military officials to slander the ability of black military personnel. Even though most black papers opposed disobedience to military orders —including discriminatory ones—they maintained a lively interest in the plight of the convicted black "mutineers" until these men were ultimately released.

The black press was less successful in formulating a consistent wartime policy for the black community. Throughout the defense build-up of 1939–40, most black papers considered segregation in the military a *fait accompli,* and they accepted segregation and called for proportional representation in all branches of the service.

During the immediate prewar years, these papers were often willing to support mass action such as the MOWM, and gave wide coverage to those blacks who refused to be drafted because of military discrimination. The press soon shifted course and began to object to the quota system and segregation. At the same time, it reversed its previous approval of mass action and individual resistance to the draft.

With the outbreak of war the black press adopted a position that black people should insist upon the right to fight because their wartime performance would determine the postwar status of blacks in the country. The press, therefore, had reverted to an old idea that black leaders had embraced in the Civil War and World War I. Since the position of the press reflected the views of most of the black leadership during the war, one can conclude that black leaders took a conservative course rooted in the past. Despite the stirring of the black masses and the militant rhetoric of the black leaders, the war years cannot be considered the beginning of the "black revolution." It would be more accurate to describe these years as the last effort of the old order.

After waiting more than a decade without any sign of white gratitude for their wartime loyalty, blacks took to the streets and organized direct action, mass civil disobedience movements to demand their rights. Segregation laws were violated and discrimination patterns ignored. The advances blacks made during the 1960s came by the very actions that the black press opposed and worked to avoid throughout World War II. It was resistance rather than rhetoric, action by the masses, not pleas by the leaders, that forced concessions from a reluctant white society.

If we seek the roots of the "black revolution" of the 1960s in the World War II era, a study must be made of the black masses, not their leaders. There were, indeed, stirrings among the black people. Anger and resentment often led to open conflict and widespread racial violence. On the other hand, black leadership—including the press, which was considered the most radical—was definitely anti-revolutionary. When historians are selective and simply extract the militant statements of the press and leadership, they can create a picture of revolutionary proportions. The militancy of the rhetoric, though, was usually in denouncing discrimination. This cannot be considered either radical or new to the World War II years. The black press began denouncing discrimination with the first copy of *Freedom's Journal* in 1827 and continued to do so throughout the years until World War II. The "black revolution" began when new action was called for. The approach taken by the black press during World War II offered little that was new to its readers. It substituted militant rhetoric for its lack of innovative direction.

Bibliography

Newspapers
(Nineteenth Century)

Douglass' Monthly.
Frederick Douglass' Paper.
Freedom's Journal.
The North Star.

(1939–1945)

The Afro-American (Baltimore).
California *Eagle.*
Chicago *Defender.*
Gazette (Cleveland).
Journal and Guide (Norfolk).
New York *Age.*
New York *Amsterdam News.*
New York Times.
New York *World Telegram.*
People's Voice (New York).
Pittsburgh *Courier.*
PM
Savanah *Tribune.*

Organizational Publications
(1939–1945)

The Black Worker.
Congress Vue.
The Crisis.
Equality.
Interracial News Service.
Interracial Review.
The March.
NAACP Annual Report.
NAACP Bulletin.
NAACP Press Service: News Releases.
National Bar Journal.
Opportunity.
Our Fight.
The Southern Frontier.

Periodicals and Magazines
(1939–1945)

The Brown American.
Headlines.
Journal of Negro Education (Editorials).
A Monthly Summary of Events and Trends in Race Relations.
National Negro Printer and Publisher.
The Negro: The Journal of Essential Information.
Negro Digest.
The Negro History Bulletin.
Negro Quarterly.
PEP: Negro Publisher Editor and Printer.
Phylon ("A Chronicle of Race Relations").
Pulse.

Manuscript Collections

Committee on Participation of Negroes in the National Defense Program Papers. Moorland-Spingarn Collection, Howard University Library, Washington, D.C.

Wayne Coy Correspondence. Franklin D. Roosevelt Library, Hyde Park, New York.

NAACP Papers, Library of Congress.

William Pickens Papers. Schomburg Collection, New York City.

Franklin D. Roosevelt Papers. Franklin D. Roosevelt Library, Hyde Park, New York.

Walter White Correspondence. James Weldon Johnson Collection, Yale University Library, New Haven, Connecticut.

Unpublished Material

Alexander, Will W. "The Reminiscences of Will W. Alexander." Oral History Research Office, Columbia University.

Byers, Jean. "A Study of the Negro in Military Service." Washington, D.C.: Department of Defense, 1950. (Mimeographed, Schomburg Collection.)

Committee on Fair Employment Practice. "Seventh Hearing." Birmingham, Alabama, June 18, 1942. (Typescript, Schomburg Collection.)

Council for Democracy. "Memorandum to the Board of Directors." November 15, 1940. (New York Public Library.)

———. "Negro Press Conference." May 7–8, 1943. 2 vols. (Typescript, Schomburg Collection.)

Dalsimer, Marlyn H. "Samuel E. Cornish: Negro Newspaper Editor in New York City, 1827–1839." Master's thesis, New York University, 1967.

Fleming, G. James. "The Negro Press." Research memorandum prepared for the Carnegie-Myrdal Study, September, 1942. (Typescript, Schomburg Collection.)

Gladieux, Bernard L. "The Reminscences of Bernard L. Gladieux." Oral History Research Office, Columbia University.

Kifer, Allen Francis. "The Negro Under the New Deal." Ph.D. dissertation, University of Wisconsin, 1961.

Lynn, Conrad. "Autobiography." (Typescript, in possession of author.)

Pride, Armisted S. "Register and History of Negro Newspapers in the United States." Ph.D. dissertation, Northwestern University, 1950.

Schomburg Vertical Files. Lynn Case.

———. Miscellaneous.

———. Negro Labor Victory Committee.

———. Newspapers: I, II, III.

———. United States Army: Negro Troops.

———. United States Army: Women's Army Corps.

———. World War, 1939–1945: Lynn Case.

———. World War, 1939–1945: Navy Mutiny Trial.

———. World War, 1939–1945: Negroes.

Schuyler, George S. "The Reminiscences of George S. Schuyler." Oral History Research Office, Columbia University.

White, Walter. "Memorandum to the War Department from Walter White, War Correspondent for the New York *Post*, and Secretary of the National Association for the Advancement of Colored People." (Mimeographed, Schomburg Collection, 1944.)

Wilkins, Roy. "The Reminiscences of Roy Wilkins." Oral History Research Office, Columbia University.

Public Documents and Government Publications

Fair Employment Practice Committee. "Chronological Summary of Developments in Philadelphia Transportation Co. and PRT Employees' Union Case." (Smith Committee, Exhibit No. 462, Mimeographed, Schomburg Collection.)

———. *First Report. July 1943 - December 1944*. United States G.P.O., 1945.

———. *Final Report, June 28, 1946*. United States G.P.O., 1947.

Federal Security Agency, Social Security Board, Bureau of Employment Security, Division of Research and Statistics. *Negro Workers and the National Defense.*

Lee, Ulysses. *United States Army in World War II. Special Studies. The Employment of Negro Troops*. Office of the Chief of Military History, United States Army. Washington, D.C., 1966.

Office of War Information. *The Negro Looks at the War: The Attitude of New York City Negroes Toward Discrimination Against Negroes*. Survey, April 11 - May 11, 1942.

———, Magazine Section. *Magazine War Guide*. Monthly Summary of Information Suitable for Use in Magazines.

Owen, Chandler. *Negroes and the War*. Office of War Information, 1942.

Selective Service in Peacetime. First Report of the Director of Selective Service, 1940–1941. (From September 16, 1940–December 8, 1941.) United States G.P.O., 1942.

Selective Service in Wartime. Second Report of the Director of Selective Service, 1941–1942. United States G.P.O., 1943.

Speech of Lawrence W. Cramer, Executive Secretary, FEPC. Presented at the Regional Meeting of the National Conference of Social Work in New York City, March 11, 1943. (Schomburg Collection).

United States Congress, House of Representatives. *Hearings before the Committee on Military Affairs on H. R. 10132, Selective Compulsory Military Training and Service.* 76th Cong., 3rd Sess.

United States Congress, Senate. *Hearings before the Subcommittee of the Committee on Appropriations on H. R. 9209, Appropriations for the Military Establishment for the Fiscal Year Ending June 30, 1941.* 76th Cong., 3rd Sess.

United States Court of Appeals for the Second Circuit United States of America *ex rel. Winfred William Lynn.*

United States Department of Commerce, Bureau of the Census. *Negro Newspapers and Periodicals in the United States: Negro Statistical Bulletin No. 1.* Washington, D.C., August 29, 1946.

United States Selective Service System. *Special Groups.* Special Monograph No. 10. 2 vols. United States G.P.O., 1953.

United States War Department. *Army Talks:* "Negro Platoons in Composite Rifle Companies—World War II Style." Washington, D.C., April 12, 1942.

Interviews

Angell, Ernest. October 1, 1969.

Lynn, Conrad. October 16, 1969.

Books, Memoirs, Pamphlets, and Yearbooks

Adams, Julius J. *The Challenge: A Study in Negro Leadership.* New York: Wendell Malliet and Co., 1949.

American Council on Race Relations. *The Negro Press and the Issues of Democracy.* First Annual Dinner of the Capitol Press Club, Washington, D.C., June 21, 1941.

AYD Fights Jim Crow. Report of the American Youth for Democracy Campaign for Equal Participation of Negroes in the Armed Forces, and Report of the Youth Delegation to Washington on April 30 - May 1, 1944. New York City, 1944.

Ayer & Sons. *American Newspaper Annual and Directory.* Philadelphia, Pa., 1940–1945.

Booker, Simeon. *Black Man's America.* Englewood Cliffs, N.J.: Prentice-Hall, Inc., 1964.

Broderick, Francis L. *W. E. B. DuBois: Negro Leader in a Time of Crisis.* Stanford, Calif.: Stanford University Press, 1959.

Brooks, Maxwell R. *The Negro Press Re-examined: Political Con-*

tent of Leading Negro Newspapers. Boston: Christopher Publishing House, 1959.

Brown, Earl, and Leighton, George. *The Negro and the War*. Public Affairs Pamphlets, Number 71, 1942.

Bundy, M., and Stimson, H. L. *On Active Duty in Peace and War*. New York: Harper and Bros., 1947.

The Commission on Interracial Cooperation. *The Durham Statement; The Atlanta Statement; The Richmond Statement*. Atlanta, 1943.

Conrad, Earl. *Jim Crow America*. New York: Duell, Sloan and Pearce, 1947.

Council For Democracy. *Brief Statement of Aims and Activities*.

———. *Censorship*. 1942.

———. *First Annual Report of the Council For Democracy*.

———. *The Negro and Defense: A Test of Democrary*.

Carter, Hodding. *Southern Legacy*. Baton Rouge: Louisiana State University Press, 1950.

Dalfiume, Richard M. *Desegregation of the U.S. Armed Forces: Fighting on Two Fronts*. Columbia, Mo.: University of Missouri Press, 1969.

Detweiler, Frederic G. *The Negro Press in the United States*. Chicago: University of Chicago Press, 1922.

Douglass, Frederick. *Life and Times of Frederick Douglass*. Hartford, Conn.: Park Publishing Co., 1882.

Drake, St. Clair, and Cayton, Horace. *Black Metropolis*. 2 vols. New York: Harcourt, Brace and Co., 1945.

DuBois, W. E. B. *The Autobiography of W. E. B. DuBois*. Edited by Herbert Aptheker. New York: International Publishers Co., Inc., 1968.

Durr, Robert. *The Negro Press*. Paper read at the Southern Regional Council, 1947.

Embree, Edwin R. *13 Against the Odds*. New York: The Viking Press, 1944.

Field, Marshall, III. *The Negro Press and the Issues of Democracy*. Chicago: American Council on Race Relations, 1944.

Fleming, G. James, and Burckel, Christian E., eds. *Who's Who in Colored America*. Yonkers, N.Y.: Christian E. Burckel and Associates, 1950.

Foner, Philip. *Frederick Douglass.* New York: The Citadel Press, 1964.

Ford, James W., ed. *Negroes and the National War Effort: An Address by Frederick Douglass.* New York: Workers Library Publishers, Inc., April, 1942.

———. *The War and the Negro People.* New York: Workers Library Publishers, Inc., January, 1942.

Franklin, John Hope. *From Slavery to Freedom.* 3rd ed. New York: Alfred A. Knopf, 1967.

Frazier, E. Franklin. *Black Bourgeoisie.* Glencoe, Ill.: The Free Press, 1957.

———. *The Negro in the United States.* New York: Macmillan, 1949.

Garfinkel, Herbert. *When Negroes March: The MOWM in the Organizational Politics for FEPC.* Glencoe, Ill.: The Free Press, 1959.

Gore, George W. *Negro Journalism.* Greencastle, Ind.: Journalism Press, 1922.

Guzman, Jessie P. *Negro Year Book: A Review of Events Affecting Negro Life 1941–1946.* Tuskegee: Tuskegee Institute, 1947.

Hampton Institute Conference on the Participation of the Negro in National Defense. *Findings and Principal Addresses.* Hampton, Va., 1940.

Hastie, Wm. H. *On Clipped Wings: The Story of Jim Crow in the Army Air Corps.* NAACP, 1943.

Hill, Roy H. *Who's Who in the Negro Press.* Dallas: Royal Publishing Co., 1960.

Johnson, Charles S. *To Stem This Tide: A Summary of Racial Tension Areas in the United States.* Boston: The Pilgrim Press, 1943.

Kolko, Gabriel. *The Politics of War: The World and United States Foreign Policy, 1943–1945.* New York: Random House, 1968.

Logan, Rayford W., ed. *What the Negro Wants.* Chapel Hill, N.C.: University of North Carolina Press, 1944.

Lowenstein, Ralph, and Fisher, Paul, eds. *Race and the News Media.* Eighth Freedom of Information Conference, University of Missouri, 1966. New York: Frederick A. Praeger, 1967.

MacDonald, Dwight. *The War's Greatest Scandal! The Story of Jim Crow in Uniform.* New York, 1943(?).

MacLeish, Archibald. *American Opinion and the War*. The Rede Lecture, Cambridge University, 1942. New York: The Macmillan Press, 1942.

Mandelbaum, David G. *Soldier Groups and Negro Soldiers*. Berkeley: University of California Press, 1952.

Meier, August. *Negro Thought in America, 1880–1915*. Ann Arbor, Mich.: University of Michigan Press, 1966.

Merrill, Francis E. *Social Problems on the Homefront: A Study of Wartime Influences*. New York: Harper and Brothers, 1948.

Moton, Robert R. *Finding A Way Out*. New York: Doubleday, Page and Co., 1921.

Mott, Frank Luther. *American Journalism: A History of Newspapers in the United States through 250 Years, 1690–1940*. New York: The Macmillan Co., 1941.

Murray, Florence, ed. *The Negro Handbook*. New York: Wendell Malliet and Co., 1942.

Myrdal, Gunnar. *An American Dilemma*. 2 vols. New York: McGraw-Hill, 1964.

National Association for the Advancement of Colored People. *Mutiny? The Real Story Behind How the Navy Branded 50 Fear-Shocked Sailors as Mutineers*. New York, 1945.

National Negro Congress. *Negro People Will Defend America*. Text of Resolution Adopted at Emergency Meeting of the National Executive Board of the National Negro Congress. Washington, D.C., n.d.

National Urban League. *The Negro and National Defense*. New York, n.d.

———. *Racial Conflict, A Home Front Danger*. New York, 1943.

Nelson, Dennis D. *The Integration of the Negro into the U.S. Navy*. New York: Farrar, Straus and Young, 1951.

Nichols, Lee. *Breakthrough on the Color Front*. New York: Random House, 1954.

Oak, Vishna V. *The Negro Newspapers*. Yellow Springs, Ohio. Antioch Press, 1948.

Odum, Howard W. *Race and Rumours of Race: Challenge to American Crisis*. Chapel Hill: University of North Carolina Press, 1943.

Orlansky, H. *The Harlem Riot: A Study in Mass Frustration*. Social Analysis Report No. 1, 1943.

Ottley, Roi. *Black Odyssey: The Story of the Negro in America.* New York: Chas. Scribner's Sons, 1948.

———. *The Lonely Warrior: The Life and Times of Robert S. Abbott.* Chicago: Henry Regnery Co., 1955.

———. *"New World A-Coming": Inside Black America.* Boston: Houghton Mifflin Co., 1943.

Ovington, Mary White. *Portraits in Color.* New York: The Viking Press, 1927.

Penn, I. G. *The Afro-American Press and its Editors.* Springfield, Mass.: Willey and Co., 1891.

Powell, Adam C., Jr. *Marching Blacks.* New York: Dial Press, 1945.

Quarles, Benjamin. *Black Abolitionists.* New York: Oxford University Press, 1969.

Record, Wilson. *Race and Radicalism: The NAACP and the Communist Party in Conflict.* Ithaca, N.Y.: Cornell University Press, 1964.

Reddick, L. D., ed. "The Negro in the North During Wartime." *Journal of Educational Sociology* 17 (January 1944).

Rose, Arnold M. *The Negro's Morale.* Minneapolis: University of Minnesota Press, 1949.

Ross, Malcolm. *All Manner of Men.* New York: Reynal and Hitchcock, 1948.

Ruchames, Louis. *Race, Jobs and Politics: The Story of the FEPC.* New York: Columbia University Press, 1953.

Saunders, John, and Parker, Albert. *The Struggle for Negro Equality: Program of the Socialist Workers Party.* New York: Pioneer Publishers, 1943.

Schuyler, George S. *Black and Conservative.* New Rochelle, N.Y.: Arlington House, 1966.

———. *Fifty Years of Progress in Negro Journalism.* 1950.

Scott, Emmett J. *The American Negro in the World War.* Chicago: Homewood Press, 1919.

Smith, Bruce; Lasswell, Harold D.; and Casey, Ralph. *Propaganda, Communication and Public Opinion.* Princeton: Princeton University Press, 1946.

United Urban League Service Fund. *On The Same Team.* N.p., 1944 or 1945.

Villard, Oswald G. *The Disappearing Daily*. New York: Alfred A. Knopf, 1944.

Watson, Goodwin, ed. *Civilian Morale*. Second Yearbook for the Society for the Psychological Study of Social Issues. New York: Houghton Mifflin Co., 1942.

Weaver, Robert C. *Negro Labor: A National Problem*. New York: Harcourt, Brace and Company, 1946.

White, Walter. *A Man Called White*. New York: The Viking Press, 1948.

White, Walter, and Marshall, Thurgood. *What Caused the Detroit Riot?* New York: NAACP, 1943.

Wilkerson, Doxey A. *The Negro People and the Communists*. New York: Workers Library Publishers, Inc., 1944.

Wilson, James Q. *Negro Politics*. Glencoe, Ill.: The Free Press, 1960.

Yensor, Thomas, ed. *Who's Who in Colored America, 1941–1944*. Brooklyn, N.Y.: Who's Who in Colored America Corp., 1945.

Articles

Alexander, Will W. "Our Conflicting Racial Policies." *Harper's Magazine* 190 (January 1945): 172–79.

Anderson, M. Margaret. "Open Letter to the *Reader's Digest*." *Common Ground* 3 (Spring 1943): 107–8.

Barnett, Claude A. "The Role of the Press, Radio, and Motion Picture and Negro Morale." *Journal of Negro Education* 12 (Summer 1943), 474–89.

Baynton, J. A., and Bell A. "An Explorative Study of the Negro Press." *Journal of Negro Education* 20 (Winter 1951): 8–15.

Bennet, Lerone, Jr. "Founders of the Negro Press." *Ebony* 19 (July 1964).

Berlack-Boozer, T. "*Amsterdam News:* Harlem's Largest Weekly." *The Crisis* 45 (April 1938): 105–6.

Birnie, Wm. A. H. "Black Brains Trust." *The American Magazine* 135 (January 1943), 36–37, 94–95.

Bond, Horace Mann. "Should the Negro Care Who Wins the War?" *The Annals of the American Academy of Political and Social Science* 223 (September 1942): 81–84.

Boyd, James. "Strategy for Negroes." *The Nation* 156 (January 26, 1943): 884–87.

Brewer, James H. "Robert Lee Van, Democrat or Republican: An Exponent of Loose Leaf Politics." *Phylon* 8 (Second Quarter, 1947): 100–102.

Brown, Earl. "American Negroes and the War." *Harper's Magazine* 184 (April 1942): 545–52.

———. "The Negro Vote 1944: A Forecast," *Harper's Magazine* 189 (July 1944); 152–54.

Brown, Warren H. "A Negro Looks at the Negro Press." *Saturday Review of Literature* 25 (December 19, 1942): 5–6.

———. "A Negro Warns the Negro Press." *Reader's Digest* 42 (January 1943): 32.

Browning, Chas. P. "Negro Press Serves Democracy." *Editor and Publisher* 86 (February 7, 1953): 55.

Burma, John H. "An Analysis of the Present Negro Press." *Social Forces* 26 (December 1947): 172–80.

Cayton, Horace R. "The Negro's Challenge." *The Nation* 157 (July 2, 1942): 10–12.

Clark, Kenneth B. "Morale of the Negro on the Homefront: World Wars I and II." *Journal of Negro Education* 12 (Summer 1943): 417–28.

"Cleveland's *Call and Post*." *The Crisis* 45 (December 1938): 391, 404.

Cohn, David L. "How the South Feels." *The Atlantic Monthly* 173 (January 1944): 47–51.

Dabney, Virginius. "Nearer and Nearer the Precipice." *The Atlantic Monthly* 171 (January 1943): 94–100.

———. "Newspapers and the Negro." *The Quill* 31 (November-December 1943): 3, 14.

———. "Press and Morale." *Saturday Review of Literature* 25 (July 4, 1942): 5–6, 24–25.

Dalfiume, Richard M. "The Forgotten Years of the Negro Revolution." *Journal of American History* 55 (June 1968): 90–106.

Daniels, Jonathan. "New Patterns for Old." *Survey Graphic* 31 (November 1942): 485–87, 561.

Davenport, Walter. "Race Riots Coming." *Colliers* 122 (September 18, 1943): 11, 79–83.

Davis, John W. "The Negro in the United States Navy, Marine Corps and Coast Guard." *Journal of Negro Education* 12 (Summer 1943): 345–49.

Davis, Ralph N. "The Negro Newspapers and the War." *Sociology and Social Researches* 27 (March-April 1943): 373–80.

De Armand, Marjorie. "Pacific Scottsboro." *New Masses* (October 11, 1944), pp. 9–10.

Dungee, Roscoe. "Tis The Set of the Sail." *The Crisis* 63 (January 1956): 24.

"Field Asks Attack on Enemies of Democracy." *Editor and Publisher* 75 (June 13, 1942): 8.

"Fortune Press Analysis: Negroes." *Fortune* 28 (Spring 1945): 233–38.

Fortune, T. Thomas. "The New York Negro in Journalism." *Official Souvenir Program of the National Negro Exposition,* Richmond, Va. (July 1915).

Garlington, S. W. "The Negro Press." *New Masses* (March 9, 1943), p. 10.

Gosnell, Harold F. "Obstacles to Domestic Pamphleteering." *Journalism Quarterly* 23 (December 1946): 360–66.

———. "Symbols of National Solidarity." *The Annals of the Academy of Political and Social Science* 223 (September 1942): 157–61.

Graham, Shirley. "Negroes Are Fighting For Freedom." *Common Sense* 12 (1943): 45–50.

Granger, Lester B. "Negroes and War Production." *Survey Graphic* 31 (November 1942): 469–71, 543.

Graves, John Temple. "The Southern Negro and the War Crisis." *The Virginia Quarterly Review* 18 (Autumn 1942): 500–517.

Gross, Bella. "*Freedom's Journal* and *The Rights of All.*" *The Journal of Negro History* 15 (July 1932): 241–86.

Hamilton, Albert. "The Black Cabinet." *Common Sense* 12 (March 1943): 97–98.

Harrison, Wm. "William Monroe Trotter—Fighter." *Phylon* 7 (Third Quarter 1946): 237–44.

Hastie, Wm. H. "The Negro in the Army Today." *The Annals of the Academy of Political and Social Science* 223 (September 1942): 55–59.

High, Stanley. "How the Negro Fights for Freedom." *Reader's Digest* 41 (July 1942): 113–18.

Houston, Charles H. "Critical Summary: The Negro in the United

States Armed Forces in World Wars I and II." *Journal of Negro Education* 12 (Summer 1943): 364–66.

Johnson, Campbell C. "The Mobilization of Negro Manpower for the Armed Forces." *Journal of Negro Education* 12 (Summer 1943): 298–306.

Johnson, Chas. S. "The Present Status of Race Relations." *Social Forces* 23 (October 1944): 27–32.

Johnson, Ernest E. "The Washington News Beat." *Phylon* 7 (Second Quarter 1946): 120–29.

Jones, Clifton R. "The Negro Press." *One World*, ed. Brown and Rourek. New York: Prentice-Hall, Inc., 1952. Pp. 401–15.

Jones, Lester M. "The Editorial Policy of the Negro Newspapers of 1917–1918 as Compared with that of 1941–1942." *Journal of Negro History* 29 (January 1944): 24–31.

Kesselman, Louis C. "The Fair Employment Practice Commission in Perspective." *Journal of Negro History* 31 (January 1946): 30–46.

Krieghbaum, Hiller. "The Office of War Information and Government News Policy." *Journalism Quarterly* 19 (September 1942).

Lawson, M. M. "The Adult Educational Aspects of the Negro Press." *Journal of Negro Education* 14 (Summer 1945): 431–36.

Lewis, Alfred Baker. "Racism at Home." *Common Sense* 11 (June 1942): 194–95.

Lewis, Roscoe E. "The Role of Pressure Groups in Maintaining Morale among Negroes." *Journal of Negro Education* 12 (Summer 1943): 464–73.

Lewis, Theophilus. "The Negro Press Is a Racial Advocate." *America* 67 (September 19, 1942): 655–56.

———. "The Negro Press Was Born of a Necessity." *America* 67 (September 12, 1942): 627–28.

Lochard, Metz T. P. "Negroes and Defense." *The Nation* 152 (January 4, 1941): 14–16.

———. "Robert S. Abbott-Race Leader." *Phylon* 8 (Second Quarter 1947): 123–32.

Locke, Alain. "Color: The Unfinished Business of Democracy." *Survey Graphic* 31 (November 1942): 455–59.

Long, Howard H. "The Negro Soldier in the Army of the United States." *Journal of Negro Education* 12 (Summer 1943): 307–15.

"The Luckless 92nd." *Newsweek* 25 (February 26, 1945): 34.

"Lynching Bee." *Time* 44 (November 20, 1944): 67.

Lynn, Conrad. "Brief For Relator: United States District Court Eastern District of New York. United States of America ex rel. Winfred Lynn, Relator against Colonel John W. Downes, Commanding Officer at Camp Upton, New York, Respondent." Reprinted in *Politics* 1 (February 1944): 23–26.

Martin, Louis. "Blood, Sweat, and Ink." *Common Ground* (Winter 1944), pp. 37–42.

———. "Prelude to Disaster: Detroit." *Common Ground* 4 (Autumn 1943): 21–26.

MacDonald, Dwight. "On the Conduct of the Lynn Case." *Politics* 1 (April 1944): 85–88.

———. "The Novel Case of Winfred Lynn." *The Nation* 156 (February 20, 1943): 263–70.

———. "Supreme Court's New Moot Suit." *The Nation* 159 (July 1, 1944): 13–14.

McAlpin, Harry. "The Negro Press and Politics." *The New Republic* 111 (October 15, 1944): 493.

"Meet the George Schuylers." *Our World* 6 (April 1951): 22–25.

Meier, August. "Booker T. Washington and the Negro Press: Special Reference to the *Colored American.*" *Journal of Negro History* 38 (January 1953): 67–90.

"Monopoly Trend Noted." *Editor and Publisher* 81 (June 24, 1944): 22.

Morrison, Allan. "The Crusading Press." *Ebony* 18 (October 1963): 204–10.

Morton, Mary A. "The Federal Government and Negro Morale." *Journal of Negro Education* 12 (Summer 1943): 452–63.

Murphy, Carl. "The Afro: Seaboard's Largest Weekly." *The Crisis* 45 (February 1948): 44–46, 50.

"Mutiny on Mare Island." *Time* 44 (October 2, 1944): 66.

"Negroes Ask About Democracy." *Propaganda Analysis* 4 (August 26, 1941): 1–11.

"Negro Paper Has Writer in Africa." *Editor and Publisher* 75 (December 26, 1942): 26.

"The Negro Press." *The New Republic* 109 (October 18, 1943): 540–43.

"The Negro Press 1955." *Time* 46 (August 13, 1955): 64, 66.

"Negro Press Holds a Meeting in New York." *Editor and Publisher* 81 (March 6, 1944): 18.

"Negro Publishers." *Time* (June 15, 1942): 70–71.

"The Negro's War." *Fortune* 25 (June 1942): 77–80, 157–58, 160, 162.

Nesbitt, George B. "The Negro Race Relations Expert and Negro Community Leadership." *Journal of Negro Education* 21 (Spring 1952): 148–60.

Nixon, Raymond B. "Propaganda and Censorship in America's Next War." *Journalism Quarterly* 16 (September 1939): 237–44.

Oak, Vishnu V. "What About the Negro Press?" *Saturday Review of Literature* 52 (February 1943): 4–5.

Ottley, Roi. "The Good Neighbor Policy at Home." *Common Ground* 2 (Summer 1942): 51–56.

———. "Negro Morale." *The New Republic* 105 (November 10, 1941): 613–15.

———. "The Negro Press Today." *Common Ground* 3 (Spring 1943): 11–18.

———. "A White Folks War?" *Common Ground* 2 (Spring 1942): 28–31.

Partington, Paul G. "*The Moon Illustrated Weekly*—The Precurser of *The Crisis*." *Journal of Negro History* 48 (July 1963): 206–16.

Perry, Samuel. "In Defense of the Negro Press." *Harvard Guardian* 7 (December 1942): 15–19.

"The Philadelphia Strike." *The Nation* 159 (August 12, 1944): 172–73.

Powell, Adam C. Jr. "Is This a White Man's War?" *Common Sense* 11 (April 1942): 111–13.

———. "A Big Stride Forward." *Spotlight* 2 (April 1944): 3–4.

Poston, Ted. "The Negro Press." *The Reporter* 1 (December 6, 1949): 14–16.

Prattis, P. L. "The Morale of the Negro in the Armed Services of the United States." *Journal of Negro Education* 12 (September 1943): 355–63.

———. "Racial Segregation and Negro Journalism." *Phylon* 8 (December 1947): 305–14.

———. "The Role of the Negro Press in Race Relations." *Phylon* 7 (Third Quarter 1946): 273–80.

Pride, Armisted. "Negro Newspapers: Yesterday, Today, Tomorrow." *Journalism Quarterly* 18 (Spring 1941).

Puttkammer, Chas. W. "William Monroe Trotter, 1872–1934." *Journal of Negro History* 43 (October 1958): 298–316.

Reddick, L. D. "Letters From a Jim Crow Army." *Twice A Year* 14–15 (Fall—Winter 1946—1947): 371-82.

———. "The Negro in the Navy During World War II." *Journal of Negro History* 32 (April 1947): 201–19.

———. "The Negro Policy of the United States Army." *Journal of Negro History* 34 (January 1949): 9–29.

———. "The Negro Policy of the American Army Since World War II." *Journal of Negro History* 38 (April 1953): 194–215.

Redding, J. Saunders. "A Negro Speaks for His People." *The Atlantic Monthly* 172 (March 1943): 58–63.

———. "Southern Defensive." *Common Ground* 4 (Spring 1944: 34–42.

"Report on the Negro Soldier." *Time* 45 (March 26, 1945): 22.

Robbins, Richard. "Counter Assertion in the Negro Press." *Phylon* 10 (Second Quarter 1949): 126–33.

Rudwick, Elliott. "W. E. B. DuBois in the Role of *Crisis* Editor." *Journal of Negro History* 43 (July 1958): 214–40.

Rutledge, Archibald. "The Negro Problem Reaches a Crisis: What if the South Should be Right." *The American Mercury* 59 (December 1944): 680–86.

Sale, J. Kirk. "The *Amsterdam News*." *The New York Times Magazine* (February 9, 1969), pp. 30–31, 37, 39–40, 42, 44, 46, 49, 52.

Sancton, Thomas. "The Negro Press." *The New Republic* 106 (February 8, 1942): 176–78.

———. "The Negro Press." *The New Republic* 108 (April 26, 1943): 557–60.

———. "The South Needs Help." *Common Ground* 3 (Autumn 1942): 12–16.

Saunders, Scott J. "I Worked for a Negro Newspaper." *The Crisis* 57 (January 1950): 4.

Schuyler, George S. "The Negro Problem Reaches a Crisis: More

Race Riots Coming." *The American Mercury* 59 (December 1944): 686–91.

Scott, E. J. "The Participation of Negroes in World War I." *Journal of Negro Education* 12 (Summer 1943): 288–97.

Siebert, F. S. "Federal Information Agencies—An Outline." *Journalism Quarterly* 19 (March 1942): 29–32.

"The South's Greatest Newspaper." *Negro Digest* 7 (July 1949): 39–40.

Thompson, Chas. H. "The American Negro and the National Defense." *Journal of Negro Education* 9 (October 1940): 547–52.

———. "The American Negro in World War I and World War II." *Journal of Negro Education* 12 (Summer 1943): 263–67.

———. "Mr. Dabney and the Precipice." *Journal of Negro Education* 43 (Spring 1943): 141–43.

Thornbrough, Emma L. "More Light on Booker T. Washington and *The New York Age*." *Journal of Negro History* 43 (January 1958): 34–49.

Thurston, T. "The Call: Leader in the Southwest." *The Crisis* 45 (June 1938): 173–74, 187–88.

Townsend, Willard. "Note on Criticism by W. C. Couch of an Essay on *What The Negro Wants*." *Twice A Year* 12–13 (Summer 1945): 293–301.

"Trials End." *Time* 44 (November 6, 1944): 68.

"Uncolored News." *Headlines and Pictures* 2 (January 1946): 34–37.

Villard, Oswald G. "Negroes Not Allowed." *Common Sense* 10 (July 1941): 199.

Wechsler, James. "A Pigeonhole For Negro Equality." *The Nation* 156 (January 23, 1943): 121–22.

Werner, Ludlow. "The New York *Age:* Lusty Veteran." *The Crisis* 45 (March 1938): 74–75, 91–92.

White, Walter. "Its Our Country Too." *The Saturday Evening Post* 213 (December 14, 1940): 27, 61, 63, 66, 68.

———. "The Negro Waits to See." *The Nation* 159 (October 21, 1944): 466–67.

———. "Race Relations in the Armed Services of the United States." *Journal of Negro Education* 12 (Summer 1943): 350–54.

———. "The Right to Fight for Democracy." *Survey Graphic* 31 (November 1942): 472–74.

———. "What the Negro Thinks of the Army." *The Annals of the Academy of Political and Social Science* 223 (September 1942): 67–71.

Wilkerson, Doxey. "FEPC—The Alphabet of Hope." *New Masses* 45 (October 20, 1942): 5–8.

———. "The Negro Press Today." *Journal of Negro Education* 14 (Fall 1947): 511–21.

Wilkins, Roy. "The Negro Press." *Opportunity* 6 (December 1928): 362–63.

———. "The Negro Press Hits Back." *Magazine Digest* (April 1943), pp. 3–7.

Winslow, Henry F. "George S. Schuyler: Fainting Traveller." *Midwest Journal* 5 (Summer 1953): 24–44.

Wolseley, Roland. "The Vanishing Negro Press." *The Commonweal* 52 (September 22, 1950): 577–79.

Young, Consuelo C. "A Study of Reader Attitudes Toward the Negro Press." *Social Forces* 26 (December 1947): 148–52.

Young, P. B. "The Extent and Quality of the Negro Press." *The Southern Workman* 62 (August 1933): 323–29.

"The Youngs of Norfolk." *Headlines and Pictures* 2 (January 1946): 16–21.

Zoerner, Cyril E., and Beard, Richard L. "Associated Negro Press: Its Founding, Ascendency and Demise." *Journalism Quarterly* 46 (Spring 1969): 47–52.

Index